PANDEMIC
MEDICINE

Advances in International Political Economy

PANDEMIC MEDICINE

Why the Global Innovation System Is Broken, and How We Can Fix It

Kathryn C. Ibata-Arens

LYNNE
RIENNER
PUBLISHERS

BOULDER
LONDON

Published in the United States of America in 2021 by
Lynne Rienner Publishers, Inc.
1800 30th Street, Suite 314, Boulder, Colorado 80301
www.rienner.com

and in the United Kingdom by
Lynne Rienner Publishers, Inc.
Gray's Inn House, 127 Clerkenwell Road, London EC1 5DB
www.eurospanbookstore.com/rienner

Library of Congress Cataloging-in-Publication Data
Names: Ibata-Arens, Kathryn C., author.
Title: Pandemic medicine : why the global innovation system is broken, and
   how we can fix it / by Kathryn C. Ibata-Arens.
Description: Boulder, Colorado : Lynne Rienner Publishers, Inc., 2021. |
   Series: Advances in international political economy | Includes
   bibliographical references and index. | Summary: "Analyzes the rise and
   decline of the global innovation system for new drug development and
   proposes a policy framework for fast-tracking the implementation of new
   discoveries and preparing for future pandemics"— Provided by publisher.
Identifiers: LCCN 2021015856 | ISBN 9781626379695 (hardcover) | ISBN
   9781626379718 (paperback)
Subjects: LCSH: Drug development. | Medical policy. | Drugs—Quality
   control. | Medical innovations—Social aspects.
Classification: LCC RM301.25 I23 2021 | DDC 615.1/9—dc23
LC record available at https://lccn.loc.gov/2021015856

British Cataloguing in Publication Data
A Cataloguing in Publication record for this book
is available from the British Library.

Printed and bound in the United States of America

The paper used in this publication meets the requirements
∞ of the American National Standard for Permanence of
Paper for Printed Library Materials Z39.48-1992.

5 4 3 2 1

For my mother, Janie C. Ibata

~

Her nurturing spirit lifts us

Contents

Acknowledgments

This book follows from my book *Beyond Technonationalism: Biomedical Innovation and Entrepreneurship in Asia* (2019). Research support was provided by Fulbright, Japan Society for the Promotion of Science, and the University Research Council of DePaul University. Research assistance was provided by Benjamin Bui, Abbas Dahodwala, Naixin Kang, Wanlin (Mia) Lu, Shweta Surawanshee, Dolma Tsering, Shaokun Wang, and Qing Wang. A special thanks goes to Wenjing Wang, whose research assistance and overall support throughout the writing process has been invaluable. Two anonymous reviewers provided critical feedback, pushing me to refine my argument and polish the case study narratives in the book. Advances in International Political Economy series editors Alex Nunn, Sophia Price, and Stuart Shields offered ongoing feedback on several drafts. I thank Lynne Rienner for her enthusiasm early on about my vision for the book and her prodding me to remain on task to completion (almost) on time.

Extensive fieldwork in Asian countries from 2016 to 2020 with government officials, policy advocates, community organizations, and social entrepreneurs would not have been possible without the kindness of many. For example, I am grateful to the late Ezra Vogel for his introductions years ago in China and his spry mirth that inspired me to pursue my ambitious goals for the book. Likewise,

Shelly Ochs shared her insights and expertise as a doctor of traditional medicine, including her contributions to the Covid-19 pandemic treatment efforts in China. I am indebted to Changhua Liu for the countless ways he informed and illuminated my understandings of healing medicines and the intersections of tradition and modern medicine in China. In India, Sulakshana Sen facilitated important introductions and offered keen insights from her own expertise in international relations and India's health diplomacy. Vinod Baliga kept me abreast of entrepreneurial initiatives in Indian biopharmaceuticals. Anthony D'Costa provided perspectives on innovation trends in Asian economies and its study in the field of international political economy. In Japan, Eiichi Kodaira shared his wisdom and scientific knowledge about plant medicinals and their potential for new drug discovery. Michie Hisada, then at Takeda Pharmaceutical Company, and Chieko Ikeda of the Japan Ministry of Health, Labour, and Welfare connected me to entrepreneurs and innovators in new drug discovery in Japan, as well as offered their seasoned perspectives on private-sector innovations and national and global health policy. Julia Yongue of Hosei University deepened my understanding of the history of medicines in Japan. Masaki Kuroki, Ritsumeikan University, kindly hosted me as a visiting researcher and inspired me with his expertise on social entrepreneurship. Linda Grove, professor emeritus, Sofia University, and Nicole Restrick Levit, Social Science Research Council, invited me to present at convenings of science and technology experts in Japan and the United States. The archivists and staff at the Ford and the Rockefeller Foundation archives and Takeda Pharmaceutical Kyoto Garden archives helped me track down documents instrumental in understanding the histories of various initiatives. Any errors or omissions remain my own.

I thank friends and colleagues who invited me to present my work in progress to their students and faculty, including Katherine Chen, City University of New York; Erin Chung, Johns Hopkins University; and Mary Alice Haddad, Wesleyan University. I am grateful for feedback from colleagues at the Midwest Japan Seminar, sponsored by the Japan Foundation; the Catalyst Workshop on Policymaking in East Asia, Wesleyan University, sponsored by the Center for Global Partnership, Japan Foundation, and hosted by Mary Alice Haddad; and the Center for Global Partnership–sponsored 21st Century Japan Politics and Society Initiative, Indiana University, hosted by Adam Liff. Support from the Maureen and Mike Mansfield Foundation was important in exploring pan-Asian and national security aspects of innovation in Asian economies. At the Institut d'études politiques de Paris, Martha Zuber and Étienne Nouguez, as well as colleagues in the Centre de sociologie des organisations shared their feedback on early stages of this research. Participants in the Society for the Advancement of Socio-Economics 2020 miniconference "Regulation, Innovation, and Valuation in Markets for Health and Medicines" asked insightful questions about the conceptual framing and provided feedback, prompting me to extend my analysis to make it more approachable for a broader audience. Likewise, hosts of and participants in the Governance of Socio-Ecological Systems (GOSES) workshop at East China Normal University, Shanghai (2019), and at the meeting of the International Association for the Study of Traditional Asian Medicine (IASTAM) in conjunction with the Association of Asian Studies, Washington, DC (2018), shared perspectives on sociocultural aspects of natural medicines.

This book owes its existence to health care professionals, including medical doctors and nurses, scientists, and other stakeholders, who have dedicated their lives to improving human health.

An Innovation Commons: The Global System for New Drug Discovery

What happened to the global innovation system that makes us—government officials, company executives, patients, and advocates—less prepared than we should be for viral pandemics and such other threats to human health as antibiotic-resistant bacteria and killer parasites? Chronic (noncommunicable) conditions, including asthma, cancer, diabetes, and heart disease, have also risen to epidemic levels. The noblesse oblige of pioneers of modern medicine—the sharing of discoveries in the commons as a communal resource for all humanity—was the norm in the early twentieth century. This open sharing of medical innovations, the introduction of such new goods and services as medicines and treatments to society, was the basis for modern medicine. Prior to the rise of patent-centric intellectual property rights (IPR), novel discoveries had been shared in what can be called an innovation commons.[1] An innovation commons has two key characteristics. First, knowledge flows across institutional and other boundaries, and access is free and open. Second, knowledge and innovation stakeholders often share a sense of civic duty—that is, a sense of responsibility to the community to seek solutions for the common good.

For most of the twentieth century, lifesaving medicines and medical treatments were shared in the innovation commons for the public good. These shared innovations in medicine have included insulin, saving millions from the debilitating and deadly disease diabetes (1921); the first antibiotic, penicillin (1928); the polio vaccine (1955); and monoclonal antibodies (1975), which have been essential in cancer treatments (Hager 2019).[2] It is noteworthy that these innovations were all natural biologics—that is, natural medicines derived from living things (e.g., plants, microbes). Unfortunately, the innovation commons of shared discoveries in natural medicine has since morphed into a global juggernaut of drugmakers working with synthetic (i.e., non-natural) chemicals that have intentionally closed off the innovation commons with patent monopolies.[3] Patented synthetic chemical drugs have indeed been important in the alleviation of symptoms of chronic conditions and have also been effective in the treatment of infectious disease, although their safety and efficacy had declined by the end of the twentieth century. This innovation decline is examined in Chapter 2.

That is not to say that prior to the twentieth-century (and current) system of monopoly patented drugs, life was idyllic for most. Infectious disease of epidemic and pandemic proportions sickened and killed large swaths of the human population on a regular basis. Certainly, pharmaceutical companies have been effective in producing drugs and vaccines at scale, reaching millions of consumers and patients worldwide. Nevertheless, previous sharing of medicine discoveries in the public commons has been eclipsed by the global race among private companies to dominate markets. Patient health has become subjugated to the drive for profit (Raghupathi and Raghupathi 2018). Human health on the whole has suffered. As a result, the global innovation system for the discovery and development of new medicines is failing to keep up with pandemics and other threats to humanity. To be sure, private actors in international markets are not expected to serve the common good. Nevertheless, when the health of humanity is at stake, incentive mechanisms must be in place to encourage private and state actors to work together in seeking remedies. Such global health crises as pandemic disease expose the failure of private markets to provide opportunities for actors to collaborate in providing social returns on investment. The cost to humanity of this market failure has been catastrophic during the global coronavirus pandemic that began in 2019. The toll has been measured in millions of lives lost, billions of taxpayer dollars spent on pandemic responses that could have been allocated elsewhere, and trillions of dollars in lost economic activity.

In this book I explain how the global innovation system for medicine development became broken in the twentieth century and propose a way to fix it. Absent a complete overthrow of the current patent-centric global intellectual property rights regime—which some argue undermines the potential for disruptive innovation—state and private-sector experiments underway may offer an answer. These include creating spaces of inclusivity in innovation practice that are neither entirely state nor purely private-sector solutions. I call these (innovation) sandboxes and (intellectual property) pools.

Sandboxes and Pools

Transformational change in the way the world innovates for new drug discovery can be explained by innovation sandboxes and shared intellectual property pools within a framework that I call the typology of innovation system architectures (TISA). Sandboxes and pools representing open innovation architectures are situated within the TISA. Innovation sandboxes aim for new discoveries through open exchange within structured play. Examples include transnational collaborative new drug discovery found in India's Open Source Drug Discovery analyzed in Chapter 4. Innovation pools promote sharing between select groups of stakeholders of old knowledge, evident in the competitive collaboration in sharing drug compound libraries for new drug development in Japan's Global Health Innovative Technology Fund (GHIT), explored in Chapter 5. The TISA framework reflects the degree to which interactions aiming for innovation are open or closed and the degree to which the innovation output itself is novel or not. Further, analyzing innovation activity through the framework of the TISA exposes how the current global innovation system architecture for the discovery and development of new medicines has become enclosed into fenced-in spaces. An apt metaphor for this enclosure is a cage, since innovations become trapped and cannot be shared in the commons. These enclosures or cages are secretive, reflecting the efforts of private interests to protect patentable findings from competition. Once caged in, innovation activity tends to become less innovative over time, then stagnates, falling Icarus-like from the novel heights of innovative activity into an enclosure. Closed innovation architectures tend to lead to silos, becoming walled off to information exchange with the outside (except the one-way extraction of knowledge resources inward). Reliance on old discoveries means that outside ideas that could refresh and renew innovation activities can't get inside. Collectively, innovation cages and innovation silos comprise the anticommons, the opposite of architectures designed to share in the open innovation commons. Figure 1.1 outlines the relationships between open and closed system architectures and the level of market and product novelty. Chapter 2 details and explores the typology of innovation system architectures in light of the rise and decline of innovation in new drug discovery within the global pharmaceutical industry.

As the case studies in subsequent chapters show, removing regulatory barriers is not enough to engender an open innovation commons characterized by sharing of medicine knowledge and resources for the greater good. It is about not only removing the fences and cages enclosing the sandbox of innovative activity but also inviting a greater variety of stakeholders to play in it. Pools of shared medicine knowledge have reduced both transaction costs and redundancy in collaborations for new drug discovery (Nair 2010). In the absence of a global intellectual property rights regime ensuring a global innovation commons, intermediate but nevertheless transformational ways of pursuing innovation for essential medicine discovery and development in sandboxes and pools offer insights into possibilities for the future. Analyzing these trends across countries at the state–private-sector nexus offers a lens on how states and others within the global innovation system have risen to the challenge of promoting innovation for the public good. Findings indicate an offensive strategic nationalism in China, caging in new innovations and preventing them from being shared widely; a global commons, sandbox-guided defensive posture in India; and a middle ground of shared intellectual property pools through international health diplomacy in Japan.

This book is also about the potential for a new, emergent kind of global innovation architecture, presenting successful case study models of new drug discovery and innovation inclusive of certain stakeholders. An inclusive innovation architecture is one structuring incentives for open innovation that benefits (private) firms and (public) states while reducing the burden on national governments and ultimately taxpayers and citizens. This involves improving governance of the global innovation commons (Ostrom 1990), discussed below,

Figure 1.1   Typology of Innovation System Architectures (TISA)

Products and Markets	Closed	Open
High novelty	Cages	Sandboxes
Low novelty	Silos	Pools

while structuring incentives for private-sector actors to act in the interest of human health. This change would help in preparing for future pandemics and also in healing chronic conditions—as opposed to treating their symptoms—through investments in developing novel medicines heretofore neglected by the pharmaceutical industry. The crisis in innovation precipitated by the coronavirus pandemic presented an opportunity to innovate the global innovation system.

Innovation Crisis in the Covid-19 Pandemic

A novel coronavirus erupted in Wuhan, China, in late 2019, spreading rapidly around the world by early 2020. The resulting Covid-19 disease has killed millions and sickened millions more. The pandemic has also disrupted the global innovation status quo. That status quo was one of patents for profit, characterized by private competition to bring drug treatments and vaccines to market. Collaboration under a sense of the general good was all but absent, save existing initiatives by a handful of private foundations.[4] During the initial response to the coronavirus in early 2020, the global drug discovery and development system was ill prepared, with tragic consequences for human health worldwide. Academic institutions had been conducting pandemic health policy response prior to the coronavirus pandemic, though the United States, for example, at a national level had been retreating from its previous role in funding basic science at universities and public research institutions. The fragmented international response led to an innovation crisis in which national attempts to bring innovative diagnostics, drugs, and therapies to patients were hampered by conflicting national and state policies, as well as different levels of competency in national leadership and international cooperation. National governments worldwide scrambled to identify and develop diagnostic and vaccine candidates, costing the global economy many trillions of dollars in lost economic activity.[5] The World Bank (2020) estimated that global GDP shrank in 2020 between 5 and 8 percent due to the Covid-19 pandemic. Initial estimates for 2021 anticipated a drop in global growth by about 1 percent amid ongoing uncertainty (Hannon 2020). In an innovation crisis scenario, actors trade away efficiency in an urgent search of perceived, but untested or unproven, effectiveness.

From the 1990s, the global pharmaceutical product pipeline for drugs and diagnostics had spread across the globe, its "supply chain" stretching from research and development (R&D) centers in cities like Boston and Chicago, to component suppliers in Europe, information technology centers in India, and production that became heavily dependent on mainland China. The world had also become dependent on China for raw biological materials and materials for active pharmaceutical ingredients. While patients were dying in hospitals around the world during the Covid-19 pandemic, the production of test kits was slow as a result of quarantining and the shutdown of the global transportation system. A dismayed epidemiologist noted that the swabs needed for test kits in the United States had been produced almost exclusively in Italy, while Italian researchers with important data and samples had been shut out of their labs, unable to access critically needed information for the pandemic response (*Reset* 2020). Had the intellectual property and tacit know-how been held in an innovation commons, other stakeholders in the research, development, and production of potentially lifesaving drugs and diagnostics could have stepped in to help more quickly and efficiently. Unfortunately, the global innovation commons had become dangerously fragmented, closed behind national and institutional borders—an anticommons.[6] During the Covid-19 crisis, pharmaceutical firms competed to be the first to market with a vaccine.

In addition to making the unprecedented move of circumventing standard scientific reporting procedures, instead announcing their clinical testing findings in press releases aimed at boosting their stock prices, Pfizer/BioNTech and Moderna told their investors that the companies would be profiting handsomely from the sale of the Covid-19 vaccine, including earning billions of dollars in government vaccine contracts. The first-to-market Covid-19 vaccines benefited from decades of government-funded research and development, and further, during the pandemic these pharmaceutical companies received cash infusions from public funding to the tune of billions of dollars (Pfizer and Moderna, United States), pounds (AstraZeneca, United Kingdom), and euros (BioNTech, Germany) (Mazzucato, Li, and Torreele 2020; Baker et al. 2020; Hiltzik 2020). Further, Galkina Cleary and colleagues (2018) have noted the role of the US National Institutes of Health in all drugs approved by the Food and Drug Administration between 2010 and 2016 as part of more than $100 billion in government funds benefiting drugmakers. Political oversight or lack thereof exacerbated the fragmentation and failure to have transparency when clinical subjects became seriously ill from experimental vaccines (Zimmer, Thomas, and Mueller 2020). Part of the reason why there has been so little oversight is the success of the pharmaceutical industry in lobbying governments and multilateral institutions for preferential policies.

The billions of dollars ($306 billion in 2020 alone) spent by the drug lobby representing the interests of large pharmaceutical companies have resulted in rent seeking in which private-sector actors gain economic benefit from governments without doing the work to earn it.[7] One example of rent seeking is that these companies continue to earn profits from patents extended on old drugs, called *evergreening*, instead of bringing novel drugs to market. Since 1950, each decade has brought half as many new drugs to approval per each billion dollars spent by the pharmaceutical industry (Scannell et al. 2012). Something about the current architecture for innovation isn't working. A complete replacement of the current system may not be possible, despite the coronavirus crisis. We must, however, innovate our global innovation system for new drug discovery.

Innovation Commons and Human Health

In contrast, the innovation commons approach of the Human Genome Project (HGP) (1990–2003) provided a framework for data and information sharing across national and institutional boundaries. Because the norms and practices of sharing had been in place through the HGP when the severe acute respiratory syndrome (SARS) epidemic struck Asia in 2002, scientists managed to quickly, by early 2003, map the genomic structure of that virus, enabling effective testing and treatment. This open sharing in the innovation commons—transcending national and particularistic boundaries—helped to avert that epidemic from becoming a pandemic. The disease outbreaks of SARS (2003) and Covid-19 (2020) were both caused by coronaviruses, but in 2020 no HGP-level global collaboration architecture was in place.

The HGP is an example of how a shared goal of identifying gene targets benefited from a structured and committed international effort to bring complementary resources (data analytic technology, scientific talent) to solve common scientific questions. The HGP functioned as an innovation sandbox and intellectual property pool within an open commons framework, on the commons side of the TISA. The origins of the HGP and its impacts have been discussed extensively elsewhere and are beyond the scope of this book (Tripp and Grueber 2011). Briefly, the HGP led to numerous new medical treatments and also to a generation of new venture start-ups in biomedicine, especially in Asian countries (Ibata-Arens 2019a). However promising, the innovation commons approach of the HGP represents an anomaly. Since the 1980s the rules of the global innovation system have been written to encourage profit but discourage open innovation.

The State and the (Pharma) Firm: The Rise of the Global Patent System

To protect the health of their citizens and residents, nation-states play an important role in mitigating negative externalities of global economic competition. Governments thus have a responsibility to maintain a delicate balance between promoting private-sector economic activity (in markets) and engendering innovation that matters to their citizens and humanity (in society). In the early twentieth century, drug companies in the United States and Europe promised to research and develop medicines that improved patient health. In this regard, George W. Merck, in the early years of that eponymous company, was quoted as saying, "Medicines are for the patients . . . for the people . . . not for profit" (J. J. Li 2014). Flash-forward to the 1970s and Merck's then CEO Henry Gadsden. His interest was more in marketing than in pharmaceutical science. In his own words, changing the script from Merck's founding motto of "patients before profit," Gadsden said that he wanted "to sell drugs to everyone. I want to sell drugs to healthy people. I want drugs to sell like chewing gum" (Robertson 1976; Moynihan and Cassels 2005; see also Hawthorne 2003). Similarly, John McKeen, Pfizer chief executive in the 1950s, argued that it was not worthwhile to invest in drugs that wouldn't generate windfall revenues (Posner 2020; J. J. Li 2014).

Following in the footsteps of McKeen, Edmund Pratt, CEO of Pfizer in the 1980s, headed the coordinated lobbying effort (alongside other multinational corporations with an interest in pharmaceuticals: DuPont, Bristol-Meyers, Johnson & Johnson, and Monsanto) that led to the creation of the patent-centered global intellectual property rights regime under the World Trade Organization (WTO) discussed below (see Drahos 2010; Matthews 2002).[8] It is interesting to note that the rise of the marketing juggernaut of Pfizer and its sales of drugs on a global scale coincided with Pfizer's hiring of skilled medical advertiser Arthur M. Sackler. Sackler went on to found Purdue Pharma, whose marketing of the addictive synthetic chemical drug OxyContin contributed to the opioid epidemic in the United States in the 2000s.[9] Criminal investigations later confirmed that Purdue executives had been well aware that users would likely become dependent on the drug. After all, an addicted user is a repeat customer. Patients might suffer and eventually die, but in the meantime, pharmaceutical company profits would be guaranteed. This is not a new phenomenon.

Pharmaceutical companies grew from early-1900s purveyors of "cure-alls" (Posner 2020), often laced with cocaine or opium. These companies would go on to build a global industry based on broad-spectrum or cure-all antibiotics used in the treatment of bacterial infection, but increasingly as a prophylactic against it.[10] Contagious epidemic disease was soon replaced by noncommunicable chronic disease as the main target for drug discovery in the pharmaceutical industry. Meanwhile, finding it easier to obtain patents granting monopoly sales rights on synthetic chemicals, pharmaceutical companies moved away from developing natural medicines, which had proven more difficult to extract from the global commons unchallenged. Figure 1.2 outlines the different types of drug discovery, showing the variety of material resources within natural medicine discovery and development.

Within the global market share for drugs and medicines—the distinction between "drug" and "medicine" is explained in Chapter 2—medical discoveries based on biologics had accelerated exponentially,

Figure 1.2   Drug Discovery by Type

Natural Biologics
<ul><li>Genomics</li><li>Microbes (e.g., for antibiotics)[a]</li><li>Stem cells</li><li>(Re)discovered natural (plant, animal, fungi) chemical compounds from traditional medicine</li><li>Vaccines</li></ul>
Synthetic Chemicals

Note: a. Microbes or microorganisms include bacteria, viruses, and fungi (e.g., yeast and mold). Other microbes are algae amoebas and slime molds. Enzymes are not living things but can be produced by microbes, namely, bacteria.

particularly in genomics and stem cell therapies but also in medicines dependent on other biological materials, including those derived from plants and animals. Such synthetic drugs as the first effective HIV/AIDS treatment (azidothymidine, from sea sponges) and blood pressure medications (e.g., angiotensin-converting enzyme [ACE] inhibitors, from the Amazonian pit viper) owe their discoveries to observations of the natural world (Plotkin 2020).[11] Unfortunately, synthetic chemical drugs became central to the profits of pharmaceutical companies just as their curative potential was waning.

Medicine and Pandemics: The Need to Save Biological Materials and the Knowledge About Them

By the mid-twentieth century, global pandemics seemed rare, the memories of the 1918 Spanish flu relegated to the pages of history.[12] Then, in 1997, the S5N1 bird flu hit 18 countries, killing half of those who fell ill (estimated 455 deaths). Within a few years, in 2002, the world would battle SARS, which hit a number of Asian countries, including China. Less than a decade later, the 2009–2010 H1N1 swine flu infected 214 countries, killing hundreds of thousands of people. In 2012, Middle Eastern respiratory syndrome spread to 28 countries, killing 858, with a 34 percent death rate. Since 2012, at least five viral outbreaks have spread around the world, with the novel coronavirus emerging in 2019 to threaten the entire human population. Meanwhile, other diseases endemic to the developing world—malaria, Zika, and dengue fever, to name a few—continue to infect people of all ages, with increasing resistance to the synthetic chemical drugs on the market to treat them (Woodward and Gal 2020; Madhav et al. 2017; Landers and Inada 2020; Chotiner 2020). In sum, the world faces human health crises—including viral pandemics and rampant growth in antibiotic-resistant killer bacteria—that have exposed the curative limits of synthetic chemical compounds sold by pharmaceutical companies.

While on average more people die from chronic conditions, pandemics tend to kill quickly, especially targeting the most vulnerable, the elderly, and those with underlying health conditions. Pandemic diseases result from complex economic, political, and social factors. For example, pathogens are more easily spread among human populations in locations where people interact closely with each other (cities) and among wild and domesticated animals in smaller spaces (Lock and Nguyen 2018; Ackerknecht 2016). Epidemics (illnesses affecting large numbers of people at the same time) and pandemics (epidemics spread across wide geographic space and sickening an unusually high proportion of the population) have been around since the beginning of recorded history.[13] Why do we seem to be affected by them more now?

Both the number and the severity of viral pandemics are on the rise for the same reasons why the natural medicines with the potential to cure them are about to disappear. Natural medicines depend on biological materials living in biodiverse ecosystems. Urbanization, changes in land use (e.g., monocropping, built infrastructure), and shifts in climate are reducing biodiversity worldwide (Sala, Meyerson, and Parmesan 2009). Shrinking biodiversity is also bringing wild animals into closer contact with human populations. Of the epidemics and pandemics to threaten human health in recent decades (avian flu, SARS, Covid-19, swine flu), evidence points to their pathogens' having jumped from wild animals (bats, birds) to humans (a process called zoonosis), frequently via domesticated animals (chickens, pigs).

Bacteria, viruses, and other microorganisms that cause disease have become more virulent in less biodiverse ecosystems and, further, are more likely to invade human hosts. Cholera, Lyme disease, and malaria are among many examples of human infectious diseases whose spread worsens within destabilized natural ecosystems (Alves and Rosa 2007). The Covid-19 crisis made clear how humanity depends on biodiversity. Earth's living plants and animals (including microbes) have evolved for millions of years, keeping viral and bacterial pathogens in check within biologically diverse ecosystems (called *reservoirs*). It is in these biodiverse ecosystems that the plant (and animal) genomic resources for medicines reside.

Natural Medicines and the Innovation Commons

Natural medicines have always been an important source of both the quotidian medicine know-how and the biological materials for the development of new medicines. Microbes, for example, are the basis for many vaccines and depend on a biodiverse ecosystem for their survival. Continued availability of and access to these biological materials is dependent on plant biodiversity (cultivated varieties lack the potency of naturally occurring active ingredients), and microbes and fungi need a diverse plant ecosystem to flourish. This medicinal plant biodiversity is under threat from a myriad of factors, some outlined above. Others will be discussed in subsequent chapters in the context of efforts by local organizations to protect and conserve traditional medicine knowledge (TMK) and medicinal plant biodiversity (Center for Biodiversity and Indigenous Knowledge in China, *deo rahati* in India, and Takeda Garden for Medicinal Plant Conservation, Kyoto, in Japan). The emergent organizational case studies from China, India, and Japan offer an opportunity to explore, via grounded theory (Lundvall 2007), how national governments have risen to the challenge—or at least gotten out of the way—of promoting innovation that improves human health while navigating the thicket of rules in the global IPR regime that have prioritized private profit over the public good.

The earth's biodiversity for natural medicine depends on humanity to conserve and protect it. Unfortunately, humanity on the whole has done a poor job of doing so, to the detriment of natural ecosystems that are habitats for wild medicinal plants. Scientists have found that virulent pathogens had previously been held in check by certain microbes and plants in their ecosystems. These microbes and plants have also been critical resources in the development of drugs and treatments against pandemic disease (Grifo and Rosenthal 1997). Innovations in the discovery and development of healing natural medicines have been made for thousands of years, and these discoveries have been documented extensively in ancient medicine texts. These books of remedies evolved from doctors' notes taken by the bedsides of patients, then evolved in some countries into compendiums of codified medicine formulations. So-called traditional natural medicines are used extensively, for example, in Asian countries, on their own and also in combination with Western methods.

The definition of traditional medicine varies slightly across countries. Generally, the term refers to the holistic practice of medicine, treating a whole person's overall health rather than a narrow (allopathic) focus on a particular disease or condition. Traditional medicines are naturally derived, having no synthetic chemicals. Formulations are inherited and innovated across generations, typically through a master-apprentice training relationship. Formulations of these medicines are routinely innovated, responding to changing patterns in illness, environment, and availability of raw materials. "Traditional" refers to the way knowledge is created, preserved, and transmitted from older to younger—not the knowledge per se. In other words, traditional medicine knowledge is often dynamic and innovative, not static and rarefied (Finetti 2011). TMK stakeholders, including scholars of medicine and traditional medicine doctors, have stewarded and innovated natural medicine knowledge and treatment for thousands of years, maintaining the knowledge corpus in the innovation commons.

The Promise of Biologics: Traditional Medicines and Their (Plant) Biological Materials

As stated above not until the twentieth century did drugs become predominately synthetic chemicals.[14] From the loss of medicinal plant biodiversity follow the decline and loss of potential naturally derived chemical compounds to treat increasing numbers of disease conditions. National governments have borne the bulk of the high-cost burden of emergency treatment and containment. At the same time, growing evidence indicates that such natural medicines as those derived from wild plant species have significant healing potential (Fung and Wong 2015; Simpson, Sedjo, and Reid 1996; Srinivas 2012).[15] In fact, 85 percent of the world's population depends on plants alone for their primary health care needs (Cox 2009).[16] For instance, ginger (Chang et al. 2013) and ginseng (Im, Kim, and Min 2016) are used as antivirals in medicines made from their rootstalks, called *rhizomes*. Such fungi as mushrooms have been effective in treating bacterial infections (Jakubczyk and Dussart 2020). Other promising innovations in natural medicines are discussed in Chapters 3 to 5. Studies have noted that the greater chemical diversity found in medicinal plants is superior as measured by potency and low toxicity in disease treatment to that in synthetic combinations of chemicals (Fabricant and Farnsworth 2001, cited in Alves and Rosa 2007).

The need to protect, cultivate, and harness natural medicine resources, including medicinal plants and the knowledge about them, for future human health has been recognized by scientists and multilateral organizations, including the World Health Organization (WHO) and the United Nations (Secretariat of the CBD 2005, 2016). Table 1.1 outlines select multilateral policies related to innovations within and protection of natural medicine. Pharmaceutical firms have attempted, with some success, to exploit traditional medicine pharmacopoeia (listing medicines and their formulas and usages) from countries including China and India. Ethnobotanical research methods, combining social scientific study of human communities with observations of the natural world, have been found to be the most effective means of identifying efficacious medicines from the natural world (Cox 2009). For example, the Western field of ethnobotany, which relies on the traditional medicine knowledge of indigenous healers in guiding pharmaceutical research in natural medicine, is said to have originated in the early 1700s with the ethnographic work of Karl Linnaeus. Linnaeus had worked with Sámi healers in northern Lapland, located across the northern provinces of Finland, Norway, and Sweden.

The search for inspirations in new drug discovery has also included data mining of traditional medicine texts and "bioprospecting" for raw materials in such biodiverse countries as China and India (Dalton 2000; Utkarsh 2003; Watal 2000). Critics call this "biopiracy" of indigenous assets and a serious threat to maintaining global biodiversity (Bender 2003; DeGeer 2003; Drahos 2000; Garcia 2007; Ho 2006; Latha 2009; Oyewunmi 2013; Stenton 2003). For

Table 1.1 Key Multilateral Policies Related to Natural Medicines

Year	Policy	Aim	Organization
1993	UN Convention on Biological Diversity (CBD)	Promote conservation and sustainability of biological diversity and seek fair and equitable benefits sharing in genetic resources (Convention on Biological Diversity 2020b)	UN CBD
1995	Agreement on Trade-Related Aspects of Intellectual Property Rights (TRIPS)	Institute a comprehensive, multilateral legal agreement on intellectual property (WTO 2020)	WTO
2000	WHO Traditional Medicine Strategy 2002–2005	Outline WHO's role and strategy for traditional medicine in health care systems (WHO 2002)	WHO
2001	Doha Declaration on the TRIPS Agreement and Public Health	Reaffirm right of WTO members under the TRIPS Agreement in order to protect public health and enhance access to medicines (WHO 2020b)	WTO
2003	Cartagena Protocol on Biosafety	Ensure biosafety from potential risks of handling, transporting, and using living modified organisms (Convention on Biological Diversity 2020a)	UN CBD
2008	Global Strategy and Plan of Action on Public Health, Innovation and Intellectual Property	Promote new thinking on innovation and access to medicines (WHO 2020e)	WHO
2009	WHO Traditional Medicine Strategy 2014–2023	Help member states to develop and implement policies and plans to strengthen the role of traditional medicine in health care systems (WHO 2013)	WHO
2010	Strategic Plan for Biodiversity 2011–2020	Promote the implementation of the objectives of the CBD (Convention on Biological Diversity 2020e)	UN CBD
2011	WIPO Re:Search	Support early-stage research and development against neglected tropical diseases, malaria, and tuberculosis (WIPO 2020)	WIPO
2014	Nagoya Protocol on Access and Benefit Sharing	Promote benefit sharing of genetic resources in a fair and equitable way (Convention on Biological Diversity 2020c)	UN CBD
2018	The Nagoya–Kuala Lumpur Supplementary Protocol on Liability and Redress to the Cartagena Protocol on Biosafety	Provide international rules and procedures in the field of liability to promote objectives of the CBD (Convention on Biological Diversity 2020d)	UN CBD

Note: World Health Organization (WHO), World Intellectual Property Organization (WIPO), and World Trade Organization (WTO).

millennia, natural medicines have been integral to human health in these societies, and, further, research and development into medicines has been shared in the public commons.

Consequently, knowledge about and innovations in these ancient traditional medicines have been maintained in an innovation commons, transcending national and institutional boundaries. Traditional medicine knowledge encompasses the theories and practice of medicine concerned with caring for holistic human health (the overall health of a person) and the prevention, diagnosis, treatment, and cure of illness. It is often contrasted with "modern" or "Western" medicine in that the latter tends to focus on treatment of disease after a person has already become sick. Traditional medicine is also called natural medicine as it avoids the use of synthetic chemicals and focuses on the body's natural immune response in the treatment of disease. The origins of natural medicine predate Western medicine by thousands of years and therefore focus on natural nonsynthetic chemical medicines. In the span of human history, synthetic chemical drugs are a relatively recent phenomenon in treating illness.

As discussed below, a handful of drug manufacturers—synthetic chemical pharmaceutical companies together called Big Pharma (so named due to their market dominance, high profits, and political influence)—have captured the global market for medicines. Part of this market capture has included creating a global intellectual property rights regime supposedly promoting innovation, arguing that without many decades of monopoly protections on patented drugs, investments into developing new medicines would not otherwise occur. Unable to patent nature, though not for want of trying, companies have opted to alter and manipulate naturally occurring chemical compounds into synthetic chemical drugs. The easiest way to copy natural chemical active ingredients is by observing how natural medicines have been used in treating patients, either directly or via referencing ancient medicinal texts. Also common has been the extraction of requisite biological materials from their natural ecosystems while bypassing stewards of the sustainable use of these materials. In the biological material extraction process, exploiting youth in poor rural communities has been problematic in India, as discussed in Chapter 4. For example, bioprospectors, in their search for biomaterials, typically pay local youth who might know the location of wild medicinal plants but lack the training to harvest sustainably or knowledge about why these materials are important community assets to be protected from unfair outside exploitation. Historical victims of this exploitation of resources in the commons include vast tracts of wild plants and ocean animals worldwide (Aoki 1998). More recently, in 2020, during the race to develop a Covid-19 vaccine, the world's population of sharks was threatened in the search for the adjuvant squalene, which stimulates immune response. Squalene is abundant in shark livers (Meneguzzi 2020).[17] As analyzed in the chapters that follow, rather than being protected and conserved, natural medicine knowledge and material resources have been extracted from the commons and used with impunity by Big Pharma.[18] The drive to maintain monopoly patents is behind this exploitation.

Patents in Perpetuity

The global market has failed to keep the innovation commons open and inclusive of knowledge stakeholders or to invest in the development of curative medicines. That the global pharmaceutical industry, as of this writing, on average invests 75 percent of research and development into miniscule, literally molecular-level, incremental changes to existing synthetic drugs exposes the fact that the current global innovation system is producing very little radical innovation in medicines, leading to stagnation. Instead, pharmaceutical companies are focusing on obtaining patents in perpetuity for drugs developed decades ago, themselves thanks ultimately to natural medicine and original sharing of discoveries about biologics in the innovation commons. In sum, under the pressure of market competition, unless they can patent it for profit, companies lack incentive to bring discoveries to society. With the increasing potential of biologics, we are in urgent need of innovation system reform, since ceding power over life itself by allowing nature to be patented would have dire consequences for the (plant medicinal) biodiversity of this planet and consequently for humanity. As Drahos (1999) has put it, "The scope of patentability is expanding while the role of moral standards in the operation of the patent system is being increasingly limited."

At the same time, poor and low-income households either cannot afford and/or lack access to Western mass-produced synthetic drugs, and persistent commodification of traditional herbal remedies puts upward pressure on prices and has led to overharvesting of medicinal plants. The future biodiversity of the earth from which healing medicines can be derived, therefore the stability of human health, is at stake. A number of investigative journalistic publications have exposed how so-called Big Bad Pharma uses its powerful political influence on national governments' foreign economic policies as well as within multilateral organizations like the World Trade Organization. In other words, powerful corporate interests use these fora to set the rules of the innovation game in their favor (Posner 2020). In this regard, the WTO became the arbiter of who gets to claim monopoly profit rights over innovation outputs. This has been in effect since the mid-1990s, as discussed below.

In response to market failure, national governments, especially in the developing world, face the dual challenges of supporting biopharmaceutical research and development to discover healing remedies and at the same time protecting national assets, including biodiversity in plant and other biological materials (Boldrin and Levine 2009). These challenges transcend national borders and have led countries to seek transnational and multilateral solutions—often in direct response to the capture of the WTO by Big Pharma.

For example, the voice of stakeholders in developing countries was excluded from the design of the WTO Agreement on Trade-Related Aspects of Intellectual Property Rights (TRIPS), discussed in detail in Chapter 2. The TRIPS fused international trade (i.e., access to US and European markets) to an IPR regime reifying exclusionary patents.[19]

In response, a transnational effort, led by nonprofits, community health organizations, and national governments representing developing countries in the Global South, led to amendments to the TRIPS allowing flexibilities in compliance with the agreement so that at-risk communities could access essential medicines at affordable prices.[20] Essential medicines are those necessary for basic health care needs of the population—for example, antibiotics and vaccines (WHO 2020c).[21] The movement also led to the establishment of public-private partnerships (PPPs) for essential medicine drug discovery and development. For example, the Medicine Patent Pool under the World Health Organization is one such PPP. TMK stakeholders have also turned to the United Nations.

Under the UN Convention on Biological Diversity (1993), pharmaceutical companies would have to disclose the origin of the plant genetic materials of compounds extracted from nature and natural medicines, while acknowledging the contributions of traditional medicine knowledge stakeholders. Efforts within the World Intellectual Property Organization have also been attempted. Unfortunately, without the carrot and stick of market access or exclusion afforded by the WTO, these efforts have had limited impact in stimulating investments into drug discovery inclusive of natural medicines and their stakeholders. Consequently, the global IPR regime resides de facto within the WTO under TRIPS (Sengupta 2019).

The global innovation system has thus become fragmented into issue areas controlled by multilateral organizations each claiming domain. These supranational organizations purportedly represent the interests of all nation-states and thus humanity writ large. Some have argued that the WTO in particular instead protects the vested interests of a small number of multilateral corporations (Drahos 2010; Matthews 2002). As discussed below, the study of innovation that is inclusive of the needs of human health transcends disciplinary boundaries. For example, national and multilateral politics and policy often guide and regulate the global system governing new drug discovery. Likewise, access to knowledge about natural medicines depends on the protection and conservation of TMK and plant medicinal biodiversity. Further, as the knowledge about traditional medicines is lost (discussed in Chapters 3 and 4), so is resistance to unsustainable use of plant medicinal materials. Figure 1.3 illustrates these disciplinary intersections and overlapping issue areas.

The current structure of the global innovation system reflects the increasing power of patent-centric IPR as governed by the WTO TRIPS. Meanwhile, we are witnessing a steady creep of patents further into the natural world. Namely, patents have been granted for biologics, extracting them from the public commons of material natural resources. This extraction benefits pharmaceutical companies mostly while neglecting overall human health.[22] As outlined in Figure 1.3, the complexity of the challenge of creating spaces for inclusive innovation is evident in the interconnectedness between policies governing the protection and conservation of medicinal plant biodiversity, access and benefit sharing in intellectual property rights, and the development of essential (natural) medicines for better human health. This study is at the center of the overlapping issue areas of biodiversity, human health, and intellectual property rights in a global context. For

**Figure 1.3   Natural Medicines in the Innovation Commons:
Issue Areas (multilateral organization domain)**

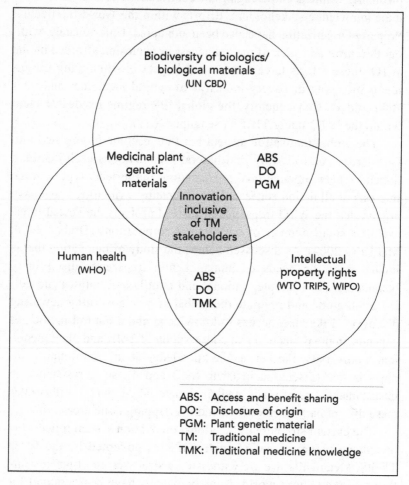

ABS: Access and benefit sharing
DO: Disclosure of origin
PGM: Plant genetic material
TM: Traditional medicine
TMK: Traditional medicine knowledge

example, biodiversity-related issues include such genetic materials as medicinal plants. The boundary-spanning issues of concern also relate to intellectual property rights in terms of who gets enriched at the expense of whom within a patent-centric global innovation system governed by IPR within the WTO TRIPS system.

In a November 2020 open letter to the WTO TRIPS Council, a transnational network of sixty-seven scientists, politicians, scholars, and activists called on the WTO member states to approve a waiver to TRIPS, granting permission to developing countries to access the patented vaccines at fair and equitable prices. Further, they called upon pharmaceutical firms to share the tacit know-how to produce Covid-19 vaccines and other critically needed Covid-19 diagnostics. Without this waiver, millions of people would die unnecessarily from Covid-19 (Baker et al. 2020). As of May 2021 lobbyists representing Pfizer and other pharmaceutical firms continued to block these appeals in the WTO (Fang 2021).

Among the key findings of the 2019 Global Innovation Index (Dutta, Lanvin, and Wunsch-Vincent 2019) was the need for more investment into medical innovation for health, as well as greater diffusion of existing innovations. The report further noted that while medical innovations were critical in reducing disparities in who gets access to health care on a global level, pharmaceutical research and development had continued to decline (Dutta, Lanvin, and Wunsch-Vincent 2019). Meanwhile, China had become the most prolific patentor in pharmaceuticals. The United States, China, and Japan led in biotechnology patent publications. At the same time India grew increasingly specialized in pharmaceuticals relative to other kinds of patents within its domestic innovation system.[23] The report speculated that the decline in medical innovations, despite the rising need for them, might reflect "fundamental structural problems within the biomedical innovation system and incentives facing public and private sector researchers" (Dutta, Lanvin, and Wunsch-Vincent 2019). In other words, the global structure for innovation had broken; it was not just a market failure but a global system failure.

Innovation Systems

An innovation system is comprised of the institutions and people creating and producing new goods and services for society and markets. Healthy innovation systems have certain features—for example, a capacity to generate new ideas. This activity should be self-sustaining over time. New ideas in the innovation system for drug discovery and development ideally contribute to improving quality of life, stimulating new investment, encouraging a healthy, stable workforce, and improving quality standards in new drug development.[24] Institutions within innovation systems include the rule of law, regulations, government policies, and so forth. Institutions and practices within healthy innovation systems operate at various levels: local, regional, national, transnational, and global. Healthy innovation systems are open to tacit knowledge exchange, learning by doing, and other ways in which knowledge is shared in an open and inclusive innovation commons. An innovation architecture is how structures cohere together and function to support innovation activities. For example, the nation-state has autonomy to make innovation policy decisions within domestic economies. States are limited by competition from other states within the international system as well as constrained by supra-national organizations, including the WTO, as mentioned previously.

Underexamined is how public- and private-sector actors, through collaborative spaces in emergent organizations (emergent in the sense that they are unique and not a copy of preexisting forms), some of them PPPs while others are more loosely networked, have sought to innovate our global innovation system for new drug (re)discovery. Leading transformative change in the global innovation system, thus improving innovation outcomes that serve human health, has been a priority for a variety of global actors. These include transnational networks of civic-minded actors through best-practice innovation architectures. PPPs, defined in detail in Chapter 2, are providing powerful lessons. These lessons are explored in historical-institutional detail in Chapters 3 (China), 4 (India), and 5 (Japan).

Research has found that certain transnational actors—those that have ample financial and human capital resources and also normative influence, for example, through their humanitarian vision—might be a basis for transformational change at the global level (Binz and Truffer 2017). It is at this intersection of the structures within the global political economy and the agency of individual national and transnational organizations that the study of inclusive innovation resides. That is, individuals and organizations pursuing innovation activity inclusive of human health and humanity in both outcome (who benefits) and process (who gets to participate) must navigate system-level rules and often powerful entrenched interests bent on maintaining exclusionary structures. Exclusionary practices are evident in the building of enclosures around innovation activities, the TISA anticommons outlined above. This includes Big Pharma attempts to patent nature, thereby fragmenting the global innovation commons. This behavior is not new.

Beginning in seventeenth-century England, privatization of land that had been underway for centuries was codified by Parliament in a series of "Enclosure Acts." Traditional rights to access lands shared in the commons for grazing animals were eliminated.[25] The enclosure of such modern intellectual property rights as codified in patents and copyrights is likewise the closing off of a resource from sharing within a public commons (Yu 2007; Boyle 2003; Runge and Defrancesco 2006).

Enclosure attempts are evident under the original version of the WTO TRIPS. Savvy business executives know that influencing the global standard setting—in other words, the rules of the game—of innovation is an effective way to ensure the longevity of their products and their sales revenues in global markets (e.g., through drug patent "evergreening"). Under the WTO TRIPS, for example, companies and countries unable or unwilling to comply with the patent monopolies on high-priced drugs and antibiotics can be excluded from exporting their goods and services to WTO member markets.[26] The WTO markets together make up most of the global economy. Ideally, the world needs a sui generis global innovation system comprised of an innovation commons for essential medicines.[27] Realistically, possible in the near term are meso-level improvements, including the inclusive innovation approach (sandboxes and pools within the TISA commons) exemplified by case studies of emergent organizations, including certain PPPs, analyzed herein. At the same time, the coronavirus pandemic has created an interstice of opportunity in the emergence of alternative ways of thinking about and doing innovation, which the emergent organizations analyzed herein exemplify. As such, their impact might prove closer to a Schumpeterian gale of creative destruction rather than leaving the system as is, in a state of innovation decline, by continuing to prop up the institutions of the status quo (Schumpeter 2005 [1942]). In other words, these emergent actors have become agents of change for the global structure of innovation. How are ideas about system transformation and actions to make it happen related?

First, the lens of emergent organizations, including PPPs in new drug discovery for natural medicines (biologics), is a way to reflect on the state of the field of the study of innovation in global context. Second, it shows the challenges nation-states and domestic actors are facing in succeeding, but sometimes failing, in the pursuit of innovation that matters for human health. The emergent organizations analyzed in subsequent chapters are focused on developing and rediscovering biologics that show promise to cure a range of diseases and conditions. It need not be mentioned that synthetic chemical drugs, comprising the vast majority of drugs on the market and in the R&D

pipeline of global pharma, have not lived up to the promises made by industry lobbyists.[28] Data on this is outlined in Chapter 2.

Toward an Open Architecture of Innovation

Since the twentieth-century rise of the global pharmaceutical industry, we have been conducting innovation for new drug discovery in separate, fenced-off spaces, the cages and silos of the TISA. Efforts to include local TMK stakeholders, for example, in bioprospecting for (new) natural drug compounds, have had a spotty track record. In the 1990s Costa Rica's national government was a first mover in this regard, bringing in Merck Pharma to bioprospect for natural chemical compounds in its biodiverse rainforest (Hammond 2015). Initially, the partnership received positive reviews in international media. After a time, it was found that the local stakeholders who were supposed to benefit had been excluded (Grifo and Rosenthal 1997). Within a decade, the project had collapsed. Observers speculated that the availability of substitute sources of biodiverse bio assets in other countries made the costs of Costa Rica's arrangement unattractive (Simpson 2019). Likewise, the US start-up Shaman Pharmaceutical and the WTO/WHO InBio had both gone defunct within a few years after launching, reflecting the difficulty of making local stakeholder inclusion economically viable. These high-profile failures make even more noteworthy the emergent inclusive innovation architectures in place within the case studies in natural medicine and new drug discovery analyzed in this book.

Multilateral (WTO, UN, WHO) and multinational (corporate social responsibility) activities often receive the most international press attention. Meanwhile, emerging transnational actors and networks—for example, those with global reach, including such partners as the Bill & Melinda Gates Foundation and the Wellcome Trust—may be having important impacts, without fanfare on the ground, with local communities in capacity and resilience building, establishing network synergies that lead over time to sustainable economic practices and even democratization, going beyond popularized "ecosystem services"[29] and the like. These and other philanthropies have held "grand challenges" to incentivize research and development into essential medicines. Similar efforts by other grassroots and transnational actors, illustrated by the case studies of inclusive innovation in the chapters that follow, provide insight into the local and global dynamics of stakeholder inclusion that is more than distributive in outcome.

Since so many of the most impactful discoveries of medicine were made by accident (e.g., penicillin), usually by bringing some outside knowledge, experience, or person to the project—a sandbox, not a silo—it follows that for a new generation of drugs and medicines, it makes sense to provide incentives to set various different talented minds to the tasks and to related activities from which novel, serendipitous discoveries can occur. In sum, the inclusion of diverse stakeholders in the innovation process can lead to new discoveries. Including more people in innovation sandbox activities is a first step.

The second way to coax players within the global innovation system into sharing a bit more in the innovation commons is creating shared pools of patented and proprietary libraries of compounds.[30] Japan's Global Health Innovative Technology Fund, discussed in Chapter 5, is a recent example of how to do this. Briefly, GHIT is a PPP backed by leading Japanese pharmaceutical firms in partnership with government ministries. GHIT researchers benefit from access to shared pools of heretofore underutilized and off-patent compounds. Participating researchers from around the world can access these resources in new drug discovery research and development. GHIT is focused on bringing new drugs and diagnostics to the developing world to treat endemic diseases, called neglected tropical diseases because they have attracted little attention from major pharmaceutical companies. They are "neglected" by Big Pharma because discovering treatments and cures for these diseases is unlikely to reap significant, if any, return on investment. The noblesse oblige of the global pharmaceutical industry died long ago, if it ever existed at all. Major multinational companies are discovering, however, that doing good actually does, in some cases, lead to doing well as first movers (see CIPLA in Chapter 4 and Takeda Pharmaceutical in Chapter 5). In other words, the right kinds of corporate social responsibility have on occasion led to serendipitous discoveries and thus improvements to the bottom line of profits (Falck and Heblich 2007; Preuss 2011).

An innovation boom in biopharmaceuticals has been underway in Asia as that region continues to grow into the center of the global economy (Baur et al. 2019). The empirical case studies focus on China,

India, and Japan for two reasons. First, China and India are both mega-biodiverse and have among the world's oldest documented histories of traditional medicine practice and scholarship, drawing from vast national natural medicine biological resources and deep medical knowledge. Second, despite these similarities, they have varied in their policies toward incorporation of their ample natural medicine expertise and plant genomic resources into modern drug discovery. Both China and India have launched new drug discovery policies incorporating TMK into R&D domestically and health diplomacy internationally. However, they have differed substantially in their approach to protection and conservation of the tacit knowledge and biological materials for natural medicine. Japan's small geographical size in comparison makes it resource dependent. Nevertheless, it also has a long lineage of traditional medicine. Its *kampo* (literally "Chinese drug") medicines depend almost entirely on plant materials from China. Japan's policy responses have thus been very different from those of China and India.

The TISA innovation sandboxes and resource pools outlined above in the context of discoveries in biologics have proven their viability on a limited scale, as evidenced by the case studies in the chapters that follow. Tackling the challenges involved in protecting and conserving the earth's living system biodiversity is beyond the scope of this book. Nevertheless, on a more limited scale, this book also explores ways in which local communities have partnered with national governments, supported by private foundations and firms, in collaboration with multilateral organizations to save our planet's critical natural plant medicinal resources for future generations of drug discovery. Before outlining the chapters in this book, I will provide a brief overview of the methods employed in this research.

Methods

The methods of this research include historical-institutional analysis of policies supporting open and inclusive innovation in new drug discovery, complemented by original case studies in Asia. Semi-structured interviews were conducted from 2016 to 2020 with government officials, representatives of non- and quasi-governmental organizations and foundations, entrepreneurs, and investors. I also engaged in participant observation at policy-related meetings, with PPPs, and in local community organizations, as well as with traditional medicine practitioners and inside medical clinics.

Interviews with local stakeholders, including natural and traditional medicine doctors, nonprofit organization founders, funders, community activists, government officials, and so forth, were conducted in the national languages of each country (directly by me in Japan; aided by interpreters and document translators in China and on occasion in India), supplemented with secondary sources including archival research (e.g., held by international foundations and in local repositories).[31] Limits of the analysis include lack of familiarity with indigenous dialects and languages of China and India, which would surely have added greater depth to the analysis. Other limitations include the absence of national-level, publicly available aggregate data on the total number of similar TMK-biodiversity-focused organizations, projects, and network activities, as well as a lack of standardized reporting of statistics of funds expended at regional and local levels on these activities, numbers of personnel involved, and to what degree this reflects national-level interest in these matters.[32] Nevertheless, local stakeholder perspectives are integral to the pursuit of effective policy and practice that is more substance than statement. This book attempts to fill some of these conceptual and empirical gaps.

Chapter Previews

Chapter 2 reviews the rise and fall of innovation in the pharmaceutical industry with reference to prior attempts at explaining how the current structure of global innovation came to exist and has since faltered in producing novel innovations. It then outlines the TISA framework to analyze innovation systems by their architecture (the way they are structured) and their contributions to developing new, novel products, including drugs and medicines. Subsequent chapters provide empirical context to apply the inclusive TISA innovation sandboxes and pools framework on the ground, evident within emergent organizations, in collaboration and sometimes conflict with the state.

The empirical chapters present organizational case studies of inclusive innovation in China, India, and Japan as a lens to analyze national-level policies contextualized within the global innovation system. Doing so provides a way to analyze, in a limited empirical context, nested levels of innovation—local, regional, national, and international—within a global system of innovation while at the same time transcending national and institutional boundaries. Chapters 3 to 5 (country-level empirical case studies) have the following layout. First, the chapters begin with a brief overview of the historical inter-relationships between natural (or "traditional") medicine and modern medicine discovery and development. I have written extensively else-where about the role of the national government in stimulating inno-vation in modern pharmaceuticals (Ibata-Arens 2019a). Here the focus is on the innovation (and pandemic preparation) potential of incorpo-rating biologics, including traditional medicinal stakeholders and stew-ards of medicinal plant biodiversity, into drug (re)discovery and devel-opment. Second, each chapter outlines how the state and private-sector actors have dealt with protection and conservation of medicinal plant biodiversity—and essential knowledge about it—for the purpose of maintaining plant genetic diversity in material resources for drug development and discovery. Third, through fieldwork-based original case study analysis, the role of innovation sandboxes and pools in structuring inclusive innovation practices is analyzed. Particular focus is on how local efforts have benefited from engagement inter-nationally, including with transnational-boundary-spanning actors connecting stakeholders with multilateral organizations and multina-tional corporations. The chapters conclude with possibilities for the future of inclusive innovation in and by the subject country. As such, a TISA analytical lens represents a meso-level step toward or founda-tion for reestablishing a global innovation commons for essential medicines.

The chapters that follow focus on looking forward in identifying and analyzing promising new intersections of people and institutions seeking transformative change in the way we innovate. Chapter 2 offers a glimpse back to how we got here, reviewing explanations for why we find ourselves in this situation of market and innovation fail-ure in the face of a global pandemic. The past is important for under-standing our present, and learning from it is a step toward transfor-mative change within institutions and calls to action to innovate for what truly matters for human health and by extension humanity.[33]

It might be that in looking forward we will see the possibilities for new innovation architectures or sui generis regimes that are neither purely private markets nor entirely public entities. What are the best practices in stimulating sustainable innovation in essential medicines? The cases analyzed herein reflect on three distinct approaches: working within the current system (accepting the structure as is) of prizes and grand challenges; proposals, as change agents, for a return to a global innovation commons or the creation of other sui generis systems; and something in between, a hybrid emergent organizational experiment evident in certain PPPs. Is it possible that hybrid organizational forms (emergent kinds of PPPs) between markets and states are the best option moving forward? Further, what is the role of such transnational actors as foundations, philanthropists, and nongovernmental organizations in facilitating these emergent processes? Analysis of the innovative organizational forms in Chapters 3, 4, and 5, followed by a call to action in Chapter 6, are helped by a look back in Chapter 2 to the rise and fall of innovation in twentieth-century drug development—namely, the global pharmaceutical industry and its relation to systems of innovation. The story begins with drugs.

Notes

1. The word *patent* derives from the Latin *patere* ("to lay open"), referring to a letter from a monarch granting some exclusive right. A letter of patent would be made available for the public to view.

2. Insulin was discovered by three scientists who donated their patent to the University of Toronto (selling their stake for $1 each for a total of $3). Eli Lilly repatented insulin in the United States (see Thompson 2018).

3. Pharmaceutical companies have also attempted to patent nature for monopoly profit, as will be discussed below.

4. A number of international collaborations were established to jointly develop treatments and/or vaccines for the coronavirus in 2020. Incentive mechanisms proposed to stimulate investments in vaccine development included megafunds, which were supranational to distribute investment risk (Vu et al. 2020). Other efforts included procurement (guarantees to purchase vaccines produced) (Paun 2020).

5. Not to mention defection from multilateral collaborations, exemplified by the United States' defunding of the WHO in 2020 (BBC 2020).

6. Anonymous sources in pharmaceutical companies confirm that given the race to patent and commercialize synthetic chemical drugs, the industry culture is one of secrecy (anonymous interviews 2018, 2019).

7. According to OpenSecrets.org, in 2020 the pharmaceutical industry spent more than $306 million lobbying US government officials. See "Pharmaceuticals/Health Products, Industry Profile: Lobbying, 2020, Graph, Annual Lobbying on Pharm/Health Prod, Total for Pharmaceuticals/Health

Products" (OpenSecrets.org 2021). Totals included $306,226,988 spent on behalf of 467 clients, represented by 1,502 lobbyists.

8. Historians have noted the role that patent agents, in their own pursuit of profit, had in persuading drugmakers to focus on obtaining patents (see also Moser 2013).

9. The differences between founding and successor generations of pharmaceutical industry leaders reflect the shift in innovation for medicines from a focus on patients to one that puts patient health secondary to profits.

10. The spread of antibiotic-resistant killer bacteria (e.g., methicillin-resistant staphylococcus aureus) was in part a result of the improper use and overuse of broad-spectrum antibiotics.

11. ACE inhibitors lower blood pressure by relaxing veins and arteries.

12. The Spanish flu of 1918–1919 killed up to 50 million people; in comparison, the viral disease HIV/AIDS, which has yet to have a vaccine, has killed up to 35 million since its outbreak in 1981 (LePan 2020).

13. One could say that pandemic disease has always afflicted human populations, intensifying with the movement of peoples across space, especially along trade routes (LePan 2020). The black death of the fourteenth century, a bacterial pandemic spread via rats and fleas, is estimated to have killed more than 200 million people, possibly 50 percent of the entire population of Europe at the time (Berezow 2014).

14. Synthetic drugs ingested by humans make their way into the water supply via sewage systems, with detrimental effects on wildlife.

15. For example, during the SARS1 pandemic (2002–2003) in China, Guangdong province was found to have the lowest mortality rate due to its reliance on traditional Chinese medicine–based treatment of patients.

16. Natural biologic medicines also include those derived from animals and microbes, as defined below.

17. Indicating the interest in the study of sustainable resource management of the commons, the *International Journal of the Commons* has published a number of articles on the subject (e.g., Lucchi 2013).

18. See Hoareau and DaSilva (1999) for a review of the use of medicinal plants in the pharmaceutical industry (Mgbeoji 2014).

19. See Boldrin and Levine (2008) for a discussion of IPR as stifling innovation and creativity.

20. See Karl Polanyi, *The Great Transformation*, for a historical-institutional analysis of societal response to state and market failure in times of crisis and volatility.

21. The WHO maintains a list of essential medicines.

22. For an overview of institutions involved in the governance of global health, see Harman (2012).

23. See Table T-1.1 in the 2019 Global Innovation Index for an overview of the top origins of health patent publications between the years 2010 and 2017 (Dutta, Lanvin, and Wunsch-Vincent 2019).

24. It need not be said that healthy workers are productive workers.

25. See "Enclosures," chap. 3 in Polanyi (1944).

26. Defenders of the TRIPS have argued that there was always economic disparity in who gets access to essential medicines and that the TRIPS system did not worsen it (Khair 2016).

27. Brown and Susskind (2020) discuss public health in the context of the Covid-19 pandemic as a global public good, or "GPG," that should be provided for through international cooperation.

28. Annually in the United States alone, the pharmaceutical industry spends more money on influencing politics in Washington, DC, and by extension Geneva, the seat of the WTO, than any other industry. Pfizer has been at the top of the list in this regard, spending more than $4 billion since 1998 (Frankenfield 2020).

29. So-called ecosystem services have been a way to incorporate the protection and conservation of the earth's biodiversity into liberal economic discourse—for example, how having a biodiverse ecosystem "services" our access to clean water.

30. Thaler and Sunstein (2008) refer to this as "nudging" (see also Thaler and Sunstein 2003).

31. Scholars of traditional medicine and the history of medicine have been instrumental in tracing the lineage of ancient, premodern, and modern medicine (see, for example, Ackerknecht 2016).

32. In most Western medical systems, traditional medicine is often referred to as alternative or complementary medicine, thus implying that Western medicine is the standard around which traditional medicine varies or that it supplements. As discussed in subsequent chapters, the definitions of traditional versus modern are more comprehensive in Asian countries.

33. For example, there is no doubt that Asian countries' experience with colonialism profoundly affected developmental innovations and trajectories, but this is beyond the scope of this book.

2

Twilight of the
(Big Pharma) Gods:
The Rise and Decline
of Innovation

The word *drug* is said to derive from the Old French *drogue* by way of the Middle Dutch *droghe vate*, which referred to barrels for storing dried medicinal herbs, an important trade good brought to Europe from Asia on Dutch trading vessels in the seventeenth century. Even today the majority of drugs on the market worldwide derive from natural medicines or are synthetic mimics of the active ingredients found in natural medicines (Chivian and Bernstein 2008; Escohotado 1999; Neergheen-Bhujun et al. 2017; Riddle 2002; Kong, Li, and Zhang 2009; Buhner 2002). For example, 50 percent of all drugs introduced to market between 1981 and 2006 were of natural origin (Kingston 2011). This includes 60 percent of anti-cancer and 75 percent of anti-infective drugs approved between 1981 and 2002 (Patwardhan and Vaidya 2010). Despite these natural origins, by the end of the twentieth century the global pharmaceutical industry had focused research and development (R&D) increasingly on synthetic chemical drugs, which have been easier to patent. Profitable synthetic chemical drugs are patented again and again in seeming perpetuity—a widespread tactic to extend patent monopoly profits with minimal additional investment. These repatented drugs are virtually identical copies of themselves. With this practice, firms are responding to the incentives of the patent system, which grants monopolies and thus extended profits on old innovations. In sum, the global innovation

33

system for drug development rewards incremental innovation, weakening the capacity and drive for novel radical innovations in medicines. Drug discovery and development has largely fallen into a predictable pattern of innovation siloing evident in the lower-left quadrant of the typology of innovation system architectures (TISA), characterized by low novelty and low openness (see Figure 1.1). The next section provides a brief overview of modern drugs and medicines, noting the rise and decline of innovation output in the global pharmaceutical industry since the mid-twentieth century.

Global Pharmaceutical Industry

"The best way to get a long-lasting blockbuster [drug] is to make sure it doesn't cure anything."[1]

An old marketing adage says that you either create new products for existing markets—or create new markets for the products you have on hand. In nineteenth-century Germany, the manufacturing process for making colored dyes for the textile industry produced numerous synthetic chemical by-products. German industrialists hit upon the idea that some of these chemicals might have potential as drugs for human consumption (Sneader 2005; Jones 2011). From this, the modern Western pharmaceutical industry was born.[2] Peruse most books written in English about medicine, and it would seem that all medicine, the practice of it, and the drugs and treatments within it originated in the Western world (Sneader 2005). In truth, the written record of the use of such medicines as medicinal plants goes back to West Asia circa 3000 BCE in Sumerian texts.[3] Since then, a vibrant intellectual tradition in medicine discovery and development has been documented throughout East, South, and West Asian civilizations.

The origins of medicine can be traced even farther back to prehistoric Mesopotamia (8000 BCE) in West Asia (including parts of modern-day Syria, Iraq, and Iran), where plants and other biological materials were formulated to heal a variety of identified disease conditions. This holistic healing focus continued for 10,000 years. This changed quite recently in the time span of human history (in the 1900s CE). By the twentieth century, in search of new markets, mostly German, French, and American drug companies were making a panoply of synthetic chemical compounds—then searching for potential disease conditions that could be treated with them. These markets matured over time, and by the turn of the twenty-first century, pharmaceutical companies were working with doctors and the US Food and Drug Administration (FDA) to create such new diagnoses (of previously unnamed or nonexistent medical conditions) as attention deficit/hyperactivity disorder and "anxiety disorder," which could be "treated" with their synthetic drugs (Hager 2019).[4] Some argue that for most of the twentieth century, pharmaceutical companies had been developing drugs and then inventing medical diagnoses for which the drugs could be prescribed (Moynihan and Cassels 2005). Profiting from real and imagined human sickness, pharmaceutical companies have also had advantageous relations, albeit not as extreme as in the United States, with drug regulators in Europe and elsewhere. Wherever there is money to be made on the sale of their drugs, you can find pharmaceutical industry lobbyists influencing national state policy.

A number of books have been written to explain how the global market for drugs, which by the 1990s was led by multinational companies producing drugs for high-income economies, has lost its innovative spark. Despite its growing profits and international political influence, the industry on the whole has failed to bring cures to market (Posner 2020), while being very good at selling drugs that mask symptoms of underlying conditions (Angell 2005; Moynihan and Cassels 2005; J. J. Li 2014). Others have warned about increased manufacturing quality problems since the production capacity for making drugs has shifted to countries including China and India for essential medicines like insulin (Gibson and Singh 2018; Eban 2019; Ibata-Arens 2019a).[5] Critics (Stiglitz 2006) have pointed out that most of the money supposedly spent on pharmaceutical research and development is instead put into marketing campaigns.[6] These include the direct-to-consumer advertising discussed below and also seminars to "teach" doctors about drugs to prescribe to their patients as medications, typically held in sunny, luxurious tropical resorts, convened during the dreary months of winter.[7]

By the 2000s, the focus of the Western pharmaceutical industry was on selling so-called lifestyle drugs (Ibata-Arens 2019b). Viagra for "erectile dysfunction" has made drugmaker Pfizer tens of billions of dollars since it was launched in 1998, and generations of Americans have taken Adderall and other amphetamines in part because they are perceived to be performance enhancing (Schwartz 2016; Mukherjee 2018).[8] In the United States, the only country other than New Zealand to allow direct-to-consumer drug marketing, patients ask their doctors for prescriptions of specific drugs by name, having heard about them via "infomercials" on the television or in print advertisements. Likewise, doctors read about new drugs in product-placement articles in industry journals and magazines, paid for by pharmaceutical companies (Posner 2020). The United States has been described as unique in the monetizing of each stage of the disease and related drug development pipeline. For example, rather than cures being offered for chronic conditions, symptoms are masked with analgesics, and when they eventually manifest as acute life-threatening conditions, they are then treated with high-priced specialty care.

Analyses of the drug pipeline have found that less and less innovation in new drug development is occurring with synthetic chemical drugs (J. J. Li 2014; Angell 2005), the mainstay of pharmaceutical industry drug research and development since the mid-twentieth century. In contrast, since the 1990s innovations have grown rapidly in biologics, including in the areas of genomic-based medicines, stem cells, and "reverse pharmacology." The latter is a misnomer because rather than contribute to new discoveries, it entails rediscovery of natural compounds proven effective in treating disease (Patwardhan 2005; Patwardhan and Gautam 2005).[9] As mentioned above, these natural medicines have been documented in traditional medicine texts (also referred to as books of remedies or pharmacopoeia) and practices going back millennia, when medicines were developed at patients' bedsides. These newly rediscovered medicines have potential to treat both chronic and acute illness with less toxicity than chemical drugs, for example, during the 2002–2003 severe acute respiratory syndrome (SARS) epidemic and the Covid-19 pandemic underway in 2020 (Ochs and Garran 2020; Rapaka et al. 2014).[10] Natural medicines also hold promise for treating neglected tropical diseases (NTDs) endemic to poor countries. As mentioned in Chapter 1, the "neglected" in NTDs refers to the fact that Big Pharma ignores the diseases of poor populations because they are unprofitable (Grover et al. 2012).[11] This neglect of patients in need, in favor of patients who can pay, is in marked contrast to the ethos of the pioneers of modern medicine, who shared their discoveries in the open, public commons by forgoing the opportunity to profit from them through monopoly patents. When asked why he did not seek to patent his discovery of the polio vaccine, Jonas Salk said that it belonged to the people, concluding with the oft-quoted "Could you patent the sun?"[12] In sum, the microbes for the polio vaccine are part of the natural world, to be shared with humanity, not patented for profit. For Salk, to do otherwise went against the natural order.

Meanwhile, affluent patients are traveling to medical spa resorts in places like Costa Rica, India, and Thailand. For less cost than a luxury vacation, Americans and Europeans are returning home with tans—and new knees, facelifts, and even babies born by surrogates (Kelley 2013). Scientific advances in stem cells and genomic-based precision medicine have sped the growth of medical tourism, replete with personal concierges and personalized medical treatments. In a perverse fashion, drug and medicine development has come full circle, returning to a focus on curing disease and improving overall health, but only for affluent patients. One could argue that if it had not been for the sharing in the global innovation commons of such revolutionary discoveries as insulin, penicillin, and vaccines, which were then commercialized and manufactured on a mass scale by pharmaceutical companies, the drug industry might have never become Big Pharma. Its industry size (companies with money to spend on lobbying for preferential government policies) and scope (global market dominance) mean that it is able to set global rules about who gets enriched by incrementally changed, marginally innovative innovations. Figure 2.1 shows the disparity in access to medicines.

Some argue that the US Orphan Drug Act (1983), which was intended to stimulate investments in innovation for rare diseases, has led to the creation of a "boutique medicine" industry, where patients receive curative therapies—but at extremely high cost (e.g., upward of millions of dollars per stem cell "dose"). "Orphan drug" designation allows, compared to other drugs, faster FDA approval and more years of monopoly patent protection. While 98 percent of drug compounds never get commercialized, those having "orphan drug" designation have become very profitable. In 2017 alone, 44 percent of all new FDA drug approvals had "orphan drug" designation, up from

Figure 2.1   Access to Medicines: Who Can Afford What?

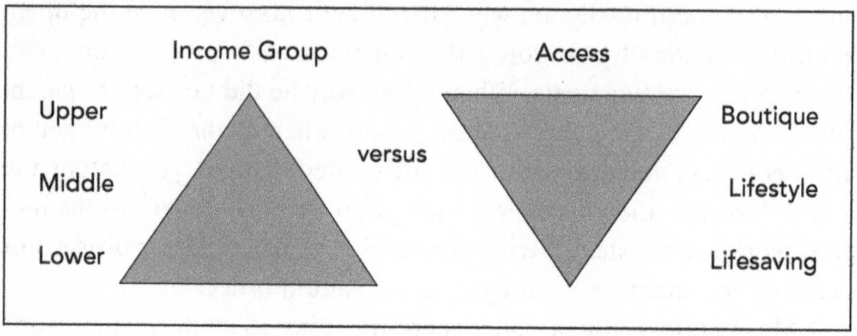

10 percent in 1998. In the meantime, the cost to patients rose considerably, from an average of $7,136 in 1998 to a whopping $186,758 by 2017 (Alsever 2020). Consequently, global pharmaceutical firms have responded to this market-based incentive by focusing on more profitable boutique medicines for patients who can afford them, with fewer investments in drugs for other kinds of patients—namely, the poor.[13] In sum, markets have failed to incentivize research and development for drugs for impoverished patients and, for that matter, for the majority of the world's population. The plight of the poor in the developing world has heretofore not prompted significant national investment.

After 1980, legislation encouraged in part by US pharmaceutical companies supported the enclosure of drug discovery into an anticommons, allowing monopoly owners to exclude others from accessing previously shared resources (Heller and Eisenberg 1998; Heller 1998). Extreme privatization in the anticommons increased transaction costs, as those wanting access to patented entities would have to pay, reducing access to potentially innovative and lifesaving information (Raghavan, Jain, and Jha 2013; see also Ostrom 1990). Global pharmaceutical firms have often been accused of violating business ethics in using their monopoly patents to charge high prices for medicines by extending patent monopolies via "evergreening" (also referred to as "me-too") tactics.

Typical justifications in support of patent-based intellectual property rights (IPR) argue that (pharma) firms need to protect their substantial investments into new drug development through patents that grant them a (typically twenty-year) monopoly on product sales.

Without patent-granted monopoly rights, the argument goes, firms would not invest in potentially lifesaving new drug development. The market tells a different story.

The largest growth in global pharmaceutical sales, reflecting the foci of R&D investments, has been in analgesics, including opioids, and oncology drugs. The first mask symptoms of underlying medical conditions, while the latter prolong life. Both create an extended time-line of repeat customers, the golden rule in ensuring firm longevity. Neither, on the whole, offers cures. Other studies have indicated that supposed investments into new drug research and development have instead been spent on marketing (minor molecular modifications of) existing drugs (Thompson 2018; J. J. Li 2014; Angell 2015).

International scandals, including Mylan's price increase, from $100 to $600, of the lifesaving EpiPen, manufactured by Pfizer and used for emergency treatment of allergic reactions and asthmatic attacks, and so-called patent troll Martin Shkreli's 2015 "overnight" price increase, from $13.50 to $750, of the antiparasite drug Daraprim (Shkreli was later jailed for fraud on a separate charge), have drawn scrutiny of the current patent-centric IPR regime, which has led to price gouging and, further, to fragmentation of the innovation com-mons (Holtz 2016; Kozarich 2016; Walters 2016).[14] The tide of public opinion began to turn against the image of a pharmaceutical industry no longer reified as a lifesaver.

Big Pharma Lobby Versus Humanity

Fearing the destabilizing effects of transformative change, private industry first attempts to maintain the status quo in its position within global power hierarchies. PhRMA, the industry lobbying organization of the global pharmaceutical industry, has exerted its influence in Washington, DC, and in the World Trade Organization (WTO). Even so, the power of public voices with a moral compass in the court of public opinion has, on occasion, with the agency of activists and organizations, forced Big Pharma to retreat. This occurred in 1998 when Nelson Mandela, then head of state of South Africa, was sued unsuccessfully by Pfizer and a reported thirty-eight other (pharmaceutical) companies for trying to purchase HIV/AIDS antiretrovirals at affordable prices. To sue a humanitarian leader for trying to save lives crossed a normative line (Nilsson 2017). Further, the debacle demonstrated that the privatized, global patent-centric intellectual property rights regime was at odds with public health.

A 2013 joint report by the World Health Organization (WHO), World Trade Organization, and World Intellectual Property Organization (WIPO) noted the need for effective transnational innovation networks to help build domestic innovation capacity in medicines within developing countries. The report noted that the African Network for Drugs and Diagnostics Innovation was one example of such a transnational innovation network (WHO, WTO, and WIPO 2013). Stiglitz (2006), in an essay on inclusive innovation, pointed out that 90 percent of the R&D by (big) pharmaceutical firms has been for lifestyle drugs (e.g., Pfizer's Viagra), serving the "needs" of the top 10 percent of wealthy consumers, mainly in advanced industrialized countries. Meanwhile, the investment pyramid hierarchy shows that the health of the poorest 90 percent of the world's population has been ignored. Neglected diseases (e.g., tuberculosis) disproportionately affecting people in low-income countries receive little R&D attention, and existing drugs (e.g., HIV/AIDS drugs) are not made available at affordable prices to those countries. The 2013 WHO-WTO-WIPO joint report cited a 2011 study (Stevens et al. 2011) finding that nearly all vaccines introduced in the previous twenty-five years had resulted from initial research results shared in the public innovation commons by public-sector research institutions. In the United States, even the so-called blockbuster drugs (those with high sales and profits) depended on National Institutes of Health and other government funds for their very existence. That is, instead of innovating themselves, pharmaceutical companies have obtained new drugs via acquisition of national-government-funded university innovations and small start-ups (Angell 2005). Discussing vaccines, the 2013 report also noted that since immunity is typically obtained with a low number of doses, ongoing (repeat customer) profits are limited; thus vaccines have been ignored by Big Pharma, the Covid-19 pandemic notwithstanding. Despite these limitations within the market, societal groups have responded, lobbying their national governments and multilateral organizations for access and benefit sharing in the development of new medicines.

Promises and Limitations of Current Research

How can we explain the precipitous decline in innovation per dollar spent in the global pharmaceutical industry? This book uses case studies as a lens to explain this lack of inclusive innovation and proposes ways to build it.[15] Relevant to understanding the origins of the global innovation system for new drug discovery, but beyond the scope of this book, are studies of the history of medicine, its bifurcation over time into traditional and modern (Apffel-Marglin and Marglin 1990), and the displacement of indigenous health and medicine practices resulting from colonialism (Connor and Samuel 2001; Kanagarathinam 2018; Yip 2009; Brimnes 2004). There is also a diverse legal literature on the intersection of law with multilateral treaties and governance of resources in the public commons (Maskus 2000; May 2009; Sell 2002).

A body of research has questioned assumptions that patents encourage innovation (Heller and Eisenberg 1998; Jaffe and Lerner 2011; Mansfield 1986; Shapiro 2000) and, more broadly, whether the patent-centric closed innovation system architecture is good for radical innovation (McManis 2009; Crampes and Langinier 2009).[16] Others have criticized how the current global IPR regime reinforces inequality, as the poor cannot afford today's commodified health technologies (Sell and Williams 2020). In the past patents had been granted exclusively to synthetic—that is, not naturally occurring—new molecular entities. In recent decades, patenting has crept into the natural world. This privatizing of the global commons sustaining natural resources includes attempts to monopolize the use of naturally occurring compounds (as long as they are "artificially" extracted), including vitamins and parts of whole persons (e.g., genetic markers).

Further, the present architecture of the global IPR regime reflects power asymmetries as much as, or more than, it provides a framework to enable innovation, though patents are often used (by me included) as a proxy to measure innovative output. Patents grant temporal monopolies of exclusive right to profit from an innovation recognized as "novel." In a sense, the current structure in terms of the rules of the global IPR regime contradicts the tenets of both competition and innovation. Antitrust law, for example, is said to facilitate competition by preventing and breaking up monopolies. Patents grant them. Further, patent-centric IPR undermines the innovative process. It is a sequential decision process on the part of existing innovators who have been granted patent protection (incumbents), limiting access on the part of new entrants. The system is thus rife with "intertemporal inconsistency" (Crampes and Langinier 2009). New entrants demand that the doors be open in terms of the open sharing of information, but once a patent is granted, they demand that the protective door of patented IPR be shut tightly behind them. It follows then that keeping the doors open would enhance innovation flows, creating the ideal sandbox for flourishing innovative activity in the global innovation commons.

Innovation Architecture

Meanwhile, the idea of innovation architecture has gained attention in the fields of engineering (Gawer 2014), information science (Fishenden and Thompson 2013; Wareham, Fox, and Giner 2014; Boudreau 2010), and network theory (Tsujimoto, Matsumoto, and Sakakibara 2014; Fowler and Christakis 2010; Christakis and Fowler 2013; Shu et al. 2012). Similarly, Ibata-Arens (2019a) proposes an innovation typology for developing economies of mitigated openness within a "networked technonational" framework reflecting a Janus paradox of either being open and exposed to global competition or closed and left behind in the race to innovate.

Heeks, Foster, and Nugroho (2014), in a citation analysis of publications about inclusive innovation, found that not only did they lack a specific conceptual lens or theoretical framework, but only a handful of studies to date had been published prior to 2007, and the number of studies overall peaked in 2013 (at 164 total publications). According to Saha (2016), in early studies that took place in the 1970s, inclusive innovation became a focus of research at universities in Europe. These early research collaborations resulted in some of the first publications to address the relationship between innovation and development (Singer et al. 1970). Forty years would pass before a follow-up volume was published from this research initiative (STEPS Centre 2010).

Scholars across disciplines have identified best-practice models of inclusion, while making policy recommendations to development organizations. These works were represented in two special issues in the journal *Innovation and Development* (K. J. Joseph 2014a, 2014b). Included in the issues are evaluations of top-down and bottom-up approaches to inclusion. Multilateral organizations, including the Organization for Economic Cooperation and Development (OECD), have also examined inclusivity in relation to innovation, growth, and development (OECD 2012). The 2012 OECD report "Innovation and Inclusive Development," distinguishes innovation for the poor (bottom of the pyramid [BOP]) from that by the poor, noting that "frugal" or "inclusive" innovation pertains to the former, while "grassroots" innovation reflects the latter.

Likewise, Rauniyar and Kanbur (2010) distinguish inclusive growth from inclusive development, as the former comprises income, while the latter includes distribution and improvements in other dimensions of social well-being, including access to food, clean water, and health care. In an article evaluating inclusive innovation models, Botha, Grobbelaar, and Bam (2016) take an applied approach and offer a meticulous and comprehensive literature review and typology of methods. Again, the authors find most inclusive innovation efforts to date target customers at the bottom of the pyramid (e.g., with cheaper, stripped-down, or "lean" versions of existing mobile phones and computers). BOP consumerism is contrasted with developmental approaches that empower and provide opportunities to improve well-being at the base of the pyramid (e.g., micro lending for small-scale entrepreneurship). Responding to the observation that much of the extant research has focused on inclusiveness as distributive to the poor and marginalized, rather than empowerment by the poor, Heeks, Kintu, and Shah (2013) and Heeks, Foster, and Nugroho (2014) propose a hierarchy of levels, or "ladder," of inclusive innovation (Heeks, Foster, and Nugroho 2014, Figure 2). The ladder is aspirational in that, at lower rungs, the basis for inclusivity is the intention of a given innovation to address the needs of marginalized groups. At mid-tier rungs, inclusion of heretofore excluded groups in the process (i.e., the research and development) of innovation is key. At the top of the ladder is an inclusive structure of innovation, as well as inclusivity in the discourse about innovation.

Heller and Eisenberg (1998) note that the "tragedy of the commons," or overuse of such common resources as water access, led to the increased privatization of assets that would otherwise be shared.

Likewise, patents in pharmaceuticals are removing from the innovation commons biomedical discoveries (e.g., those funded heavily in the United States by the federal government). Previously, novel contributions to science and biomedicine were shared freely in the innovation commons within the public domain (the sandboxes of the upper-right quadrant of the TISA in Figure 1.1) (Ostrom 1990; Agrawal and Ostrom 2006; see also Cole and McGinnis 2014). The aforementioned review of literature about structuring innovation activity that generates discoveries of importance for humanity rather than narrowly serving the interests of a handful of private companies is diverse and complex. How can we get from theory to practice, from thinking about the problem to actively working toward solutions? That is, in seeking transformative change, is there a better way to analyze and apply what we know about how innovation works in practice?

The Typology of Innovation System Architectures: A TISA Framework

Innovation systems can be characterized in two ways: first, how closed or open they are vis-à-vis information and resource exchange; second, how much they produce new, so-called novel contributions, for example, to economic development and improving health. This yields four main variations in the way innovation activities are structured (the architecture of innovation)—arranged across quadrants in an x-y axis typology of high to low novelty (vertically along the y-axis) and closed to open exchange (horizontally along the x-axis). The typology of innovation system architectures was introduced in Chapter 1 and illustrated in Figure 1.1.

In the lower-left quadrant lies low novelty and closed exchange (TISA silos), resulting, for example, in the aforementioned patent evergreening and "me-too" drugs. The twentieth century held such promise in so-called new molecular entities derived from synthetic chemical compounds that were supposed to cure life-threatening cancer and chronic conditions including diabetes. Instead, the use of patents to wall off potential knowledge exchange from the commons has led to less innovation in bringing healing medicines to market and deincentivized research into developing cures for the ailments affecting most of the world's population. For example, generic medicine manufacturers in India have often complained that Western pharmaceutical companies have refused to share know-how or tacit knowledge about the process of producing medicines, even after the drug patents have expired. Meanwhile, as outlined in Chapter 1, scientists have forecasted that the world will face pandemics more often while at the same time losing potential natural medicines to cure the diseases that cause them.

High novelty but closed information exchange characterizes the upper-left quadrant (TISA cages) of the innovation system typology. The cage metaphor seems apt for a quadrant where novel discoveries are prevented from being shared in the commons. Trade secret recipes or formulations are typical products in that quadrant. Proprietary formulations in traditional medicines have been tailored to individual patients and are thus difficult, if not impossible, to scale. As such, dynastic families of traditional medicine knowledge holders have struggled to maintain succession (in China, called *inheritance*), and the quotidian knowledge about medicines is dying out. Making matters worse, the plant genetic resources dependent on global biodiversity are being lost due to unsustainable overharvesting, changing land-use patterns, and shifts in climate, leading to species extinction. Chapters 3 (China) and 4 (India) offer stories of the individuals and organizations leading efforts to save this knowledge and these natural resources before they are gone forever.

The low novelty yet open exchange in the lower-right quadrant of the typology (TISA pools) is exemplified by peer-to-peer sharing of known discoveries, sometimes referred to as the sharing economy. Digital medicine and big data have been used on platforms that share patient data, enabling crowdsourcing of diagnosis for rare, difficult-to-discern disease conditions. Open-source mobile applications have enabled medical personnel in developing countries to better treat patients. In new drug discovery, sharing of compound libraries has supported research into treatments. Case studies in this regard are examined in Chapters 4 (India) and 5 (Japan).

High novelty with open exchange of discoveries characterizes the innovation commons (TISA sandboxes), situated in the TISA upper-right quadrant. Such an innovation commons approach—sharing knowledge for novel contributions for the public good—as that applied within the Human Genome Project (HGP) led directly to the innovation capacity of the China project team that was able to rapidly map the genetic sequence of the SARS virus, enabling lifesaving development of diagnostics and treatments, contributing to ending that epidemic in 2003.[17] This open innovation architecture then led to the establishment of one of China's fastest-growing start-ups, Beijing Genomics Institute (Ibata-Arens 2019a). Unfortunately, China's rising technonationalism, equating national security with technological advancement, in the years since its participation in the HGP has discouraged international collaborations. During the global coronavirus pandemic that began in 2020, lacking a global commons approach, countries for the most part competed instead of collaborated in disease response, mitigation, treatment, and vaccine development. The result was to be expected: the advanced industrialized world would have access to a relatively safe and effective Covid-19 vaccine, but one that required complicated and costly storage and transportation at subzero temperatures. The Pfizer/BioNTech Covid-19 vaccine initially required storage at a temperature of $-70°C$, which is colder than Arctic winters. Less developed countries, particularly those in the sights of China's Belt and Road Initiative (Ibata-Arens 2019a), would receive the Chinese Sinovac inoculation, far more affordable than the Pfizer/BioNTech one but with questionable safety and efficacy as of this writing.

To help explain the limits of the current global innovation system architecture for inclusive innovation in new drug discovery, it is useful to start by defining concepts related to innovation and to analyzing how innovation works, or sometimes fails to work properly, in bringing new products and services to society that do more good than harm.

Clarification of Terms

The ideas behind inclusive innovation reviewed above have had applications across a variety of fields. Here are terms relevant to the study of inclusive innovation in general and innovation of drugs and medicines in particular. *Innovation* refers to the introduction of new (novel) products and services to markets and society. Innovations are considered to be "novel" if they are new or unique—for example, a newly introduced drug that did not exist before and thus can be patented and its intellectual property (IP) protected. Innovations can be radical (completely novel) or incremental, minor improvements to existing goods and services. The latter also includes process innovation—for example, improvement in the way some extant product is made. *Closed innovation* is exclusive. It refers to information and other resource exchange enclosed within a given boundary (e.g., within firms or other entities) for the purpose of developing new products or services. *Open innovation* is unfettered information and other resource exchange for the purpose of developing new products or services. Open innovation reduces barriers to participation in research and development activities (removing the fence around the sandbox).

An *innovation sandbox* is structured play. It involves creation or exchange of ideas and knowledge within a defined set of research partners, as in public-private partnerships (PPPs), for new drug discovery. An *innovation pool* is characterized by sharing between select stakeholders of old, typically codified knowledge. For example, it includes the sharing of patented compounds on a limited (e.g., nondisclosure, noncompete) basis. An innovation pool can be closed, for example, protecting the IP of secret compound libraries, or open, as in compound libraries shared in the commons. An innovation sandbox and pool framework draws from the strengths while responding to the weaknesses of the four kinds of innovation architectures, as shown in the typology of innovation system architectures.

Inclusive innovation is intentional in that in addition to reducing barriers to entry, it invites previously excluded stakeholders to participate in research and development activities, as well as sharing of the benefits from innovation (invitations to play in the sandbox). Inclusive innovation incorporates new or previously excluded stakeholders (e.g., local firms and people) in the process of innovation activities. "Inclusive" can also refer to the distribution of welfare to the needy or the targeting of low-income individuals for the consumption of new products, thereby sharing in the benefits of innovation (profits, education, capacity, and skills improvement), as discussed above. The inclusive innovation examined in this book is focused on the former: the innovation activity itself rather than the welfare-based distribution of the resulting output. Now to the specifics of inclusive innovation in the context of new drug discovery.

Biologics are typically large, complex molecules (e.g., microorganisms, plant-derived natural chemical compounds) produced only by living systems. Biologics also include genomics and related agents.[18] *Drugs* are natural or synthetic chemical compounds used to affect the physiology of the body. Examples include naturally derived opium and synthetic fentanyl. Natural drugs are large, complex molecules used as drugs, derived from plant and other biological materials. Only living systems can produce them. Examples include microbes as the base for antibiotics (e.g., penicillin), gene-based therapies in precision medicine, and opium, an opiate, which is derived from poppies.[19] Natural drugs are a type of biologic. *Synthetic chemical drugs* are small, single-molecule compounds identified through chemical synthesis. Recent studies have found that such synthetic drugs as opioids (oxycodone, fentanyl) have higher toxicity and more addictive properties than natural drugs (Editors of *Time* 2019).[20] Chemicals occur naturally in living things but remain natural only if extracted without the use of synthetic chemical methods. *Medicines* are natural or synthetic chemical compounds for treating disease. All medicines are drugs, but not all drugs are medicines.[21] Figure 2.2 illustrates these distinctions.

Pharmaceuticals refers to medicinal drugs, but in recent decades pharmaceutical drugs have been used increasingly recreationally and/or as lifestyle drugs. That is, they have been used not for treating a specific disease condition but rather to alter mood in the recreational sense. *Vaccines* are preparations of living or dead microorganisms administered to stimulate immunity to disease.[22] The word *vaccine* is from the Latin *vacca* (cow), as the first vaccine in the Western world was invented to protect from smallpox by inoculating subjects with cowpox. *Immunization*, whereby the body becomes immune to a pathogen, results from vaccination. Before applying these concepts in inclusive innovation to potential innovations in new drug discovery, it helps to situate the current state of the global innovation system within debates about sharing natural medicine discoveries in the commons.

Innovation in the Drug (Re)Discovery Pipeline: Commons and Anticommons

Innovation is discovery of the adjacent possible. In other words, it is the result of harnessing ideas and resources unknown previously (at least to the entity claiming IPR). In an innovation architecture closed off by patents, the anticommons of enclosure within the TISA, the adjacent discoverable becomes impossible to access. Shrinking biodi-

Figure 2.2   Drugs and Medicines Composition

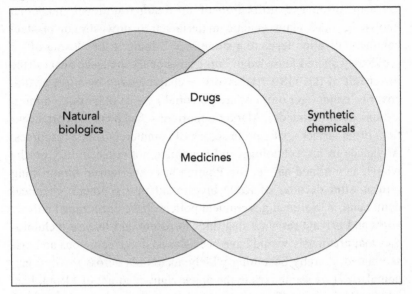

versity and increased demand by consumers in advanced industrialized economies for nonchemical, "natural" medicinals have also led to misappropriation of indigenous material and knowledge resources. As societies develop economically, access to Western medicine, in addition to provision of "modern" treatments, signals elevation in status hierarchies as these are more costly than traditional treatments. This evolution has transferred power from the healer to the medicine, reflecting the now dominant Western medical practice of allopathic (narrowly focused on disease condition) treatment, displacing previous millennia of holistic (overall patient health) treatment. In this manner, medicine has been removed from culture, its sociocultural context, and extracted from the commons (Pordié 2010). As these tangible and intangible resources of medicine and the traditional knowledge about it are lost, potentially healing discoveries are lost with them. In 2015 up to 290,000 plant species alone (other biologics include microbes) had yet to be screened, potentially yielding an estimated 653 drug candidates. Overall, 95 percent of the world's biodiversity had not been evaluated by modern scientific methods (David, Wolfender, and Dias 2015). Meanwhile, each year tens of thousands of species are vanishing forever due to biodiversity loss.

The current global intellectual property rights regime governing the acquisition and utilization of upstream traditional medicinal knowledge and plant genetic materials into downstream product commercialization leads to a silo effect. Siloing is the closing off of previously shared knowledge into exclusionary enclosed spaces (the lower left of the TISA framework is characterized by silos, as discoveries cannot get out; nor are potential new or rediscovered innovations allowed inside). Market opportunity has pushed pharmaceutical firms farther upstream in search of commercializable resources. Advances in biotechnology and genomics notwithstanding, on the whole, as outlined above, Big Pharma has experienced diminishing returns after decades of R&D investment into synthetic chemical compounds.[23] National government policies have encouraged universities and private research institutes to patent and license technologies that previously would have been shared in the commons and disseminated, thereby becoming widely accessible across institutional boundaries (via sandboxes in the upper-right quadrant of TISA). Paradoxically, in their effort to commercialize science and technology in the private sector, national governments have exacerbated fragmentation of the innovation commons by creating incentives not to share but to sell.

Findings reported in 2010 by the United Nations, describing the urgent need to reduce biodiversity loss, including that of medicinal plants, lest an "irreversible tipping point" be passed, coincided with the adoption in 2010 of the Nagoya Protocol, seeking fair and equitable benefits sharing in the use of genetic resources in order to support conservation and sustainability of biodiversity outlined in the UN Convention on Biological Diversity (Buck and Hamilton 2011; Convention on Biological Diversity 2010; Watts 2010). Since 2010, there has been mixed success in conserving biodiversity and protecting the indigenous communities of traditional medicine relying on these ecosystems. Anecdotal stories about cases of biodiversity stewardship referring to initiatives in Hawaii and Costa Rica have been cited for potential best practice in government-private-sector partnerships facilitating innovation in healing biopharmaceuticals while protecting the indigenous communities from which discoveries emerge (Jonge 2013).[24] This praise has sometimes been erroneous as the failed Costa Rica–Merck bioharvesting partnership shows, mentioned in Chapter 1.

Another infamous story in this regard is the exploitation of the bark of the tiki uba tree, indigenous to the Brazilian Amazon and used by the Urueu-Wau-Wau tribe. A 1988 *National Geographic* article about the endangered future of the tribe included a photo of the tree, noting its anticoagulant properties. While not citing a medicinal use, the article noted that hunters had used an extract from the bark on their arrows to disable prey. Someone at Merck read the article and paid the photographer to collect samples of the bark. From this, Merck got a profitable drug. The Urueu-Wau-Wau tribe went extinct, having been exposed to outside illnesses during the bioharvesting of its resources, which had been accessible to all in the commons (Dalevi 1997).

Presently, the global structure governing who gets to claim ownership of, and therefore decide on who benefits from, plant medicinal knowledge is firmly in the grip of suprastate multilateral institutions, including—as discussed above—the WTO and its Agreement on Trade-Related Aspects of Intellectual Property Rights (TRIPS) regime.[25] Despite revisions to the TRIPS, supposedly introducing flexibilities for developing countries, biopiracy of both medicinal knowledge and biological materials persists. Mgbeoji (2006) outlines how pharmaceutical and other corporations have exploited sociocultural, institutional, and legal systems in their biopiracy, not least of which is the deeply ingrained, spiritually embedded religious and cultural practice within indigenous communities of sharing their knowledge with others in an open innovation commons.

It need not be said that much of the pharmaceutical innovation in the twentieth century relied—using the terms laid out in the TRIPS—on the inventiveness, novelty, and subsequent product application of formulations from folk medicines to ancient materia medica (Stiglitz 2006). Few drug companies selling these natural medicine innovations acknowledge the contributions of traditional medicine knowledge stakeholders, and even fewer of the latter have reaped any significant financial reward for their role in improving human health. Echoing empirical findings critical of how truly innovative pharmaceutical companies have actually been, critics charge that the vast majority of so-called Western innovation has in fact been merely imitation of pre-existing medicines (Sahai, Pavithran, and Barpujari 2007).

The WTO Doha Declaration, outlining exceptions for member states under TRIPS enabling access to essential medicines, and the

UN Nagoya Protocol resulted in part from lobbying by local community stakeholders. A 2017 WHO report on access in Southeast Asia to medicines noted that it was important to remain vigilant in the face of "TRIPS-Plus" provisions extending patent terms and exclusion of local stakeholders from accessing data. The WHO has since been involved in efforts to ensure "TRIPS flexibilities" are followed in actuality, ensuring access to (generic) medicines by developing countries ('t Hoen et al. 2018).

Providing mechanisms and incentives to share data in the innovation commons is key not only for improving human health (the outcome or distributive side of inclusive innovation) but also for the incorporation of essential quotidian local traditional medical knowledge from stakeholders (e.g., dynastic families of medicinal plant cultivators, traditional medicine doctors, apothecaries) into the upstream input side—involving both credit sharing where it is due and benefit sharing of profits derived from the development of new medicines. It should be noted that scholars have criticized the commodification of traditional knowledge and medicinals as falling into the trap of a neoliberal discourse that seeks to marketize and privatize the earth in its entirety (McAfee 2003). The WHO, WTO, and WIPO (2013) have since suggested a variety of incentives to encourage inclusion of knowledge about natural medicines into modern-day drug development, including grants, prizes, tax credits, patent pools, and public-private partnerships. As such, the field is ripe for theorizing and empirical research on the efficacy of the policy experiments initiated in recent decades. Table 2.1 outlines policies by level and exclusivity versus inclusivity at various levels of the global economy.

Internationally standardized empirical data on these developments has been limited. Nevertheless, a growing body of legal studies has traced the history of international treaties governing access and benefit sharing of natural-medicine-related resources, assessed the efficacy of such treaties, and noted the power disparities between those making the rules and the local stakeholders subject to them (A. K. Gupta 2004; R. K. Joseph 2010; Kamau, Fedder, and Winter 2010; Morgera and Tsioumani 2010; Nijar 2013a, 2013b; Rosenthal 2007; Ramdas 2012; Sarnoff and Correa 2006). Some progress has been made mapping biological resource-to-patent and product-innovation links in pharmacopoeia across country contexts but has been limited by lack of funding (H. Li 2015; Utkarsh 2003). Without some kind of interven-

Table 2.1　Innovation: Levels of Policy and Practice

	Exclusive	Inclusive
Global	WTO TRIPS	Access and benefit sharing, Doha Declaration (WTO), Nagoya Protocol (UN)
National	TRIPS compliance	TMK registries, legal challenges to patents, pursuit of TRIPS flexibilities
Private/industry	Patent monopolies and trolls	Informed consent, corporate social responsibility
Local	Biopiracy (of traditional medicinal knowledge and materials)	Equitable stakeholder inclusion

tion, at the level of multilateral organizations, national policy, and/or civil action, potential cures will continue to be lost in unknown numbers. Glimmers of hope can be found in certain emergent organizations engaged in inclusive innovation for new drug discovery and plant medicinal conservation, analyzed in Chapters 3, 4, and 5.

An open and inclusive innovation system would be instrumental in protecting humanity from the next global pandemic through rapid diagnosis, response, and development of treatments.[26] Advances in the use of biologics (biological materials including microbes and stem cells) point to a potential renaissance in tapping into deep knowledge about medicinal plants—before their biodiversity goes extinct. Unfortunately, the pharmaceutical industry, opposed to an open innovation commons for new drug discovery, has lobbied fervently to keep patents and the patent-centric global IPR regime off limits to calls for innovation system reform.

To date, multilateral agreements upheld as best practice in access and benefit sharing and biodiversity conservation have been negotiated between pharmaceutical companies and such national governments as Costa Rica. While a commendable first step toward real inclusion, these agreements have since been criticized for excluding local stakeholders from negotiations over benefit sharing and therefore from profit sharing, as mentioned in Chapter 1 (Prathapan and Rajan 2011). In short, the individuals and groups with the most historical and quotidian knowledge of the plant ecosystems and use of materials in healing medicines have been the least included in the very policies purported to protect them. A next step would be to improve the governance (oversight and monitoring) allowing for bio-prospecting, including the extraction of information about herbal medicinals, while discouraging biopiracy. Findings indicate that those access and benefit sharing arrangements with an architecture inclusive of local stakeholders—traditional medicine cultivators and traditional knowledge practitioners—may represent an effective upstream-downstream relation that promotes innovation while conserving the viability of local communities of knowledge and biodiversity. The Honey Bee Network examined in Chapter 4 is one such example.

Cultural arguments have noted that traditional medical doctors hail from a history of sharing knowledge to save human lives. Tibetan doctors, for example, have been guided by their Buddhist faith not to seek profit from healing patients. Consequently, novel applications of plant medicinals are routinely shared in the public commons so that more patients can be healed. A sense of duty to serve humanity was always a guiding moral compass for traditional Asian medicine.[27] These practices relate to the *deo rahati* sacred groves protecting precious plant medicinal biodiversity, discussed in Chapter 4. These medicines are not patented by local doctors and traditional medicine knowledge stakeholders in order to obtain monopoly profits. In contrast, Western pharmaceutical companies have been criticized for profiteering from the high prices of some essential medicines (*profiteering* is defined as unreasonable profit on the sale of essential goods, especially in times of emergency). The Covid-19 crisis has demonstrated that pandemic diseases in their spread to new hosts are indiscriminate of class and national boundaries. Perhaps a sober postmortem of the global coronavirus pandemic and the specter of the next superbug threatening humanity will lead to greater international cooperation through open and inclusive innovation policies.

A Call to Action

Akin to Stiglitz's 2006 admonition to give prizes not patents, and related to Thaler and Sunstein's (2008) recommendations for "nudges" to incentivize private-sector actors to take action for the public good, calls for so-called grand challenges stimulating innovations in essential medicines have emerged (Nilsson 2017). Beyond price competition within national innovation systems, grand challenges involve collaboration worldwide on solutions to shared societal problems for the public good, including health and/or global commons biodiversity.

In the open global innovation commons, we need incentives to share creative ideas and market-disruptive discoveries for the benefit of society writ large. A related challenge is how to check or counterbalance the selfish pursuit of profit if it comes at the expense of human health. As such, the need to develop and share biologic drug discoveries worldwide at fair prices presents a kind of tragedy of the commons or prisoner's dilemma. Namely, the individual/firm-level reward for the extraction of knowledge and material resources from the global commons is high, while the costs of expropriating such resources are distributed broadly. Profits serve internal interests, while costs are externalized (hence the term *negative externalities*). That is, the cost burden is either imposed on others—for example, poor people or underdeveloped countries—or perceived to be assessed far in the future. The Covid-19 pandemic may have provided an opportunity for political and economic leaders to rethink the value to humanity of service to the public good. Change agents are facing an uphill battle (Le et al. 2020). The crux of the problem in stimulating biologic natural medicine drug discovery for the public good is that it is limited by a global innovation system regulated by mechanisms to protect private rights under the WTO TRIPS. Into this space step agents of transformative change, facing off against vested interests behind the status quo.

It is clear from research outlined above on the pharmaceutical industry that excessive and frivolous patenting has resulted from the international patent regime as manifested in TRIPS, further fragmenting the innovation commons. Examples include privatizing gene sequences without a clear product application—equivalent to multiple, overlapping dams in a single waterway—undermining the innovation ecosystem of heretofore unexploited natural resources. One possible solution is the introduction of patent pools of multiple patents that might relate to a new area of research and development, ideally reducing transaction costs of accessing any particular patent within the pool. Problems with such pools have emerged, including the tendency of upstream patent owners to overstate the value of their inventions, posing barriers to research. On the positive side, patent pools reduce transaction costs borne by individual licensees.[28] The Japan Global Health Innovative Technology Fund (GHIT) case in Chapter 5 has included a kind of pool of intellectual property in this regard.

A 2010 IBM survey of global CEOs found that even large firms most likely to have closed, proprietary innovation architectures had already shifted to a more networked, distributed innovation infrastructure—collaborating with external partners internationally. This might be an initial step toward breaking down silos and removing cages around innovation-seeking activity. National governments have pursued similarly networked innovation architectures—for example, by harnessing the talent of their global diaspora in pursuit of domestic innovation and developmental goals (Ibata-Arens 2019a). It follows that local stakeholder groups, as represented, for example, by nongovernmental organizations (NGOs) and their allies in the United Nations and WHO, might likewise benefit from such an open and networked innovation architecture.

Emergent Organizations and System-Level Transformation

Emergent organizations with potential for system-level transformative change share certain characteristics. First, emergent organizations, including PPPs, share a universal goal. That is, they are not particularistic in benefits accrued for participation. Second, they tend to be guided by a moral compass. Third, ideally they enable voice within inclusive architectures of exchange of information. Fourth, they tend to be transnational or internetworked, especially tapping into agents with global resources. Fifth, successful emergent organizations start from a narrowly and precisely defined goal, organized, for example, around a specific scientific question. As the cases that follow in the next chapters exemplify, the aim is not to cure all diseases in one swoop but to take on one or two at a time—incremental improvements to be sure, but nevertheless transformational of the status quo.

A public-private partnership is a long-term formal arrangement (i.e., contractual) between a public entity and one or more private entities for the purpose of providing a public service or developing an asset with benefits for the public. PPPs have emerged especially in fields where market mechanisms have failed to provide for such public services. Typically, the public-sector partner—for example, a national government—provides certain financial incentives, including direct funding, tax or other subsidies, and procurement agreements. The private-sector actor or actors assume certain risks. These risks include the opportunity costs of their time and effort invested into pursuing a desired outcome. Historical examples include PPPs for building nationwide transportation and other infrastructure, for example, railroads. While not immune to criticism for enriching private-sector actors and, on occasion, corruption, PPPs have advantages over purely public investments, including bringing the industry-specific and other relevant know-how to research, develop, commercialize, and market a given product or service. Government agencies and civil servants on the whole lack these private-sector skills. On the other hand, government agencies and their civil servants tend to understand the overall regulatory framework and the politics involved in pushing legislation through government and multilateral bodies, and they have acumen in establishing procedures for monitoring and compliance with safety and other laws.

PPPs as Part of the Policy Menu

After reviewing briefly the policy menu of options taken by national governments with the aim of stimulating inclusive innovation for research and development of essential medicines, I focus on recent policy experiments in PPPs. National governments, responsible for the health and welfare of their citizens and residents, have led in government interventions to encourage and incentivize private-sector actors to engage in innovation activities that benefit the public good. Of growing concern in recent decades is the rising threat of epidemic disease that increases the financial burden on welfare states and thus taxpayers, not to mention insurers and employers.[29] Epidemic disease includes the increased incidence of noncommunicable and chronic conditions, such as cancer, diabetes, heart conditions, and obesity. The aforementioned are major public health concerns mainly in the developed world but increasingly in the developing world as well. The latter is also burdened by NTDs that have been largely eradicated in the developed world and are thus of lower priority for private-sector drug developers. Pandemic viral and bacterial diseases have tended to emerge in less developed areas. A lack of resources to pay for medicines to treat these infectious diseases has led to market failure. That is, in the absence of potential (government) buyers for new drugs and treatments, private-sector (firm) actors understandably pursue research and development of other products that generate revenue.

National governments and multilateral organizations have stepped in to compensate for this failure of the market to incentivize private-sector actors to behave for the benefit of the public, namely, in the interest of human health. Purchasing is one way. For example, public-sector actors have established procurement policies promising to purchase the products that otherwise would not be made in response to market incentives. Investment into PPPs is another example. This support has taken the form of government grants to bolster private and public university research and development in basic science and also the commercializing of public institution innovations. Institutionalizing architectures of innovation is one way national governments and also private-sector actors, including private companies, NGOs, community organizations, and so forth, have stepped in to compensate for failures of the market to stimulate needed innovations in drug discovery for human health. Attempts in recent decades to counteract state and market failure have accelerated partly as a consequence of the establishment of the WTO TRIPS that solidified the hegemony of a patent-centric global IPR regime.[30] A key characteristic of these efforts to create spaces for inclusive innovation has been building transnational networks of civic-minded stakeholders (Nilsson 2017).

The Center for Biodiversity and Indigenous Knowledge, funded by the Ford Foundation in China and the GHIT–Bill & Melinda Gates Foundation partnership in Japan are two examples discussed in detail in subsequent chapters. Another example is evident in India: the Open Source Drug Discovery project with support from the Indian government. Part of the analysis herein is to map out the structures and policy relations of PPPs analyzed through the TISA framework, highlighting innovation sandboxes and pools. These exemplary open commons approaches of the TISA have stimulated drug discovery that is inclusive of stakeholders in various ways, including in the incorporation of traditional knowledge about natural medicines into the process and, on the distribution end, in terms of developing medicines essential to poor and at-risk populations. The aim is to draw policy lessons that might be useful in identifying best practice in the way PPPs are structured and function. For example, it might be that the most effective PPPs are those that focus narrowly on a particular human health problem (e.g., a specific disease condition) as a way to bring together stakeholders with the requisite interest and expertise and a shared *problématique* and language to pursue solutions jointly. This shared language—in other words, a way of thinking shared across stakeholders—also helps to build trust. That is, too many governments and foundations in the past have thrown money at problems to no avail. In sum, financial resources are necessary but insufficient in providing workable policy solutions as an alternative to failing markets. PPPs with global reach have been particularly important in the area of public health, including those concerned with access to essential medicines and treatments for diseases in developing countries. The health policy literature has provided rich descriptions of the rise of PPPs for human health as a response to state and market failures (Buse and Walt 2002; Buse, Mays, and Walt 2012). Much of this work has provided concrete policy prescriptions based on observed best and worst practice. For example, in the area of global health governance (Buse and Harmer 2007), suboptimal performance and negative externalities might be reduced through the inclusion of specific stakeholders in the decisionmaking process of said PPPs.[31]

Under the current WTO TRIPS regime, holders of traditional knowledge face a dilemma when opening up their proprietary trade secret knowledge to outside exploitation, venturing out of the innovation cages of the upper-left quadrant of the TISA into the more open architectures to the right on the x-axis. If they seek to protect their intellectual property through patents, they must overcome the legal hurdle of demonstrating novelty and invention. If, instead, traditional knowledge holders share knowledge publicly in the commons—the upper-right quadrant of the TISA—they become vulnerable to misappropriation of shared knowledge by multinational pharmaceutical firms that have the research and development resources to make incremental, but under existing patent law still considered "novel," molecular modifications and, worse, the legal resources to close off categories of knowledge into patent silos. Developing countries, including mega-biodiverse China and India, seeking access to international markets and inward foreign direct investment have had to comply with the IPR regime created by the WTO—as a price of membership. Similarly, resource-dependent Japan has had a vested interest in protecting and conserving plant medicinal resources through biodiversity conservation efforts outside Japan. Nation-states are thus constrained in pursuit of economic-development and technology-acquisition goals. At the same time, notions of inclusive innovation have been focused on normative perspectives of inclusion (for its own sake) based on concepts including human rights and diversity (George, Mcgahan, and Prabhu 2012; Zehavi and Breznitz 2017).

An alternative framing argues that an inclusive architecture of innovation leads to greater innovation gains in the long term and extends benefits to broader groups of community stakeholders, leading ultimately to sustainable economic development and contributing to overall human health. As mentioned above, studies have found that supposed innovations by drugmakers have instead merely copied prior innovations made in natural medicine (Sahai, Pavithran, and Barpujari 2007). It follows then that the preservation of the traditional knowledge and local communities whence medicinal knowledge derived is essential for future innovation in lifesaving medicines. Further, saving plant genetic samples in the model of a seed bank is necessary, as outlined in Chapter 5 in the case of the conservation efforts of Takeda's medicinal garden in Kyoto, Japan. However, seed banking is insufficient to preserve the tacit knowledge that is critical to the ability to draw from the traditional knowledge medicinal corpus in the search for new medicines. For example, had the ancient traditional medicine knowledge not been preserved in a book of remedies shared widely and preserved across generations, the world may never have rediscovered artemisinin in the 1960s. Extracted properly per the ancient codified techniques from Chinese wormwood, artemisinin has saved millions from death from malaria (Ibata-Arens 2019a).[32] In Japan, as discussed in Chapter 5, all university pharmacy schools must keep a conservation garden maintaining living herbal medicinal plants in the Japanese pharmacopoeia. As such, these are more than demonstration spaces and serve in some cases as living, curated libraries, with preservation of biological materials and contributions by scholars of natural medicine, including ethnobotanists. China and India have also established curated seed and rhizome banks.

Since we cannot know now which traditional medical knowledge or biological resources (e.g., microbes for new antibiotics) might hold the key to future lifesaving medicines, those resources must be preserved and maintained in the innovation commons. Inclusion of local, indigenous stakeholders of traditional medical knowledge and plant medicinal biodiversity as an integral part of the innovation process—upstream to downstream—is therefore essential. Unfortunately, per the previous discussion of the rise of Big Pharma in the assertion of its power to set the rules of the game within the WTO, national governments have pursued economic development within an international system structured around intellectual property right exclusivity rather than inclusivity.

In sum, powerful players in the global market for drugs and medicines have, through their agency, designed governance structures that lead to failures of the market to protect human health. Analysis of government and private-sector case studies in China, India, and Japan illuminate how organizations and states in these countries have compensated for market failures in bringing healing remedies to the world's neediest. How national governments and local organizations have transformed innovation practices in drug (re)discovery and related protection and conservation of medicinal plant biodiversity is the subject of the following chapters. The TISA framework highlighting innovation sandboxes and (patent) pools, introduced in Chapter 1 and detailed in this chapter, offers a way to compare the emergent organizations, including PPPs, across their country contexts. China, the subject of the next chapter, has taken a proactive and, in the words of President Xi Jinping, "strategic" approach.

Notes

1. A blockbuster drug is one that generates $1 billion or more in sales (Hager 2019).

2. Meanwhile, the British were commercializing natural medicines from the "British Imperium" of the Indian subcontinent—adding certain medicines to the official British pharmacopoeia of medicines (note: a materia medica is a list of therapeutic substances used in medicines). Britain also removed from its official pharmacopoeia other medicines—even though they were said to have had greater therapeutic efficacy—because their source materials lay outside the empire and were thus of less economic value for the coffers of the British nation-state (Bhattacharya 2016).

3. These records remain preserved mainly because they were carved in stone. Ancient Egyptian civilization (c. 3300–330 BCE) is believed to also have had a vibrant culture of medicine, but due to the ubiquitous use of the less sturdy papyrus, a paper, much of the historical record has been lost.

4. Insurance companies almost always require approved diagnoses and their related codes for coverage of prescription medications. At the same time, the FDA has been considered more compliant with the demands of pharmaceutical companies than counterpart agencies in Europe and Asia.

5. These criticisms belie deeper systemic geopolitics of innovation— namely, the threat to national security (i.e., in the United States) of drug development and manufacturing capacity having shifted to Asia.

6. See also Angell 2005.

7. The United States and New Zealand, as of 2020, are the only two countries in the world to allow drugs to be marketed "direct to consumer."

8. Adderall is a branded form of dextroamphetamine, sold by Shire Pharmaceuticals. Shire was a UK company established in 1986 and later acquired by Japanese company Takeda Pharmaceutical Company in 2019.

9. So-called reverse pharmacology is a misnomer since the bench-to-bedside model of the twentieth century was the anomaly: 4,000 years of written medicine history demonstrates that medicines had always been developed starting from observations at the bedside of patients, not the other way around.

10. It should be noted that natural medicines are not a panacea for avoiding toxicity; for example, the over-the-counter supplement market is under-regulated and lacks adequate quality screens for pollutants.

11. The Covid-19 pandemic tested the limits of the global innovation system. In the United States, for example, in an effort to launch potential treatments and vaccines quickly, the Food and Drug Administration lifted rules and regulations meant to protect consumers from harm. China and India, on the other hand, demonstrated that they had built up effective domestic production capacity, as well as scientific and technical talent, to bring innovations to market, albeit with weaker human-subject protections.

12. Jonas Salk, interview with Edward R. Murrow, *See It Now*, April 12, 1955 (Hewitt 1955). See also Posner (2020).

13. Novartis announced in May 2019 that it would charge $2.1 million for a gene therapy, Zolgensma, for use in infants with a deadly form of spinal muscular atrophy. Novartis had not developed Zolgensma; rather the medicine was acquired when Novartis bought the company AveXis (Bach 2019).

14. Patent trolls can be considered the inverse: seeking out and aggregating patents in order to gain windfall profits without adding any value to the original pool of patented innovations, which would entail introduction of truly new and substantively improved—not just (re)branded—products. "Excessive" price increases for Pfizer's and Roche's cancer drugs are among numerous examples of how the patent-centric intellectual property system incentivizes profiteering on essential medicines (Bell 2017; Kantarjian and Rajkumar 2015).

15. Other theories about global competition over innovation capacity have been prolific in the fields of international political economy and comparative political economy. For example, prevalent in the 1980s and 1990s, such

notions as the "developmental state" (C. A. Johnson 1982) and "technona-tionalism" (Samuels 1994) focused on explaining how East Asian countries were able to catch up to the manufacturing production capabilities of Western countries. Innovation was emphasized in these analyses in terms of the copy-ing of radical innovations of Western countries and improving on them with incremental, process innovation (C. A. Johnson 1982; Ibata-Arens 2005).

16. It is noteworthy that the modern patent system replaced the one established in Europe in the 1700s, in which the monarchy granted patents, known as royals, hence the term "royalty" payment. The difference now is that the entrenched and powerful are the multinational corporations of the pharmaceutical industry (Tomizawa et al. 2020).

17. Bacteria are independent living organisms. Most do not require an animal or human host to survive. Lyme disease and strep throat are caused by bacteria. Viruses are much smaller than bacteria and cannot survive inde-pendently of a host. They invade the cells of a host and take over cell prop-agation. SARS1 (2002), SARS2 (2019), and swine flu are examples of dis-eases caused by viruses. Identifying an agent, natural or synthetic, that can kill viruses without damaging the human host is a challenging enterprise. Other pathogens endangering human health include fungi that lead to yeast infections and parasites that cause diseases including malaria.

18. See Morrow and Felcone (2004) for a detailed definition and examples.

19. Bio.org provides definitions about biologics.

20. In the 1950s the chemical nerve agent thalidomide was prescribed to pregnant mothers in Europe and caused severe birth defects. It was later determined that thalidomide had been developed by the so-called Devil's Chemist in the Nazi concentration camp Auschwitz and that negative fetal effects were well known by the 1940s (Morris and Morris 2014).

21. The term "medicinal" is often used interchangeably with "medi-cine" but tends to be associated with natural medicines and traditional medicines. "Folk medicine" is a less used variant of noncodified tradi-tional medicine.

22. Definitions from Merriam-Webster.com and Bio.org, accessed Feb-ruary 14, 2020. Technically, the Pfizer/BioNTech and Moderna Covid-19 vaccines use molecules of messenger ribonucleic acid (mRNA), not micro-organisms per se.

23. Since the WTO amended the TRIPS to encourage more access and benefit sharing, it appears that the number of disclosures confirming bio-prospecting activities has declined. This is worthy of further investigation.

24. A 2013 failed attempt by the Indian Patent Office to protect indige-nous pharmacopoeia, which instead led to an increase in intellectual prop-erty expropriation by foreign pharmaceutical companies, provided interna-tional policy lessons. Chinese sources confirm that their current national data collection of indigenous pharmacopoeia has included strict data-sharing protocols, as they learned "what not to do" from witnessing India's struggles to protect indigenous knowledge. See also Chinese State Council (2015). Recently Costa Rica has come under criticism for excluding local holders from governance of domestic resources.

25. See Matthews (2002) for a historical chronicling of the origins of the TRIPS global intellectual property rights regime.

26. In this regard, a number of proposals and research initiatives had been launched by early 2021. For example, the WHO R&D Blueprint strategy was activated as a response to Covid-19 and prepared for infectious diseases in the future. It facilitated research and innovation of vaccines and treatments, as well as "timely and equitable access to these life-saving tools" (WHO 2020a). In Europe, a five-year EU-funded Corona Accelerated R&D program was launched with a total budget of over €75 million (around $85 million at the euro-to-dollar yearly average exchange rate in 2020). It aimed to develop therapeutics for the Covid-19 and "address future outbreaks through drug and virus-neutralising antibody discovery" (European Commission 2021).

27. See Kidd (2012) for discussion of the role of medical heritage in protecting medical knowledge.

28. Individuals and firms have been referred to as "patent trolls" when they obtain patents for the sole purpose of profiting from monopoly sales of products covered by such patents. That is, these entities on the whole do not invest in research and development of new products.

29. The economic burden of noncommunicable diseases was estimated to double from 2010 ($3.6 trillion to $22.8 trillion in 2010 USD) to 2030 ($6.7 trillion to $43.4 trillion in 2010 USD) (Harvard School of Public Health and World Economic Forum 2011). Bloom, Kuhn, and Prettner (2020) estimate that in 2016 the negative economic impact of a sample of infectious diseases was $2.687 billion to $8.062 billion in purchasing power.

30. Polanyi (1944) provides a historical-institutional analysis of the seventeenth- to nineteenth-century agricultural and industrial revolutions as leading to economic disparities and subsequent social unrest related to market and state failures.

31. See also Roberts and Siemiatycki (2015) and Reich (2002) for discussions of how governments have sometimes struggled to engage in public-private partnerships that do more than enrich private companies.

32. An example of this human health potential is the artemisinin malaria cure derived from the Chinese wormwood tree (and traditional Chinese medicine), for which its lead scientist, YuYu Tu, was awarded the 2015 Nobel Prize in Medicine. Tu had rediscovered the appropriate extraction method from an ancient text of Chinese medicine pharmacopoeia.

3

Books of Remedies: China's Drug (Re)Discovery Politics

In the midst of the global coronavirus pandemic that spread in 2020, thousands of Chinese students studying abroad at universities in Europe, North America, and around the world received boxes labeled "health care packages" courtesy of Chinese embassies and local China consulates. In addition to reassuring greetings from government officials, the boxes contained masks, alcohol wipes, and a week's supply of Lianhua Qingwen Capsule (LH, 连花清瘟胶囊, *Lianhua Qingwen Jiaonang*) (W. Xu 2020). LH is a traditional Chinese medicine (TCM) found in clinical research to be effective in symptom relief and rapid recovery from a coronavirus-caused severe acute respiratory syndrome (SARS) (Wang 2003). Covid-19 is a SARS illness and is thus often referred to as "SARS-CoV-2" or "SARS2" colloquially by scientists and medical professionals. LH had been developed by a partnership between a university and the private sector led by Dr. Wu Yiling (吴以岭), a professor of TCM at Hebei Medical University, located in Baoding, Hebei province. Below I discuss how a provincial traditional medicine doctor came to be at the center of China's private-sector contributions to the national Covid-19 medical treatment response, through Wu tapping into medicine knowledge that had been shared in the public commons for millennia. First, I review the historical-institutional background of traditional Chinese medicine and its innovative potential in pandemic preparedness and treatment in the twenty-first century.

After decades of government neglect, eventually the Chinese state began promoting strategic investments in innovation drawing from its vast traditional medicine resources. At first glance, China's current efforts at promoting innovations in natural medicine seem to be open and inclusive, in keeping with the innovation sandboxes of the typology of innovation system architectures (TISA), promoting new drug discovery. However, China's increasing technonationalism has shifted policy and government intervention to prod private-sector actors into more secretive postures (the upper-left quadrant, or cages, in the TISA).

Historical-Institutional Background

According to Ochs and Garran (2020), the historical record documents applications of traditional Chinese medicine (prior to the nineteenth century, just "medicine") as effective treatment interventions in more than three hundred epidemics from the Han dynasty (206 BCE–25 CE) to the twentieth century.[1] These include Japanese encephalitis, cholera, tuberculosis (TB), and a myriad of other acute respiratory diseases, as well as the recent pathogenetic outbreaks of the SARS1 epidemic (2003) and SARS2 (Covid-19) pandemic (2020–). Treatment of illnesses with specific medicine formulations had been codified in numerous books of remedies, the most cited in the historical record being the *Yellow Emperor's Classic of Medicine*, believed to have been written circa 300 BCE. The national state led by the Chinese Communist Party (CCP) has not always supported the use and conservation of natural medicine.

The first National Health Conference under the newly established CCP regime was held in August 1950.[2] At this conference, the CCP and the central government recognized that the number of doctors with modern (also referred to as "Western") medical training was insufficient to deal with a series of public health crises at the time. These included smallpox and diseases caused by poor sanitation (e.g., cholera). The conference proposed the "unity of traditional Chinese medicine and Western medicine" (团结中西医, *Tuanjie Zhongxiyi*) as one of its major health policies aimed at bringing Chinese medicine and Western medicine doctors to work together (NATCM 2019a). This led to support of Western medicine education and subsequent neglect of domestic medicine.

By 1986, policymakers in the CCP realized that while Western medicine education had developed and excelled in China, this had come at the cost of neglecting domestic medical traditions. As a result, the Chinese State Council established the quasi-independent National Administration of Traditional Chinese Medicine (NATCM, 国家中医药管理局, *Guojia Zhongyiyao Guanliju*). It is responsible for tasks like drawing out strategic planning for the development of traditional Chinese medicine, supervising and managing the TCM field, organizing surveys of TCM resources, and protecting endangered TCM resources and technologies for the production of TCM and its treatments (NATCM 2020). The establishment of this administration was a turning point in promoting traditional Chinese medicine as coequal to and making its management no longer subordinate to the dictates of Western medicine (NATCM 2019b).

In 1991, as China began embracing market liberalization, the CCP and the Chinese central government put "equal emphasis on traditional Chinese medicine and Western medicine" (中西医并重, *Zhongxiyi Bingzhong*) as one of the five major policies for China's health policy. Throughout the 1990s, as demand for TCM health care services increased, the TCM industry (cultivators, producers, sellers) developed along with it. The CCP and the Chinese central government continued to signal support for TCM in public policy statements (NATCM 2019c). This accelerated under President Xi Jinping, who was keen to use China's cultural assets, including its medicine, to assert its newfound geopolitical position in the world economy.

In 2012, at the 18th National Congress of the Communist Party of China, President Xi noted the importance of "revitalizing and developing traditional Chinese medicine" (着力推动中医药振兴发展, *Zhuoli Tuidong Zhongyiyao Zhenxing Fazhan*). Since then, several policy outlines related to the development of TCM have been issued, including the "Outline of 'Healthy China 2030' Plan" ("健康中国 2030" 规划纲要, *"Jiankang Zhongguo 2030" Guihua Gangyao*) and the "Outline of the Strategic Plan on the Development of Traditional Chinese Medicine (2016–2030)" 中医药发展战略规划纲要 [2016–2030年], *Zhongyiyao Fazhan Zhanlve Guihua Gangyao [2016–2030]*). The latter raised, for the first time in official CCP records, the development of TCM as a national strategy. The new strategy included the inheritance (referring to the succession of the practice of TCM across generations and also the passing on of the knowledge itself) and innovation of TCM within modern medicine discovery and development. Table 3.1 outlines the chronology of key national measures in this regard.

TCM and SARS/Coronavirus

Part of the effort to incorporate knowledge and innovations drawn from traditional natural medicines would be to document with clinical case data the safety and efficacy of the use of TCM in modern medical treatment. In 2016, the white paper "Traditional Chinese Medicine in China," released in conjunction with the "Outline of the Strategic Plan on the Development of Traditional Chinese Medicine (2016–2030)," noted that TCM treatment had made contributions to the prevention and control of epidemics, such as influenza A virus subtype H1N1 and in the treatment of HIV/AIDS.[3] For example, several research reports published by Chinese scholars indicate that the intervention of TCM combined with antiretroviral therapy can extend the quality of life of AIDS patients (Jin et al. 2015). A few researchers have claimed boldly that TCM has "the potential to become a functional cure for HIV/AIDS" (Wang et al. 2017).

The coronavirus pandemic led to a redoubling of central government efforts, for the SARS1 epidemic in 2003 foreshadowed what was to come in 2020. When the first SARS outbreak occurred in China at the end of 2002, also the result of a coronavirus, medical practitioners all over the country used a combination of TCM and Western treatments for that acute respiratory condition. At the same time, a growing body of international peer-reviewed scientific literature using Western methods of evaluation was concurring with the findings of safety and efficacy within China.

In May 2003, the Chinese State Council appointed a group for the prevention and treatment of SARS. The group convened Chinese medicine experts, who recommended that Chinese medicine be fully incorporated into the treatment interventions for SARS. This led to the state-approved use of integrated TCM and Western medicines (Chinese Academy of Sciences 2003). That year, of 5,327 patients with confirmed SARS infection in China, 58 percent received TCM

Table 3.1   Innovation Policies for New Drug Discovery in China

Year	Name (English)	Name (Chinese)
2012	The 12th Five-Year Plan of TCM Development	中医药事业发展"十二五"规划
2012	The 12th Five-Year Plan of Information Construction of TCM	中医药信息化建设"十二五"
2015	Strategic Plan for the Protection and Development of Chinese Herbal Medicines (2015–2020)	中药材保护和发展规划（2015–2020年）
2015	Chinese Medicine Health Service Development Plan (2015–2020)	中医药健康服务发展规划（2015–2020年）
2016	Outline of Strategic Planning for the Development of Traditional Chinese Medicine (2016–2030)	中医药发展战略规划纲要（2016–2030年）
2016	The 13th Five-Year Plan of TCM Development	中医药发展"十三五"规划
2016	The 13th Five-Year Plan of Information Construction of TCM	中医药信息化发展"十三五"规划
2016	"Healthy China 2030" Plan	"健康中国2030"规划纲要
2017	The 13th Five-Year Plan of Scientific and Technological Innovation of TCM	"十三五"中医药科技创新专项规划
2017	Poverty Alleviation Action Plan of Chinese Herbal Medicine Industry (2017–2020)	中药材产业扶贫行动计划（2017–2020年）
2018	Regulations on the Administration of Simplified Registration and Approval of TCM Compound Preparations	古代经典名方中药复方制剂简化注册审批管理规定
2019	Opinions of the CCP Central Committee and the State Council on Promoting the Inheritance, Innovation, and Development of TCM	中共中央 国务院关于促进中医药传承创新发展的意见
2021	Policies and Measures on Accelerating the Development of Traditional Chinese Medicine	关于加快中医药特色发展的若干政策措施

(WHO 2004). Government approval is important in the affordable access to medicines, and the national insurance scheme would subsequently cover these natural medicines (discussed below under "Health Insurance Coverage").

Chinese patent medicines such as Lianhua Qingwen Capsule and Compound Biejia Ruangan Tablet (复方鳖甲软肝片, *Fufang Biejia*

Ruangan Pian) were used to treat patients' fevers in the early stages and, in later stages, pulmonary inflammation and pulmonary fibrosis caused by SARS (Wang 2003). Several research reports about using TCM and Western medicine for treatment of SARS showed that TCM had functions in ameliorating symptoms and, further, that the use of integrated TCM and Western medicine had more advantages in patient recovery than using Western medicines alone (WHO 2004).

In 2020, during the Covid-19 pandemic, TCM was used in integrated treatment in various ways (Ochs and Garran 2020). Of all patients in China with confirmed infection with Covid-19, 92 percent received TCM. In Hubei province, the epicenter of the initial coronavirus outbreak, clinical observations found that the intervention rate and the effective rate of TCM to improve symptoms were reported to be 90 percent (State Council Information Office of the People's Republic of China 2020). In this regard, "three medicines and three prescriptions" were most commonly used as treatments: LH, Jinhua Qinggan Granule (金花清感颗粒, *Jinhua Qinggan Keli*), and Xuebijing Injection (血必净注射液, *Xuebijing Zhusheye*), which are common in the treatment of fever.[4]

Three prescriptions were given for convalescence outside a clinical setting. Qingfei Paidu (清肺排毒方, *Qingfei Paidu Fang*) is used in preventing worsening of symptoms; after taking it as directed for six days, 93 percent of patients' pulmonary lesions showed reduction. The other two prescriptions were Huashi Baidu (化湿败毒方, *Huashi Baidu Fang*), used to reduce viral load in lung tissue by 30 percent, and Xuanfei Baidu (宣肺败毒方, *Xuanfei Baidu Fang*), used to control inflammation (Yu et al. 2020). The unique advantages of TCM for Covid-19 treatments are also mentioned in the white paper "Fighting COVID-19: China in Action," not least of which was confirmation of fewer negative side effects than with the use of synthetic chemical drugs in treatment (State Council Information Office of the People's Republic of China 2020). This advantage has not gone unnoticed by the national government.

China's Health Diplomacy

For the Chinese nation-state, a flourishing TCM industry would not only support the aims of "Healthy China" (健康中国, *Jiankang Zhong-*

guo) but serve as a form of soft power in its international influence through China's global health diplomacy. Its State Council Information Office is also known in domestic circles as the Foreign Propaganda Office. In recent decades, as part of China's global health diplomacy, China has sent medical groups to provide health assistance to African countries, which have been key sources of China's foreign material resource expansion. Treatments applied by these medical groups include TCM and the integration of TCM and Western medicines. During the Covid-19 pandemic, China sent groups of TCM doctors and donated Chinese patent medicines (中成药, *Zhongchengyao*). Lianhua Qingwen Capsule was a patent medicine provided to Italy and other countries (Yu et al. 2020). Italy had recently signed on as the western edge of the Belt and Road Initiative (BRI) infrastructure development project. Chinese patent medicines are ready-to-use forms of traditional Chinese medicine. This is discussed below under the Yiling Pharmaceutical (以岭药业, *Yiling Yaoye*) case.

Health Insurance Coverage

In 2018, the overall out-of-pocket health expenditure was 1.7 trillion yuan (around $255 billion).[5] The average out-of-pocket health expenditure was around 1,212.00 yuan (around $183.08) (Chinese National Bureau of Statistics 2020). On January 1 of that year, China had launched a new version of the "Catalogue of National Basic Medical Insurance, Industrial Injury Insurance, and Maternity Insurance Drugs" (国家基本医疗保险、工伤保险和生育保险药品目录, *Guojia Jiben Yiliaobaoxian Gongshangbaoxianhe Shengyubaoxian Yaopin Mulu*). According to the catalogue, the national insurance schemes cover the costs of 1,322 Western medicines, 1,321 Chinese patent medicines, including 93 so-called ethnic medicines (a special designation of TCM), and 892 prepared traditional medicines (i.e., separated into pieces). Only 398 Western medicines (e.g., aspirin) and 242 Chinese patent medicines, such as Lianhua Qingwen Capsule and Banlangen Granule (板蓝根颗粒, *Banlangen Keli*), are considered "Class A medicines" (甲类药品, *Jialei Yaopin*), which are necessary drugs for clinical treatments, with government-negotiated prices fully reimbursable by the national insurance scheme. In contrast, the remaining "Class B medicines" (乙类药品, *Yilei Yaopin*) are considered supplemental or optional drugs for clinical treat-ments. As such, their prices are relatively higher than those of Class A drugs, and they are covered only partially by national health insurance (National Healthcare Security Administration of the PRC 2019). In order to meet the health care needs of China's large popu-lace, state and private-sector actors have partnered in the face of deficiencies of the state and weaknesses in the market in addressing health care needs.

State-Owned Enterprises and Public-Private Partnerships

Despite the aforementioned support from the central government in recent decades, including specific policies to stimulate investment in TCM development and coordination with the national health insur-ance scheme for affordable access, precious TCM knowledge and critical raw materials continue to disappear. On the one hand, there is a lack of inheritance, or succession of the knowledge and practice of TCM. According to an investigation by a group of Chinese scholars in 2015, among fifty-four items of TCM intangible cultural heritage, a shocking 48 percent had no inheritors to carry on the knowledge to future generations. In China's millennia-old medical tradition, the main means of inheritance have been apprenticeship and family suc-cession. A modern college education consists instead of learning medicine primarily through book reading, only an auxiliary path to succession. This is because the critical quotidian tacit knowledge of how to use TCM in particular clinical settings is lost in modern book-based learning (Yang et al. 2015). On the other hand, the sustainable development of TCM has suffered from declining quality in raw materials due to loss of biodiversity and poor cultivation methods among younger generations, themselves impacted by changing land-use patterns, pollution, and shifts in climate conditions.

To resolve these challenges, besides carrying out related policies and strategic plans, in December 2016 the 25th Session of the Stand-ing Committee of the 12th National People's Congress passed the Law of the People's Republic of China on Traditional Chinese Med-icine. The law was officially implemented on July 1, 2017. China would establish a national database to protect traditional knowledge (TK) of TCM. This law confirms that inheritors have rights to inherit and use TK of TCM and share benefits with others to acquire and use their TK of TCM (Standing Committee of the National People's Congress 2016). This is related to the National Registry for Traditional Chinese Medicine (NRTCM) project, being implemented by a group of TCM scholars in Beijing and Guangzhou for a number of years, discussed below.

In May 2018, the Chinese National Medical Products Administration issued "Regulations on the Administration of Simplified Registration and Approval of TCM Compound Preparations" (古代经典名方中药复方制剂简化注册审批管理规定, *Gudai Jingdian Mingfang Zhongyao Fufang Zhiji Jianhua Zhuce Shenpi Guanli Guiding*) to discover and collect ancient TCM compound preparations and reduce the costs and time needed for innovations in and clinical research about TCM. A health policy analysis by Zhang and Huang (2020) found that the new strategic policies in place had stimulated innovations within TCM, combining the ancient prescriptions with modern technology through research into the origins of ancient prescriptions, historical developments, and modern scientific methods. Figure 3.1 outlines the state ministries overseeing the integration of natural medicine into new drug discovery.

For example, in 2013 state-owned enterprise Chongqing Taiji Industry (Group) Co., Ltd. (重庆太极实业 [集团] 股份有限公司, *Chongqing Taiji Shiye [Jituan] Gufen Youxian Gongsi*) began exploring potential modern uses for ancient formulations. Taiji and five other TCM pharmaceutical companies (Dou 2018) began receiving subsidies under the Major New Drug Creation and Technology Project administered by the Chinese Ministry of Science and Technology.[6] Private-sector actors have been more entrepreneurial, while remaining subject to changing national government policies in China's one-party state: Yiling Pharmaceutical, the Global Health Drug Discovery Institute (GHDDI), the Center for Biodiversity and Indigenous Knowledge (CBIK), and the National Registry for Traditional Chinese Medicine. Each of these emergent organizations is examined in turn, reflecting China's contradictions within its quest to become innovative in medicine discovery when politics get in the way.

Figure 3.1 Inclusive Innovation in New Drug Discovery: China State and PPPs

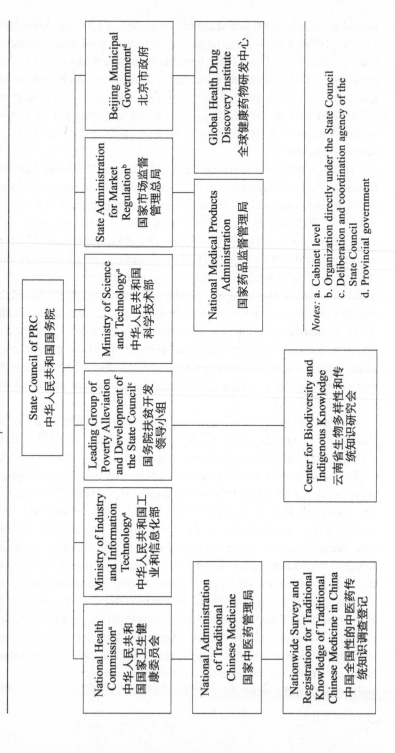

Notes: a. Cabinet level
b. Organization directly under the State Council
c. Deliberation and coordination agency of the State Council
d. Provincial government

Yiling Pharmaceutical

Lianhua Qingwen Capsule, mentioned above and innovated by Yiling Pharmaceutical, is also based on ancient prescriptions. Hebei province is about a 1.5-hour drive southwest of Beijing. A Chinese medicine doctor by training, Dr. Wu Yiling was an entrepreneur on the side.[7] Dr. Wu had founded Shijiazhuang Yiling Pharmaceutical Company, Ltd., in 1992. On June 16, 1992, Wu resigned from Hebei Chinese Medicine Hospital—it was a risky move to give up his hard-earned so-called iron rice bowl post—and founded an institute of medicine with the stated purpose of bringing more medicines to more patients. The institute later became Yiling Pharmaceutical. At the time Wu was reported to have said to himself, "Suppose during the period from my age of thirty to sixty, from graduation to retirement, I see 50 patients every day on average. Even if I don't do anything else in my life (only focus on treating patients), I can treat 300,000 patients at most. However, transforming effective prescriptions into innovative Chinese medicines can relieve the pain of more patients [我从30岁研究生毕业到60岁退休，平均每天看50个病人，就算一辈子不干其他任何事，顶多能诊治30多万个病人。把有效处方转化成创新中药，就能为更多的患者解除病痛]" (Zhao 2014). Wu had launched Yiling Pharma with funding from a personal loan of 100,000 yuan, implying that he did so in the typical "family and friends" model of angel investment—not thanks to government largesse. In the process, company lore says that he refused funding from a Hong Kong businessman, concerned that he would have to disclose his trade secrets (proprietary formulations) to foreign business interests.

After completing his university studies, Professor Wu Yiling pursued research into the traditional Chinese medicine specialty of "collateral disease" (中医络病, *Zhong Yi Luo Bing*). Collateral disease is an extension of concepts in the study of the relationship between meridians (for the flow of qi, or life force in the body, corresponding to Western measures of immune system responses, including white blood cells, lymphocytes, and so forth) (Shen-Nong Limited 2020). Dr. Wu is considered in China as the founder of that clinical specialty and a senior contributor to research and development (R&D) of new drugs under the guidance of the collateral disease theory. Dr. Wu is a recognized expert in the application of high technology to innovations in natural-medicine-based drug development. Even before the SARS1 outbreak in 2002, Wu held a number of drug patents, mainly for the treatment of kidney, lung, and heart diseases and other chronic conditions. His formulations are based on those documented in premodern medical texts, including those of his father. At one point, he was named one of the top 100 Chinese private entrepreneurs for his contributions to scientific discoveries.[8] Since the 1990s, the point at which China began its greatest market privatization since its independence, Professor Wu and collaborators have developed more than ten new drugs that hold national patents.

Wu was born in 1949 into a TCM family (医药世家, *Yiyao Shijia*) in Hebei. Mao Zedong's Cultural Revolution began when Wu Yiling was a high school freshman. Soon thereafter, his father was "locked in a bullpen," a euphemism for imprisonment during Mao's purge of the Chinese literati.[9] Being the son of a political prisoner ended Wu Yiling's prospects for a government career. The junior Wu was quoted as saying at the time, "If [I] cannot be a good minister, then [I will] be a good doctor [不为良相, 便为良医, *Buwei Liangxiang, Bianwei Liangyi*]." Wu started to teach himself traditional medicine from his father's medical books. Many Chinese entrepreneurs of that generation found themselves taking a path different from the one originally intended, since a number of years of education were lost forever, putting them behind others who were able to continue their studies (those with the financial means to avoid falling behind by emigrating abroad). The college entrance examination, which had been canceled under the Mao regime in favor of CCP-approved "political education," resumed in 1977 (Ibata-Arens 2019a). Wu took the examination and was accepted into Hebei Medical University, then trained at Nanjing University of Chinese Medicine for his master's in 1979.[10]

In 2010 Dr. Wu established the Yiling Academician Workstation, a new drug discovery consultancy. The investment was $65 million, and a reported thirty academicians work for the consultancy. In addition to providing LH for the aforementioned student health care packages sent globally in 2020, the company by mid-2020 had donated hundreds of thousands of boxes through the Red Cross Society of China to countries including Iraq and Italy (Yiling Pharmaceutical 2020c). Both were hot spots of the Covid-19 outbreak early in 2020 and also key trading partners with China as part of the Belt and Road Initiative. Iraq happens to be an important supplier of saffron, a raw material for Chinese natural medicine.[11] For thousands of years, ingredients that are both safe and effective have been easily identified in Chinese codified (classical TCM texts) and tacit (practitioner day-to-day techniques and application) knowledge about traditional medicine. Such formulations as LH and artemisinin resulted from innovation processes occurring over thousands of years in a national innovation commons. These include proper extraction methods—for example, the temperature and even the time of day at which a particular ingredient should be harvested for maximum potency.[12] These innovations in medicines have been shared in the Chinese public commons for thousands of years. This open innovation architecture included both shared pools of traditional medicine knowledge (TMK) for practitioners and innovation sandboxes within which new formulations emerged. For Covid-19, preliminary clinical studies (Hu et al. 2020; see also Wang 2003 for clinical use in SARS1) indicated LH capsules were effective in treatment "by improving the recovery rate of symptoms and shortening . . . the recovery time" and, most significantly, healing lung lesions.

The successful use of TCM in the 2003 SARS1 epidemic in China led to a renewal of positive public attention to traditional medicine. This happened after Guangdong Traditional Chinese Medical Hospital collected detailed clinical data on its experience of using integrated traditional Chinese and Western medicines in the treatment of that severe acute respiratory syndrome. On April 10, 2003, the Chinese National Administration of TCM published a clinical guide for the safe use of TCM in SARS1 treatment: "Technical Solution of Chinese Traditional Medicine Prevention and Treatment for SARS" (非典中医药防治技术方案, *Feidian Zhongyiyao Fangzhi Jishu Fang'an*). It was used to guide medical practitioners in the proper use of natural medicines in SARS1 treatment.

By May of that year, it was apparent that in comparison to other regions, especially Beijing (the seat of political power in China), the mortality and morbidity rate in Guangdong had been substantially lower. As a result, the national State Council led a government task force for the prevention and treatment of SARS, hosting a symposium of Chinese medicine experts. It resulted in the recommendation that Chinese medicine be fully integrated into the treatment protocol for SARS. The integration moved swiftly as a result of this central state intervention—it should be noted, within a command-and-control implementation structure unlike the fragmented and uncoordinated national, state, and local efforts in the United States in 2020. By mid-May 2003, most patients throughout China had been treated to some extent with integrated traditional Chinese and Western medicine (Chinese Academy of Sciences 2003). It was around this time that Wu Yiling began to experiment with formulations that would eventually become LH.

In the early stage of SARS in 2003, people knew very little about the disease. Wu Yiling had prescribed preventive TCM on the basis of patients' symptoms (Shi 2014). This approach—focusing on treating underlying body system weaknesses that lead to, for example, inflammation when the body is exposed to an external pathogen—is typical in TCM. Later a team of academicians and experts from the Yiling Institute of Medicine (以岭医药研究院, *Yiling Yiyao Yanjiuyuan*), established in April 2001, launched a spin-off project, a TCM R&D organization (中药科研组, *Zhongyao Keyanzu*). After the outbreak of the SARS epidemic in 2003, the team studied the occurrence and development of the coronavirus causing SARS in Guangzhou, Guangdong, and, based on their clinical experience, formulated the Lianhua Qingwen prescription. Following the development of LH by Wu Yiling and his team, a public-private partnership (PPP)–level laboratory of the Chinese Academy of Military Medical Sciences confirmed in a replicated study that LH was effective in alleviating the symptoms of SARS. By May 2004, LH had passed the review of the Chinese National Medical Products Administration and obtained new drug certification and approval for production at scale (Yiling Pharmaceutical 2020d). The novel coronavirus pandemic, or SARS2, has brought renewed attention to modern innovations in traditional Chinese medicine—namely, the integration of natural medicines into the national pandemic treatment response.

In May 2020 Wu Yiling had a net worth reported at $2.2 billion and had been designated a "self-made" billionaire by *Forbes* magazine (*Forbes* 2020). His riches were said to have been made on the sale of pharmaceuticals, including the Covid-19 treatment LH. In 2019, Yiling Pharma's income was up 21 percent to $820 million versus $678 million in 2018. By mid-2020 Yiling had 9,618 employees (Tianyancha 2020), and the company, as mentioned above, had donated hundreds of thousands of boxes, both directly and through the Red Cross Society of China, to the countries, including Iraq and Italy, hardest hit by the coronavirus (Yiling Pharmaceutical 2020a, 2020d, 2020e, 2020f).[13]

Chinese Communist Party officials would hardly allow Beijing, the seat of political power in China, to be left out of this newfound international natural medicine innovation by that country.

Global Health Drug Discovery Institute

The Boao Forum for Asia (BFA), established in 2001, is China's answer to Davos. Fashioned in the style of the World Economic Forum, hosted annually in Davos, Switzerland, the Chinese version is held in Boao, Hainan province, China. BFA was nominally initiated by the governments of Australia, Japan, and the Philippines in 1998. BFA's permanent secretariat is in Beijing. The forum has come to be called the "Asian Davos," reflecting its high-profile state and private-sector participants.

At the 2015 BFA, Xi Jinping met with Bill Gates in the latter's capacity as the cochair of the Bill & Melinda Gates Foundation and his/its interest in supporting organizations engaged in public service for human health (Ministry of Foreign Affairs of the People's Republic of China 2015). One outcome of this meeting was the establishment of the Global Health Drug Discovery Institute (全球健康药物研发中心, *Quanqiu Jiankang Yaowu Yanfa Zhongxin*). In 2016, a joint partnership was established between the Bill & Melinda Gates Foundation, Tsinghua University (清华大学, *Qinghua Daxue*), and the Beijing Municipal Government (BMG, 北京市政府, *Beijingshi Zhengfu*) (GHDDI 2020c). Each pledged $100 million toward the partnership's funding (Dahl 2017). By the end of 2019, it had eighty-five full-time employees and total assets of 437 million yuan (around $63 million).[14] According to Dahl (2017), GHDDI would be a part of "China's long-term strategy to build up its pharmaceutical industry" and expand its political influence in global health issues. Meanwhile, the BMG has been "promoting pharmaceutical innovations in small molecule drug [*sic*], Chinese traditional medicine, biologics and medical devices by providing significant financial, regulatory and talent development support" (GHDDI 2020b).

For Chen Jining (陈吉宁), the mayor of Beijing in 2018, the Gates-Tsinghua-BMG PPP was part of that city's three-year action plan for collaborative innovation in the biomedical and health care industry (医药健康协同创新三年行动计划, *Yiyao Jiankang Xietong*

Chuangxin Sannian Xingdong Jihua) (Beijing Municipal Science & Technology Commission Biomedicine Division 2018). Through this PPP, the Bill & Melinda Gates Foundation has sought to "promote international cooperation and improve the existing early drug development system" through cooperation with China. This institute is intended to serve as "a bridge connecting the advanced global drug research institutions and downstream clinical development agencies" (Bill & Melinda Gates Foundation 2020). As such, the partnership has functioned as both an innovation sandbox and an intellectual property (IP) pool in supporting innovations inclusive of the needs of poor patients.

According to GHDDI director Dr. Ding Sheng (丁胜), the GHDDI has been "focusing on developing modular drug discovery infrastructure and disease-specific expertise" in tuberculosis, malaria, and other neglected tropical diseases (GHDDI 2018). In 2019, the GHDDI joined the Tuberculosis Drug Accelerator partnership, which targets "the discovery of new TB drugs by collaborating on early-stage research." According to Dr. Ding, "GHDDI will be able to better collaborate with and utilize the best expertise and resources in the TB drug discovery community; at the same time, GHDDI will leverage its own unique expertise in Structural Biology, Artificial Intelligence (AI), novel target/disease biology, as well as patient samples and population in China to contribute to the global TB drug discovery community." The GHDDI has developed capacity in artificial intelligence enabling rapid selection of potential drug targets (GHDDI 2019).

Since January 2020 GHDDI has, through the "new use of old drugs" (老药新用, *Laoyao Xinyong*), identified a number of potential and effective candidate drugs for Covid-19 treatments. It also "opened internal drug R&D platforms and resources to external researchers across the globe to empower and accelerate joint research, including launching a scientific research data and information sharing portal 'Targeting COVID-19'" (GHDDI 2020a).[15] While not related directly to GHDDI, China's Sinopharm was testing a Covid-19 vaccine by the summer of that year. The goal was to have a deployable vaccine by December 2020, and Sinopharm's Covid-19 vaccine was approved officially in December that year (Brant 2020). However, it became apparent as early as August 2020 that Chinese companies had been inoculating their workers for some months, while clinical testing on "thousands of people" had meanwhile been underway around the world (e.g., Argentina, Peru, United Arab Emirates). While the GHDDI has a national and international profile, other efforts have been focused on the local level.

Community-Based Access to Medicines and Economic Development

In addition to supporting the inheritance of TCM, a TCM law enacted in 2016 and related policies emphasize the protection of wild medicinal plants and the cultivation of them. Under the law's provisions, the state designed technical specifications for the cultivation, collection, storage, and primary processing of medicinals (Standing Committee of the National People's Congress 2016). Furthermore, in September 2017 the Poverty Alleviation Action (PAA) Plan of the Chinese Herbal Medicine Industry (中药材产业扶贫行动计划 (2017–2020年), *Zhongyaocai Chanye Fupin Xingdong Jihua 2017–2020*), led by the NATCM, was implemented across China (NATCM 2017). The PAA established a new model of targeted poverty alleviation within the Chinese herbal medicine industry. For example, the PAA supported hundreds of pharmaceutical companies in building "demonstration bases" (示范基地, *Shifan Jidi*) with natural medicinal gardens (定制药园, *Dingzhi Yaoyuan*) for cultivation in poverty-stricken areas. Demonstration bases would be used to train local residents in cultivation methods through hands-on teaching by experts in the field (ethnobotanists). Efforts were made to introduce high-quality breeds able to command higher prices for "authentic" natural medicinals (道地药材, *Daodi Yaocai*) attuned to different local conditions (因地制宜, *Yindizhiyi*). Companies were incentivized with funds provided by NATCM. For example, in 2019 the NATCM subsidized twenty-two provinces with 22 million yuan (around $3.18 million).[16] The PAA established an expert group to train individuals and communities in cultivation methods for natural medicinals. The program also permits households and communities to establish cooperatives (合作社, *Hezuoshe*) and joint-stock partnerships (股份合作, *Gufen Hezuo*).

For example, Wuzhai county (五寨县, *Wuzhai Xian*) in Shanxi province has more than ten TCM pharmaceutical companies, hospitals, and markets. In this local ecosystem, the PAA supported poor households in Wuzhai in building a cooperative relationship with pharmaceutical companies by cultivating and processing natural medicinals, mainly Huangqi (黄芪). Huangqi, astralagus, or purple milkvetch plant is used in TCM for energy and immune system enhancement. In 2018, the planting area of natural medicinals in Wuzhai county was 50,000 mu (around 3333.33 hectares). A local company, Zhenghetang Chinese Herbal Medicine Company (正和堂中药材公司, *Zhenghetang Zhongyaocai Gongsi*), alone had purchased 800 tons of natural medicinals. A representative of the company said that the model of "Enterprises + Cooperatives + Bases + Poor households [企业+合作社+基地+贫困户, *Qiye + Hezuoshe+ Jidi + Pinkunhu*]" in Wuzhai county allowed local enterprises to engage in the cultivation of natural medicinals on a scale otherwise impossible while at the same time ensuring high quality in natural medicinals. The PPP structure reduces investment costs and distributes risk while supporting a basic income for local families (Q. Li 2017). In 2018, the government reported that the poverty rate in Wuzhai county decreased from 36.30 percent to an outstanding, even unbelievable, 0.5 percent within five years as a result of the partnership (*Huanqiu* 2019). As of August 2019, there were 685 Chinese herbal medicine bases in twenty-nine provinces, and the total cultivation area reached 2.95 million mu (around 196,666.67 hectares). Around 210,000 poor people had reportedly benefited from the PAA program (J. Xu 2020). These kinds of poverty alleviation through the cultivation and protection of traditional medicinals had been tried before—for example, in the groundbreaking work some decades prior of the Poverty Alleviation Board (PAB) and the Center for Biodiversity and Indigenous Knowledge, whose trials and tribulations are discussed below.

Based on observation of India's struggles, discussed in the next chapter, China's approach to the protection of traditional medicinal knowledge has been more cautious, even secretive, thus placing Chinese efforts in TISA cages as closed and secretive, yet nevertheless novel, innovations. In 2002 the Traditional Chinese Medicine Patents Database was established by the State Intellectual Property Office. The database would compile more than 19,000 records covering 40,000 TCM formulas, cross-referenced with related patent applications. In 2013, the Chinese government funded a new project to collect an additional 6,000 records comprising previously unrecorded formulas, a book of remedies for the twenty-first century. The new, or rediscovered, data was based on a nationwide ethnographic study of indigenous communities across China. This initiative is discussed below under the NRTCM case.

In 2008, the Chinese government had announced the "Outline of the National Intellectual Property Strategy." This was created to "promote the creation and utilization" of IP, to strengthen protection of IP, to improve "IP rights management and management efficiency," and to expand international cooperation in regard to IP rights. The plan has similarities to India's Traditional Knowledge Digital Library, including an information services system to help "disclose information on patents, trademarks, and copyrights" (C. Liu 2016; see also Liu and Gu 2011). While China has made efforts to improve intellectual property rights and efficiency, C. Liu (2016) finds that the "quality of patents remains poor; the protection of intellectual property rights remains inadequate; and the administrative enforcement of measures to prevent intellectual property rights infringements remains weak." The integrated approach by the Center for Biodiversity and Indigenous Knowledge is reflective of the need to link protection of traditional medicine knowledge to conservation of plant medicinal biodiversity.

Center for Biodiversity and Indigenous Knowledge

The southwestern province of Yunnan is among China's most biodiverse regions. Considered "mega-biodiverse" by the United Nations, the region comprises 0.2 percent of the total land in China, yet is home to 16 percent of its higher plant species (Hu 2003). Yunnan is also a multicultural area, said to be home to the highest number of ethnic minority tribal peoples, many of whom have been closely tied to traditional medicinal knowledge and related plant medicinal expertise.

In the early years of Deng Xiaoping's Open Door Policy, launched in the 1970s, the national Poverty Alleviation Board was open to new ideas and allowed freedom at the local level to experiment, relying in part on ethnobotanists and other stakeholders with the requisite quotidian knowledge of the plant ecosystems supporting wild plant medicinal varieties. Wild ginseng, for example, has much higher potency in its natural chemical properties (used as an active ingredient in TCM) than its cultivated version. Having visited traditional medicine markets all over Asia, I observed that a few ounces of certified wild ginseng can command prices similar to those for luxury cars, while the cultivated varieties are sold in huge barrels for pennies.

Initiated in 1978 with the goal of alleviating rural poverty, a number of projects were underway by the mid-1980s (Matsuzawa 2016). In collaboration with foreign donors including the Asian Development Bank and the Ford Foundation, in 1989 a group of twelve "units" was put together under the auspices of PAB to investigate poverty alleviation in the "poorest" rural villages. Receiving a list from Beijing of these locations, the team was allowed to work in Yunnan, which at the time had a number of the most impoverished villages in China. As an old Chinese proverb says, "The mountains are high, and the emperor is far away." CCP officials were deliberate in the selection of the distant-from-Beijing province of Yunnan. According to anonymous sources familiar with this policy initiative, any unanticipated, unwanted foreign influences on local populations' way of thinking and acting could be rooted out at any time and thus would unlikely reach the center of the national government in Beijing (anonymous interview 2017).

Junior staff assigned to small working groups were selected in part because of their English-language ability and also their ability to communicate in local dialects/languages. Mostly from government agencies, including the Academy of Social Sciences, and local universities, the teams were dispatched (after training) to engage in participatory research (under a method called *participatory rural appraisal*) in the target villages. Eventually the PAB project became the Yunnan Uplands Management (YUM) project, involving a loosely networked collaborative team from a number of local organizations, including the Kunming Institute of Botany. According to Dick Menzies, at the time a program officer for the Ford Foundation, by the early 1990s the poverty-alleviation project had expanded its focus to include ways in which indigenous knowledge, including traditional medicinal knowledge, could be harnessed to support communities while conserving the biodiversity upon which the medicinals were based (Menzies 2016).

Local community stakeholders, including ethnobotanists, teamed up with representatives of the Ford Foundation, recognizing that biological and cultural diversity were drivers of innovations that improved livelihoods—not objects to be protected and conserved per se (Menzies 2005). The idea for the CBIK, a center empowering local communities to be drivers of their own sustainable economic development, emerged out of the work of the YUM. The YUM had been funded by a grant from the Ford Foundation for the purpose of building institutional capacity for poverty alleviation. Junior researchers from university and government were trained in cohorts in participatory appraisal methods, including sponsored study in Southeast Asian countries with counterpart projects and researchers. While the original goals of poverty alleviation were not met, YUM's focus on incorporating the perspectives of local communities, including traditional knowledge holders, and creating networks among junior researchers led to a series of entrepreneurial new projects, including the CBIK.

The breadth of the participatory inclusion of the horizontally networked organizations was complemented by a deep local understanding of indigenous rights and issue areas. From this group emerged the idea for the creation of a center "dedicated to a vision of biodiversity and vibrant local culture as the key to sustainable improvements in the lives of rural people in southwestern China" (Menzies 2005). Four staff of the Kunming Institute of Botany, one of whom was on the YUM project, decided to start a new organization in 1995, the Center for Biodiversity and Indigenous Knowledge, to pursue more socially embedded research into the relationship between local communities, traditional knowledge, and plant biodiversity. CBIK was among the first nongovernmental organizations established in Yunnan province. Fortunately, the newly established CBIK was able to obtain a $90,000 grant from the Ford Foundation, a hefty sum at the time.

Over time, as successive CCP leadership and five-year plans took precedence, nongovernmental organizations came under increasing scrutiny from the central government in Beijing and by extension local CCP officials. As CBIK grew in size and reputation, the organization would come up against less informed, yet politically powerful local functionaries of the CCP, as well as conflicts of interest with the infrastructural expansion of the Belt and Road Initiative. The infrastructure projects under the BRI include the building of rail and road infrastructure in Yunnan, as part of the trade route through South Asia to Europe. As of 2018, the BRI construction had cut paths through previously undisturbed (pristine) biomass. Local informants in Yunnan note that the government has bought the silence of locals by offering to pay for "conservation" spaces—on either side of the newly built road of course (anonymous interview 2018). Money for conservation projects has meant steady (referred to by informants pejoratively as) "golden rice bowl" civil service jobs for local scientists and technicians—a step up from the previous standard iron rice bowl jobs. These are in addition to the construction jobs for the infrastructure itself. In retrospect, the CBIK should have known the risks of running afoul of the political order of things.

In the early years after its founding, CBIK invited foreign experts to serve on a voluntary advisory board to assist in field research, make (nonbinding) recommendations, and help with external grant writing. In the CBIK 2001 strategic plan, in a sentence referring to the advisory board, "board" was inadvertently translated into Chinese as "committee" (委员会, *Weiyuanhui*). The latter term has significance within the strict hierarchy of the Communist Party and rankled local CCP functionaries in the government. An anonymous informant (2018) indicated that these functionaries did not appreciate the idea that foreigners (with the luxury of funding) seemed to be making local policy. According to a person involved in the project, the group would soon begin facing difficulties in obtaining permits and approvals for its work. CCP politics got in the way (anonymous interview 2017).

In an institutional review report, Menzies (2005) noted that, paradoxically, as China develops, interest on the part of foreign donors wanes just as mounting pressures exacerbate declines in biodiversity and traditional knowledge. CBIK at one point had thirty staff, including twelve full-time professionals. By 2018, CBIK had shrunk to four total staff and was compelled to rent out most of the floor that it previously occupied in a Kunming office building. On the bright side, its ownership of the space had become a decent real estate investment.

What began as an internationally networked local initiative, replete with eager young researchers across numerous local, regional, national, and international organizations, eventually became caught up in the politics of the Chinese Communist Party. The strong reaction by party functionaries to the seemingly minor slipup in the translation of the term *board* as "committee" was an omen of the diminished future for CBIK. After the recognition of the pioneering work of Tu Youyou in (re)discovering in ancient Chinese medicine texts how to successfully extract artemisinin from Chinese wormwood for the treatment of malaria, Xi Jinping would continue to make statements about indigenizing innovation and the importance of protecting these precious cultural assets. This has translated into some additional research funds for network collaborators, including the Kunming Botanical Garden and its partners, such as Xishuangbanna Tropical Botanical Garden, though not the CBIK itself.

Political pronouncements eventually transformed into state-sponsored "active protection" efforts after calls from local activists and scholars for a sui generis regime. One reason is that despite decades of policy (pronouncements), as TCM increased in private-sector profitability, the very local communities that depend exclusively on traditional medicine for basic health care needs have increasingly struggled to access TCM. Further, according to Burke, Wong, and Clayson (2003), the more TCM becomes profitable as a result of national government policy enriching especially executives in state-owned enterprises, the less poor patients and communities have been able to access essential medicine. A government initiative in 2017 (discussed below) has attempted to alleviate this gap.

National Registry for Traditional Chinese Medicine

The China Institute of History and Literature of Chinese Medicine of the China Academy of Chinese Medical Sciences sits in a non-descript, quiet street tucked away in old Beijing. On each side of the entrance sit two three-meter-tall statues: larger-than-life figures of Sun Simiao (孙思邈, 581–682 CE) and Zhang Zhongjing (张仲景, 150–219 CE). Both are revered within the Chinese academy for their contributions to traditional Chinese medicine.

Dr. Liu Changhua (柳长华), a historian of Chinese medicine with intimate ethnographic knowledge about the practice of TCM, keeps a small office in the institute (though he retired in 2017). Dr. Liu was the lead researcher on a national government-sponsored project called the Nationwide Survey and Registration for Traditional Knowledge of Traditional Chinese Medicine in China (中国全国性的中医药传统知识调查登记, *Zhongguo Quanguoxingde Zhongyiyao Chuantong Zhishi Diaocha Dengji*). From 2005, Dr. Liu was responsible for research on the protection of the intangible cultural heritage of Chinese medicine, serving as a member of the National Expert

Committee on the Protection of Intangible Cultural Heritage. Part of this service included overseeing the entry of specific traditional medicines onto the national protection list as part of China's cultural heritage. Dr. Liu is also a recognized expert in the fields of digitalization of ancient Chinese medicine and traditional medicine as intangible cultural heritage and traditional knowledge protection.[17]

His junior collaborators on NRTCM were Drs. Song Ge and Gu Man, practicing physicians and experts in the integrated use of Chinese traditional medicine with Western medicine, particularly in oncology. Song and Gu were also familiar with the successes of applying TCM in SARS1 in 2003, having served in Guangzhou hospitals at the time. The national registry team was very familiar with the way in which India's Traditional Knowledge Digital Library (TKDL) had initially attempted to share in the public commons (called *defensive protection*) as a way to guard its own TMK from foreign intellectual piracy. The TKDL, examined in Chapter 4, was based on historical written record of medicine formulations going back thousands of years, many in the ancient language of Sanskrit. After the formulations were, according to unsubstantiated rumors, supposedly posted online without proper protections, Western researchers and pharmaceutical companies were reportedly able to exploit that information for their own research and development without compensation or credit given to India or the traditional medicine practitioners who shared the knowledge in the first place.

Observing this, Liu's project team sought to take a different approach for China. The goal would be to create a sui generis regime for the protection of TCM. By the early 2000s it had become clear that for a variety of factors internal and external to China, traditional practices and their related beliefs had "gradually [all but] disappeared" from the modern medicine canon (Song 2016). The reasons for the irrevocable loss included lifestyle changes, the influx of Western medical practice, and the shift of hospitals in China from a public service provided by the government to a privatized and profit-centric model (Ibata-Arens 2019a).

In contrast to the defensive protection model of India's TKDL discussed in the next chapter, China's model would be "active protection"—an offensive approach. That is, it would register traditional medicinal knowledge still in active use by dynastic families involved in the practice of traditional medicine. It would also continue to protect certain proprietary formulas as national "state secrets." Criteria for inclusion would be use of a formula by a given family for at least fifty years or for three generations. Protection would not be limited to medical practitioners but would also include cultivators and apothecaries (like compounding pharmacies in the West). Dr. Liu Changhua was on a mission to document and record the remaining practices still in use, not only as protection from foreign exploitation but as a way to encourage future generations of TMK stakeholders to take over the knowledge and maintain the critical quotidian tacit practice of applying the knowledge in clinical settings, reaching more patients ultimately through modern innovations that would contribute to the evolution of traditional medicine in China. Seeking these competing goals has led China to vacillate between closed, secretive TISA cages and open innovation commons sandboxes.

Dr. Liu is as much philosopher as historian of medicine and TCM practitioner. Critical of Western medical approaches that think you have to "kill everything with [synthetic] chemical drugs and antibiotics," Liu reminded me that in TCM they recognize that disease conditions are caused in two ways that work in tandem, feeding off each other and impacting the health of our bodies. First, the condition is an "inside problem," including a patient's emotional state. Second, it is an "outside problem," involving the way the world around us affects our bodies. In other words, disease is often caused by the way we respond to environmental toxins, especially the external stresses on our body, in conjunction with our emotional state at the time. The ancient text *Yellow Emperor's Classic of Medicine*, the same used by Nobel laureate Tu Youyou to rediscover how to extract artemisinin for malaria treatment (Ibata-Arens 2019a), outlined the external deficiencies (外需, *Waixu*) that affect the body's ability to defend itself from outside pathogens. Likewise, the text, published circa 300 BCE, referenced abnormal climate conditions that lead to a terrain ripe for the development of an epidemic (L. Liu 2020). For example, abnormal climate conditions might bring wild animal populations into close proximity with humans, allowing zoonotic diseases to spread to humans from animals, as happened in the coronavirus pandemic.

So, for Dr. Liu, TCM is all about promoting harmony and balance between the inside and the outside. Medicine should be used to maintain this balance, in conjunction with healthy life habits that help prevent disease in the first place (C. Liu 2016). Likewise, Dr.

Liu has been on a crusade to ensure the future of TCM, not as rari-
fied artifacts in a museum but as a living practice to be nurtured and
further developed. At the same time, he bristles at the nuisance of
having to submit to Western conceptions of medicine in the evaluation of the safety and efficacy of TCM. Liu says, "These traditional
knowledge and resources have been used for more than two thousand
years; there is no need to test and evaluate [using Western methods].
Rather it is proven by its long history in medical practice. It is also
allowed by the [Chinese] government and is legal. But to carry out
research, for example, to protect the traditional Chinese medicine
knowledge and resources in the United States, it is a matter of
national interest, and it is not easy to handle" (C. Liu 2018).[18] Other
anonymous sources noted that it was not uncommon for TCM doctors to document adverse reactions, including patient death, as having resulted from a misdiagnosis and/or an incorrect formulation prescribed by another doctor, leaving themselves blameless (anonymous
interview 2018). Dr. Song Ge, a close collaborator with Dr. Liu on
the NRTCM project, concurs with Dr. Liu's response to a question I
asked: What is the most significant challenge facing your efforts to
conserve and protect herbal medicinal plants, to ensure ongoing
access to medicinal plants?

> There are two main aspects to the protection of medicinal
> plants. The categories are material and nonmaterial protection,
> and the protection of traditional knowledge, which is connected
> with those resources, including the protection of resources and
> the protective and sustainable development of the resources
> within communities of practice. First, how can the local ethnic
> minority communities continue to hold this knowledge and
> inherit this knowledge? Second is how to share interests and
> benefits with them and how to seek the approval of the holders
> in research and development of medicines. This works as a kind
> of recognition of them and showing our respect to them.

Unfortunately, as of July 2020, the envisioned national registry
database portal had yet to be launched, contradicting the aims of Liu
and his co-investigators for an innovation sandbox and shared IP
pool of TCM formulations. Liu's aim for 10,000 new registrations
had yet to be met. By 2018, the national grant money had run out,
and the team had to wrap up the project, albeit with an impressive
approximately 6,000 validated observations. Further, and as is typi-

cal in Japan outside Tokyo, the farther away from the political capital, Beijing, the less interest in complying with national government projects—however noble the intentions of the national registry. In fact, the bulk of new registrants came from the northeast of China, in cities and regions nearest to Beijing.

Far to the southwest from Beijing is the province Chengdu, otherwise famous for its giant panda sanctuaries and Sichuan cuisine. After retiring from his post in Beijing, Dr. Liu returned as planned to Chengdu, where he had done research previously and continued his quest to preserve TCM (C. Liu 2016). An opportunity presented itself when a construction crew digging for a new subway station stumbled across what appeared to be the remains of a medical clinic from the Han period of premodern China (c. 206 BCE–25 CE). As of 2020, the local researchers led by Dr. Liu had set about the task of documenting the medicine prescriptions on slips of bamboo found in the remains of this ancient clinic. The findings were to be published as a book.

Interviewed by a journalist for his impressions of the award of the Nobel Prize to Dr. Tu Youyou in 2013, Liu was quoted as saying, "I feel happiness and sorrow." He explained that even though Dr. Tu had explicitly referred to ancient TCM texts, including the *Yellow Emperor's Classic*, in her rediscovery of the extraction method to obtain artemisinin from Chinese wormwood, the Nobel committee unfortunately had been sure to indicate in its award that it was not honoring Chinese medicine per se but the extraction method itself (I. Johnson 2015).

Referencing Tang dynasty scholar Wang Bing, Liu and Gu (2011), in an article calling for greater state and private-sector coordination in the protection and conservation of traditional medicine knowledge, conclude on the "need to strengthen the roots before irrigating seedlings." That is, comprehensive international and national institutional practices must be created through a sui generis regime for protection, conservation, and sustainable development that has resonance in local communities: "Traditional Chinese medicine is like a luxuriant tree with deep roots and flourishing leaves, but the worldwide loss and improper possession of traditional knowledge is quietly eroding the root on which the survival of traditional Chinese medicine relies" (Liu and Gu 2011, 218).[19]

In 2020, peer-reviewed clinical research began to emerge from Wuhan, site of the first outbreak of the novel coronavirus. The demonstrated safety and efficacy of the use of natural medicine in the treatment of Covid-19 precipitated a renewed renaissance—just like during the 2003 SARS1 epidemic—of scientific attention to traditional medicine as an integral part of China's global health policy. For example, Dr. Liu Lihong of the Institute for the Clinical Research of Classical Chinese Medicine recounted how in the SARS1 outbreak in 2003, treatment "was the business of Western medicine," and it was not until the later stages of the official response to that epidemic that traditional medicine (including natural medicine and acupuncture) was incorporated (L. Liu 2020). The situation was not so different in 2020 with SARS2. Dr. Liu Lihong and a team of researchers volunteered for the "front lines in Wuhan" only to find a number of obstacles, which Dr. Liu interpreted as a result of his team not being part of the "official" government response, alluding to the fact that they were not connected as CCP members. After a number of attempts in February 2020, they were finally permitted to see patients near, but not on, the actual front line, being relegated, as Liu was sure to mention, to low-ranking "People's Hospital No. 8 . . . Hemorrhoid Department No. 3."[20] It would take some months before their clinical research would attract the attention of national policymakers.

Asked about existing efforts elsewhere in China and the world to protect and conserve natural medicine knowledge, Dr. Liu Changhua noted that so far there had not been significant effort on a national level in China other than his registry project. He nevertheless remained optimistic: "These things are left by our ancestors. One day when the government finds it useful, they will know those are highly important to be protected" (C. Liu 2018). It seems the coronavirus pandemic has brought such a realization. In June 2020 the State Council announced an unprecedented change to protection, conservation, and research and development related to traditional Chinese medicine. Details were to follow in coming months (Fang 2020). Aims of the new policy included the "revitalization and development of Chinese medicine," while improving its integration with Western medicine practices and contributing to access to basic medicine in local communities through the construction of regional medical centers. The effort was to be led by top government entities the National Health Commission (国家卫生健康委, *Guojia Weisheng Jiankangwei*), the National Administration of Traditional Chinese Medicine, the National Development and

Reform Commission (国家发展改革委, *Guojia Fazhan Gaigewei*), the Ministry of Education (教育部, *Jiaoyubu*), and the Ministry of Science and Technology (科技部, *Kejibu*).

Conclusion

National CCP politics have gotten in the way of such PPPs as CBIK and NRTCM in reaching their potential for supporting inclusive innovation (through sandbox and pool architectures) that transcends nationalistic boundaries and technonational policies. Consequently, in terms of the four quadrants of the TISA framework outlined in Chapter 2, despite a history of open sharing in the innovation commons, China remains in the upper-left quadrant (TISA cages). That is, the state has been espousing sharing in the open innovation commons—for example, the GHDDI is purportedly structured like the TISA upper-right sandboxes—but as is evident in the state's national policies and keen oversight of such domestic PPPs as the CBIK and NRTCM, it operates more in keeping with the closed innovation model of the global pharmaceutical industry, albeit with a technonationalist flair. Covid-19 medicine innovations by China's Yiling Pharmaceutical have been deployed by the national government not ecumenically and openly but strategically in countries targeted by the BRI. In contrast to the international-national-local dynamics in China, efforts in India remain committed to supporting a global innovation commons in the development of new medicines.

Notes

1. This section benefits from the superb research and translation assistance of Wenjing Wang.

2. The communists took power from the nationalists in the previous year, 1949.

3. In 2016 the State Council Information Office published a white paper, "Traditional Chinese Medicine in China," in English for international audiences. The Information Office is also known as the Office of Foreign Propaganda, and the white paper referenced in this section is part of China's international health diplomacy (State Council Information Office of the People's Republic of China 2016).

4. *Jinhua Qinggan Keli* was innovated during the 2009 H1N1 pandemic.

5. 1 USD = 6.620 CNY (IRS 2020).

6. Anonymous sources indicate that state-owned enterprises have had privileged access to certain government stimulus funds. Other private-sector companies lacking ties to the CCP (e.g., in regions far from Beijing) have been excluded, despite their long history and extensive expertise in medicine development (anonymous interviews 2016, 2018).

7. It is common in China to have a new acquaintance, upon exchanging business cards, after a few minutes of conversation hand you a second card for some enterprise he or she is "doing on the side."

8. When he was recognized as a top "academician of entrepreneurs" by the Chinese Academy of Engineering in 2009, he was criticized since as an academician and therefore civil servant, he should not be engaging with "capitalism" (Shi 2014).

9. During the Cultural Revolution, so-called rightists were often imprisoned for interrogation and subsequent sentences of forced labor. These prisons were called bullpens because those targeted for purging were called "cow-devils and snake-spirits" (牛鬼蛇神, *Niugui Sheshen*) (Zhao 2014).

10. Signaling how hard he studied, Wu often shares a story about how one winter night, he had been reading all day and continued to do so late into the night under a burning gas lamp. In the middle of the night, he stood up to go to the toilet. When he went outside into the courtyard, he fell down and woke up after a while, realizing that he must have been overcome by the gas fumes and lost consciousness (Shi 2014).

11. Iran is also known for high-quality saffron for TCM. Ingredients of TCM for the treatment of respiratory conditions—including for LH—commonly include floral extracts such as honeysuckle and herbs, including ephedra. Ephedra is also known as *Ephedra sinica*, meaning Chinese ephedra (麻黄, *Ma Huang*). Other familiar raw materials include licorice and menthol, as listed on medicine box covers and the Yiling Pharmaceutical website (Yiling Pharmaceutical 2020b).

12. The ingestion method might differ across patients and conditions: teas, powders, or capsules.

13. An FDA warning in June 2020 indicated that LH being sold by other companies was an "unapproved new drug sold in violation of FDA laws" (Viswanathan 2020).

14. The yearly average exchange rate in 2019 was 1 USD to 6.910 CNY (IRS 2020).

15. Targeting COVID-19: GHDDI Info Sharing Portal (https://ghddi-ailab .github.io/Targeting2019-nCoV).

16. In 2019, 1 USD = 6.910 CNY (IRS 2020).

17. Dr. Liu was once criticized for acting like an advertiser for Hongmao liquor (鸿茅药酒, *Hongmao Yaojiu*), saying, "We need to protect nonheritable treasures like Hongmao liquor." The brand is a traditional medicinal tonic used for relaxing muscles and promoting blood circulation. Critics noted that a "Liu Changhua" was on the list of board members for Hongmao. Hongmao liquor had been designated as an intangible cultural heritage in 2014, but some scholars argued that it had not been worthy of that designation. At the time Dr. Liu was a member of the national committee of experts for the protection of intangible cultural heritage, and they questioned

whether the review standards and procedures in this instance had been entirely objective.

18. It is interesting to note that a small number of medicinal formulas are treated under Chinese law as "state secrets" (specifically the Law of the People's Republic of China on Guarding State Secrets) (Liu and Gu 2011). Formulas afforded this protection include Yunnan Baiyao (White Drug Powder), said to have been instrumental in wound healing in World War II and the Vietnam War.

19. The authors thanked then MD candidate Dr. Shelley Ochs for validation and making the article "more fluid."

20. This might have been a subtle reference to their outsider status, since the status and location of institutions, including Chinese hospitals and departments, are ranked ordinally by number. Even at the prestigious Peking University, the university health clinic was referred to by faculty as the "Western Gate" hospital, a euphemism for patients going there to die.

4

The Turmeric War: India Takes on the World Trade Organization and Big Pharma

Most every Indian household has a jar filled with a brilliant orange-colored spice derived from the rootlike "rhizome" turmeric, freshly picked or dried and powdered. Ubiquitous, like the sacred Indian neem tree, turmeric has been used for thousands of years. I am told that every Indian grandma has her own turmeric concoction for cuisine and for household care. She would mix a bit of dried turmeric powder in a bowl with some water, making a paste for use as a poultice on a child's cut to speed the healing process. Perhaps this quotidian experience is what inspired Soman Das and Harihar Kohli of the University of Mississippi in 1995 to try to patent this common and well-documented use of turmeric that has been passed down across generations for thousands of years. Around the same time in the mid-1990s, India learned, after the fact, that companies and individuals, including other nonresident Indians like Das and Kohli, were patenting for profit medicine knowledge that had been handed down generation to generation, shared freely with all traditional medicine practitioners, scholars and grandmas alike. Das and Kohli and countless others were patenting products, based on the Indian knowledge commons, to sell. In essence, they were extracting innovative ideas and material resources out of the open commons (the sandboxes of the typology of innovation system architectures [TISA]) and pulling them into enclosed spaces and seeking patent monopolies, in other words, into innovation silos on the lower left of the TISA.

Das and Kohli were not alone in attempting to commercialize knowledge already in the public commons. Enterprising individuals, their firms, and sometimes universities attempted to use patents as a way to ensure product monopolies and gain profits on their so-called inventions. Attempts were made to patent turmeric as outlined above, as well as parts of the neem tree, which is sacred in Hindu religious practice. Business interests have even tried to patent the Indian food staple basmati rice. The Indian government intervened, spending a number of years and millions of dollars to challenge the patents that had been granted by the US Patent and Trademark Office (USPTO). American patent examiners later admitted that they had granted the patents erroneously, without adequate examination of the origins of that knowledge in the Indian public commons. This shared medicine knowledge in India descends from thousands of years of diverse medical tradition, from indigenous Ayurveda to ancient, imported Unani.

Historical-Institutional Background

The Indian Systems of Medicine (ISM) has six distinct branches, Ayurveda, Yoga, Naturopathy, Unani, Siddha, and Homoeopathy (among others), known as AYUSH, most with roots in "folk medicine" (Ravishankar and Shukla 2008). The term *folk medicine* refers to an uncodified medical system whose knowledge has been passed verbally from generation to generation without being documented in writing (Sen and Chakraborty 2017). Under British colonialism (1858–1947), ISM, especially Ayurveda, were marginalized and survived only in rural regions undisturbed by colonial rule (National Ayurvedic Medical Association 2020). Despite support from Mahatma Gandhi, leader of India's independence movement, and a number of regional governments, traditional and natural medicines were neglected in India's first postindependence national health policy in 1946 (Srinivasan 1995). At the time, the "colonial culture of India perpetuated the shift to allopathic medicine," completely transforming Indian medicine (Yeola 2017).

Over time, however, evidence of the positive impact on health of "comprehensive" primary health care integrating allopathic and ISM treatments led to recommendations by various government experts to formalize the integration of ISM with Western systems of medicines (Rudra et al. 2017). It took some decades to dislodge the bias toward allopathic medicine since "modern medicines were already deeply implanted throughout the country" (Srinivasan 1995). Dr. Bushan Patwardhan, director of the Center for Complementary and Integrative Health at Savitribai Phule Pune University, said that part of the reason why Ayurveda lost ground to allopathic medicine is that it is "not typically considered a lab science" (Patwardhan 2017). Modern medicine in India and around the world is pluralistic. Yet Patwardhan agrees that doctors of so-called complementary medicine also "need to be trained in modern research methodology, scientific writing, and documentation techniques" (Patwardhan 2017). The same goes for those researchers trying to integrate Indian natural medicines into new drug discovery (NDD), including in the growing field of biologics.

The National Health Policy 1983 (NHP-1983) recognized India's diverse traditions in medical treatment, such as Ayurveda and Unani, among others. NHP-1983 explicitly promoted the integration of ISM with the modern systems by developing ISM "in accordance with its genius" in the overall health care delivery system, including its role in innovating natural medicines at affordable prices (Ministry of Health and Family Welfare 1983). Figure 4.1 outlines the government institutions involved in innovation in medicines and health.

In March 1995, the Department of Indian Systems of Medicine and Homoeopathy (ISM&H) was established to promote traditional Indian medicines; in 2003 it was renamed the Department of Ayurveda, Yoga and Naturopathy, Unani, Siddha, and Homoeopathy (AYUSH). Unani medicine originated in ancient Egypt, Greece, and other parts of West Asia. The Mughals introduced Unani to India in the sixteenth century. Even today, Unani is practiced widely in the north of India due to the fact that the capital of the Mughal sultanate was Delhi. Siddha refers to the ancient medical traditions of Tamil and Dravidian origin practiced in the southern tip of India. Among the objectives of the Department of AYUSH upon its establishment were to upgrade the educational standards of traditional Indian medicine, inclusive of its diversity of practice, and to "draw up schemes for promotion, cultivation and regeneration of medicinal plants used in these systems," particularly for innovations in natural medicines essential for basic health care needs (Ministry of AYUSH 2020a). Scholars in the Tibetan-Indian

Figure 4.1 Inclusive Innovation in New Drug Discovery: India State and PPPs

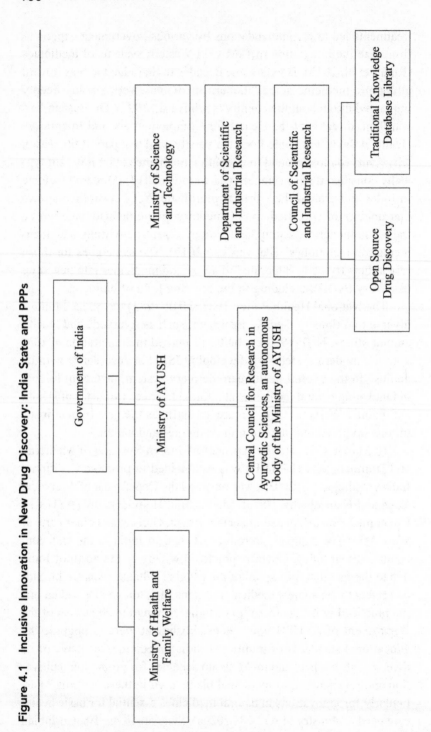

diaspora note that the *s* in AYUSH also refers to Tibetan medicine, known as Sowaricpa (*sowa*, "healing"; *ricpa*, "knowledge") (anonymous interview 2017). For political reasons (i.e., the Tibetan diaspora fled into India from Tibet after Chinese military expansion in that formerly independent nation), the role of Tibetan medicine has been obscured publicly in India. By 2018, the Ayurveda industry alone was worth $4.4 billion, $3.3 billion of which came from the sale of medicine. Projected growth was expected to be 16 percent annually to 2025 (*Economic Times* 2018; Kumar 2020).

In the National Health Policy 2002 (NHP-2002), traditional Indian medicine was noted for its contributions to basic health care access and affordability, given its "inherent advantages, such as diversity, modest cost, low level of technological input, and the growing popularity of natural plant-based products." National surveys indicated that medicines provided by AYUSH have fewer side effects and are easy to consume (Raju et al. 2016).

The NHP-2002 policy aimed to further enhance the credibility and acceptance of these alternative systems by encouraging evidence-based research and quality certification of products (Ministry of Health and Family Welfare 2002). Health and medicine policies in India are part of a broader range of policies intended to stimulate grassroots economic development through unleashing India's innovation potential with inclusive innovation policies (Dutz 2007).

Also in 2002 the National Policy on Indian Systems of Medicine and Homoeopathy was introduced. In accordance with NHP-2002, this policy aims to promote health, improve the quality of teachers and clinicians, ensure affordable ISM&H services and drugs, facilitate the availability of raw drugs, provide opportunities for the development and revival of the ISM, and so forth (Ministry of AYUSH 2002). In November 2014, the Department of AYUSH was elevated to the Ministry of AYUSH, charged with upgrading educational standards "with emphasis on epistemological strengths," conducting research based on traditional medicine knowledge (TMK) found in ancient medicine texts, implementing "quality standardization," and promoting responsible stewardship of this traditional knowledge (TK) (Rudra et al. 2017). Under the Ministry of AYUSH, the Ayurveda, Siddha, and Unani Drugs Technical Advisory Board advises the authorities on technical matters involved in the regulation of drugs derived from traditional medicine, and the Ayurveda, Siddha, and Unani Drugs

Consultative Committee advises on "uniformity in the administration of Drugs & Cosmetics Act, 1940" (Sen and Chakraborty 2017).

In 2019, the Indian government announced the establishment of a "Made in India" drug research and development (R&D) department to showcase the drug discovery capabilities of that country (Chandna 2019). The new R&D department would be under the Department of Pharmaceuticals, itself under the Ministry of Chemicals and Fertilizers.[1] The new department would seek to be a matchmaker between academic research and industry commercialization, much like similar structures in Japan, discussed in the next chapter. Challenges in making this a reality include, first, overdependence—by both India and Japan—on China for raw materials, including plant biological materials and extracted compounds, providing the basis for active pharmaceutical ingredients for biologics. Second, according to Kiran Mazumdar-Shaw, founder of India's largest biopharmaceutical company, Biocon, India is hampered by the absence of an "enabling ecosystem wherein academia generates ideas, which are incubated to proof of concept through seed and incubation funding and then taken to market through business interventions backed by venture funding" (Chandna 2019). The case studies in drug discovery and natural medicine genomic material conservation herein illustrate how public- and private-sector actors have collaborated to fill the gaps and limitations of the state and market. In doing so, the emphasis by Indian innovation agents is to share discoveries in the open commons—in other words, in the upper-right quadrant of the TISA in open and collaborative sandboxes. The cases below also reflect India's struggle to play by the rules of the game (patentable new molecular entities as the gold standard in NDD), while challenging the rules of the game in the global intellectual property rights (IPR) system (through India's positioning of traditional Indian medicine and natural medicine firmly within a global open innovation commons).

India had demonstrated previously its ability to persevere against perceived injustices in the global pharmaceutical market. For example, CIPLA's founder, Dr. Yusef Hamied, had upended the HIV/AIDS antiretroviral market in September 2002 by offering to Médecins Sans Frontières antiretroviral drugs at a tiny fraction of the then market price of up to $15,000 per year per patient. Instead Dr. Hamied offered a year's supply for less than a dollar a day, or a total of $350 a year (Odell and Sell 2003; Sen and Chakraborty 2017; see also McNeil 2001). The Big Pharma lobby did not take this well.

The imposition of the World Trade Organization (WTO) Trade-Related Aspects of Intellectual Property Rights (TRIPS) regime (outlined in Chapter 2) on the developing world was not accepted passively. With CIPLA's announcement about bringing much-needed medicines to the African continent, which had been suffering from widespread HIV/AIDS infection, India found itself at the center of a strengthening coalition of countries in the developing Global South. This coalition argued within the United Nations, World Trade Organization, and World Health Organization (WHO) that lifesaving medicines should be made available at reasonable prices and, further, that the know-how behind the drugs should be made available to generic producers. What resulted from India's activism was the Doha Declaration on WTO TRIPS and Public Health, a first step within the global IPR regime toward ensuring fair and equitable access to essential medicines. The developing country coalition had remained steadfast even in the face of intense lobbying by Big Pharma (the usual suspects: PhRMA, Pfizer, et al.) to entice individual countries to defect from the coalition (Odell and Sell 2003; see also Chaturvedi and Chataway 2009).

Despite these international successes in health diplomacy, it has proven challenging for the national government of India to integrate AYUSH into the national health delivery network and mainstream the practice of AYUSH domestically. That is, a downside to the pluralistic diversity in health care treatments and medicines is a nonstandardized national system of medicine. In 2009 the Indian National Health System Resource Centre identified a number of challenges facing the viability of AYUSH. First, despite having legal recognition, AYUSH medicines still lacked recognition in the policies and regulatory frameworks of the national health care system. This was due in part to skepticism about their scientific validation and efficacy and perceived inadequacies of AYUSH education. Second, in terms of safety, efficacy, quality, and clinical evidence base, AYUSH therapies and products lagged behind Western medicine, while at the same time there was inadequate support to generate advances in evidence-based research. Third, referring to access to medicines, biological resources critical for sustaining raw material for AYUSH remedies had been declining. Cooperation between AYUSH providers and allopathic practitioners was also weak (Saxena 2009). Another concern was the "epistemological insensitivity" and limited research focused on "theoretical foundations of the AYUSH knowledge systems." Basically, policymakers had been "blinded by the reductionist framework of modern science" with a bias toward quantitative evidence. In this case, they did not understand that "the systemic framework of AYUSH . . . cannot be measured on quantitative parameters as systemic entities can only be measured on qualitative parameters," such as the quality or impact of service or projects related to AYUSH (Saxena 2009).

The Indian government has nonetheless persevered in the aim of mainstreaming AYUSH in the national system of health. The 12th Five-Year Plan of India (2012–2017) continued the 11th Five-Year Plan's objectives associated with AYUSH systems: "mainstreaming AYUSH systems to actively supplement the efforts of the allopathic system." Subnational states have been encouraged to integrate and provide AYUSH facilities and services within all so-called modern allopathic medical facilities. It was hoped that the continued integration of AYUSH systems would prevent diseases and promote overall health, thereby reducing the welfare burden on the already overburdened state. For example, the Ministry of AYUSH led in the establishment of initiatives within the National Institute of Naturopathy in Pune, whose mission was to work with local communities in using "food as medicine." Additional measures would focus on documenting traditional knowledge of medicinal plants to contest biopiracy and bioprospecting.

To resolve lingering quality concerns about the AYUSH system, such as quality certification of raw materials and accreditation of educational programs, supplemental regulations would be imposed. For example, the modernization of pharmaceutical technology to standardize the use of natural resources and production processes was prioritized. The main difference between the 11th and the 12th Five-Year Plans was budgetary. In the twelfth plan, the total allocation for AYUSH was 10,044 crores (around $1.75 billion; one crore equals 10 million rupees). If it had been funded, the new outlay would have been more than 335 percent of the actual expenditure for AYUSH in the 11th Five-Year Plan (Planning Commission, Government of India 2013). However, the approved outlay of AYUSH was 5,186 crores (around $903.89 million), and the actual expenditure was 3,395.56 crores (around $591.83 million), which is only 33.81 percent of the original twelfth-plan outlay (National Institution for Transforming India 2017).[2] Table 4.1 outlines national policies targeting innovation in medicines and health.

During the 12th Five-Year Plan, the Ministry of AYUSH (initially still the Department of AYUSH) also implemented the National

Table 4.1   Innovation Policies for New Drug Discovery in India

Year	Name
2007–2012	Scheme for Development of AYUSH Clusters
2008	Central Sector Scheme on Conservation, Development, and Sustainable Management of Medicinal Plants
2010	Voluntary Certification Scheme for Medicinal Plant Produce (VCSMPP), revised in 2017
2012	The 12th Five-Year Plan of India (2012–2017)
2012–2017	National AYUSH Mission
2014	Scheme for Cluster Development Programme for Pharma Sector
2014	Make in India (increase domestic pharmaceutical and other intellectual and manufacturing capacity)
2017	National Health Policy 2017
2017	Vision Document 2030
2018	Pharmaceutical Promotion Development Scheme
2020	Scheme for Development of Pharmaceuticals Industry

AYUSH Mission to promote AYUSH medical systems through providing cost-effective AYUSH services; strengthening educational systems; facilitating the enforcement of quality control of Ayurveda, Siddha and Unani, and Homoeopathy (ASU&H) drugs; and ensuring sustainable availability of ASU&H raw materials. The Indian government would continue to embrace diversity in the flexibility of implementation of the programs, aiming for greater participation of the subnational quasi-autonomous state governments and union territories, the latter governed directly by the central state (Business Insider India Bureau 2019).[3] The twelvth plan also focused on the sustainable cultivation of medicinal plants, integrating medicinal plants into local farming systems, promising crop diversification, and improving the incomes of participating farmers. It would also support collective efforts at cultivation and processing in clusters through self-help groups, growers' cooperatives/associations, producer companies, and other organizations with established links to manufacturers, wholesalers, traders, and R&D institutions.[4] The Honey Bee Network (HBN), discussed below, is one such example. The National Medicinal Plants Board, established in 2000, would take responsibility for assessing the demand and supply of medicinal plants, providing guidance for the formulation of schemes, and promoting the conservation of medicinal plants (National Medicinal Plants Board 2020a). These measures have had mixed success, with national-policy-fiat-led cultivation projects doing poorly in terms of yield and sustainability compared to grassroots projects inclusive of local stakeholders with the requisite quotidian local ecosystem knowledge, as the HBN example below illustrates.

The National Health Policy 2017 continued previous policies integrating AYUSH into the mainstream. It would include measures for strengthening the farming of herbal plants with "developing mechanisms for certification of 'prior knowledge' of traditional community health care providers," enhancing their skills, and "engaging them in the conservation and generation of the raw materials required" (Ministry of Health and Family Welfare 2017). To enhance confidence in the quality of medicinal plants, the National Medicinal Plants Board also worked with the Quality Council of India to implement the Voluntary Certification Scheme for Medicinal Plants Produce, which was approved in 2010 and put into effect in 2017 (National Medicinal Plants Board 2020b). Given the intimate relationship between Prime Minister Narendra Modi, Bharatiya Janata Party politicians, and "Baba" Ramdev, founder of Ayurvedic drug behemoth Patanjali, India would continue to see national government expansion into traditional medicine protection and economic development (see Worth 2018).[5]

In 2017, the Central Council for Research in Ayurvedic Sciences (CCRAS), an autonomous body of the Ministry of AYUSH, published the "CCRAS Vision Document 2030," a fifteen-year plan in accordance with the United Nations Sustainable Development Goals. CCRAS would sponsor "development and validation of Ayurvedic drugs" by "integrating ancient wisdom with modern technology" and work "to bring Ayurveda to the people through innovations related to diagnostics, preventive, promotive as well as treatment methods and also introduce scientific research for sustained availability of quality natural resources, to translate them into products and processes and in synergy with concerned organizations to introduce these innovations into public health systems" (CCRAS 2017).

According to the report published by CCRAS in 2018, "In the recent past the Council has generated scientific evidence on safety and efficacy of approximately 82 classical Ayurvedic formulations on more than 32 diseases/conditions," and "validation of approximately 35 classical Ayurvedic formulations is continuing for generation of scientific evidence on safety and efficacy on 14 diseases/conditions," with "multicentre observational studies [undertaken] across its peripheral institute." Also, the council has been engaged in drug development. By 2018, twelve Ayurvedic products had been developed and commercialized under CCRAS projects (Dhiman et al. 2018). For example, the formulation Ayush-64 has indications in the treatment of malaria. Ingredients are natural medicinals, including saptaparna stem bark, katuki root, chirayata whole plant, and kuberaksha seed (CCRAS 2014). Another example is Ayush-82, a natural medicinal plant formulation for diabetes mellitus (IME-9 2020).

A study by CCRAS cited common reasons that lead patients to prefer traditional Indian medicines, including "lesser side effects, efficacy in chronic diseases [*sic*] management, improvement in quality of life, health promotion and preventive potential," and lack of access to allopathic medical services. The study also stated that AYUSH medicines "offer promising strategy of management in certain refractory diseases . . . liver disorders . . . [and] mental disorders" (Srikanth et al. 2015).[6]

In 2020, Ramdev, the founder of Patanjali Ayurved drug company, was accused of using his political connections to Prime Minister Modi to promote untested Covid-19 drugs. In that year Patanjali had marketed "Coronil" and other formulations, claiming they would prevent contraction of the coronavirus. Previously Ramdev had parlayed his position as Yogi, or guru, to Narendra Modi into a multimillion-dollar natural medicine conglomerate. Patanjali's natural medicines appealed to domestic Indian consumers fatigued by high prices of allopathic drugs and their side effects, and Ramdev's exhortation of *swadeshi* self-reliance in his marketing campaigns also played to a renewed Hindu nationalism (Ibata-Arens 2019a). The Ministry of AYUSH responded to public criticisms calling out the Ramdev-Modi ties as unfair and preferential, stating it had approved the Patanjali drug products only as "immunity boosters" (Pandey 2020). In 2019, Patanjali reported revenue of $1.3 billion (Findlay and Singh 2020).

During the Covid-19 pandemic, Vaidya Rajesh Kotecha, then secretary of the Ministry of AYUSH, posted an "advisory" on March 6, 2020. This advisory recommended several AYUSH drugs as prophylactics against the coronavirus, "supported with evidences for promotion of immunity and help in improving the respiratory symptoms in similar diseases" (Kotecha 2020). The Ministry of AYUSH also faced criticism after it released other advisories suggesting such homoeopathic drugs as Arsenium Album 30 could improve immunity. Shaikh (2020) noted that none of the studies proved that Arsenium Album 30 would "boost immunity in humans or in animals to protect against infectious diseases." She criticized that "homeopathy as an immune booster against COVID-19 remains . . . the most dangerous pseudo-science that the AYUSH ministry has produced during this pandemic" (Shaikh 2020). In response to public criticism about the ministry's recommendation of unproven drugs for treatment against Covid-19, the ministry appointed an "interdisciplinary task force" to investigate the claims and counterclaims. Given the lack of precise standards for plant medicinal formulations and insufficient numbers of studies demonstrating safety and efficacy, the new task force would oversee the design and implementation of studies drawing from experts within such organizations as the Indian Council of Medical Research, the Department of Biotechnology, and the WHO.

Scholars of Ayurvedic medicine have also criticized efforts to conform to Western scientific methodologies. "Ayurvedic medicine cannot be used on a molecular level. We cannot separate ingredients and use them independently. Good quality ingredients have to be used as a whole" since extracting molecules from the whole plant may cause negative side effects evidenced by the many synthetic chemical drugs that have proven problematic within the Western pharmaceutical industry (Yeola 2017).

In April 2020, the Indian government announced an "extramural research scheme" to encourage the clinical study of AYUSH treatments for Covid-19, including AYUSH-64. However, the call for proposals was open for only nine days, funding was limited to ten lakh (around $13,128.84; one lakh equals 100,000 rupees), and further research was required to be completed within six months (*The Wire* 2020).[7] The limits on funds available to validate AYUSH treatments are exacerbated by the limits on health insurance coverage for AYUSH medicines.

Health Insurance Coverage

In 2017, the WHO indicated that India's out-of-pocket expenditure per capita was $43, which was 62 percent of current health expenditure, a measure of how much individuals spend annually on health care needs (WHO 2020d). According to the Insurance Regulatory and Development Authority of India Health Insurance Regulations,

"General insurers and health insurers may endeavor to provide coverage for one or more systems covered under 'AYUSH treatment' provided the treatment has been undertaken in a government hospital or in any institute recognized by government and/or accredited by Quality Council of India or National Accreditation Board on Health" (Insurance Regulatory and Development Authority of India 2016). Fifteen insurance companies approved by the Indian government would cover AYUSH treatments, given that such treatments were received at a hospital or institute accredited by the Indian government (Ministry of AYUSH 2020b). As of 2020, 290 AYUSH treatments were covered: ninety-seven Ayurvedic, forty-nine Siddha, eighty-six Unani, twenty-seven Yoga, and thirty-one naturopathy (Ministry of AYUSH 2016, 2020d, 2020e, 2020f). Similar to the role of the central state in China in promoting the sustainable development of the traditional medicine industry, India would also seek to compensate for weaknesses in the state and market through the establishment of public-private partnerships (PPPs).

The Indian State and PPPs

The then Department of AYUSH introduced the cluster scheme in the 11th Five-Year Plan (2007–2012) and implemented it in the 12th Five-Year Plan (2012–2017). It allocated 121.75 crores (around $21.22 million) in the 12th Five-Year Plan to PPPs called special purpose vehicles (SPVs), formed by at least fifteen enterprises located in a cluster from the AYUSH sector.[8] These AYUSH enterprises were required to hold at least 51 percent equity in the SPVs, and government agencies, financial institutions, strategic buyers, and Ayurveda, Siddha, and Unani colleges would be permitted to hold the remainder. The initiative would target micro, small, and medium enterprises. A project management consultant would act as a link between the Department (then Ministry) of AYUSH and industries. Also, state governments would provide land and infrastructure resources to SPVs (Ministry of AYUSH 2020c).

To expand health care interventions across the whole country, the Department of AYUSH had promoted the concept of the AYUSH Gram (*gram* means "village," the lowest level of subdivision in India), where one village per block (the district subdivision) would be selected for AYUSH health care interventions and receive facilities, including hospitals—for example, in Karnataka—under the PPP model for a period of three years.[9] In this case, "a total of 10 Gram panchayats (village councils) in nine districts were selected," and they were handled by ten nongovernment organizations (NGOs) for "addressing health issues using traditional methods in their unique ways and approaches." For example, the SOUKYA Foundation, a charitable trust established in Bangalore by Dr. Issac Mathai in 1996, started the work with an AYUSH Gram in Jadigenahalli in 2012. The foundation provided a health care home remedies program focused on educating local residents in preventing minor illnesses at affordable cost while reducing overall the health care cost burden on households. It also trained locals in the benefits of cultivating their own medicinal gardens. According to subsequent research on the economic impact of AYUSH Gram, the farmers showed disinterest in cultivating medicinal plants due to "scarcity of water and difficulties involved in adapting to new [government imposed] cultivation options." Instead, locals were found to continue cultivation of common medicinal plants endemic to that region. It was also noted that local teachers had played a key role in educating students about reasons to protect medicinal plants. The following case studies illustrate the challenges facing India at national (Traditional Knowledge Digital Library, TKDL), international (Honey Bee Network, HBN, and Open Source Drug Discovery, OSDD), and local (reverence for *deo rahati*) levels in protecting and conserving the sustainable development of innovations in natural medicine while supporting the fair and equitable access to essential medicines, including the panoply of AYUSH medicines.

Traditional Knowledge Digital Library

The city of Pune, Maharashtra, is located in a biodiverse mountainous region between the capital of India, New Delhi, and Mumbai on the western coast. Pune, known as "Poona" under British colonialism, has a mild climate compared to the sweltering summers in New Delhi and Mumbai. The area was settled thousands of years ago and has since evolved into a community of diverse ethnicities and religious traditions. Like Kyoto in Japan, Pune is known as an education hub in India, home to numerous universities and public and private

research institutions (Mulla 2017). In addition to being the cultural
center of the Maharashtra region, Pune is also a center for training
and scholarship in Ayurvedic medicine. Regarded as the "Oxford of
the East" by some, the centuries-old Tilak Ayurved Mahavidyalaya
Center for the study of Ayurveda has over time brought leading
scholars, practitioners, and students of Indian traditional medicine to
settle in that city. These intellectual luminaries included Dr. Dinshaw
Mehta, personal doctor to Mahatma Gandhi, who tended to Gandhi
during the colonial opposition leader's imprisonment in Pune (1942–
1944). Unbeknownst to many, Gandhi studied naturopathy under Dr.
Mehta from the 1930s.[10] The Maharashtra region is also known for
its political independence and fearlessness in bucking the trends and
whims of national politics. In contrast to the fractious and violent
politics to the north, its Hindu and Muslim communities have coex-
isted in harmony, facilitating sharing of medical practices across traditions. Not surprisingly then, it was scientists from Pune, including
Ragunath "R. A." Mashelkar, who led the initial opposition to the US
turmeric patent that eventually became a national movement (Patwardhan 2017).

India's Council of Scientific and Industrial Research (CSIR) had
fought and won against the US Patent and Trademark Office's neem
and turmeric patents, ensuring that the traditional knowledge remained
in the public commons, but at significant financial cost: millions of US
dollars. In 2000, a study of data in the USPTO database revealed that
80 percent of the nearly 5,000 references in patents for products based
on 290 medicinal plants were to just seven plants of Indian origin
(Gupta and Varshney 2015; see also Gupta and Balasubrahmanyam
1998; R. K. Gupta 2003).[11] Further, out of 760 patents, 350 should not
have been granted because "prior art" was well documented in the
Indian traditional medicine literature (Chakravarty and Mahajan
2010).[12] In their response, patent examiners at the USPTO noted that
they were not aware of the Indian knowledge corpus in this regard.
India's government would have to intervene to defend Indian TMK to
ensure it remained in the public commons, in the open innovation
sandboxes described by the TISA framework.

For V. K. Gupta, then director of CSIR, this realization was "the
trigger" for the creation of the Traditional Knowledge Digital
Library. Having served in the World Intellectual Property Organization (WIPO), representing such small developing countries with rich

traditional medicine histories as Nepal and Bhutan, Gupta knew that it would be critical to organize and classify TMK in two ways. First, patent examiners in the leading patent-granting offices in the West should be able to read the TKDL in their native languages, for example, English and French. Second, metadata should be organized not by the original Sanskrit, Urdu, or Arabic names but by the Latin name of the biological plant materials—consistent with Western practice. This would present problems later in that some Indian species were unknown outside the Indian medicinal canon—and therefore untranslatable. This conformance with Western standards of classification of data on TMK would also be criticized for subordinating classical Indian materia medica to the so-called colonial mentality, very much like the enclosure effect evident in the behavior of Western pharmaceutical companies, placing them in the secretive and closed upper left of the TISA. Gupta and several hundred colleagues, including Dr. R. A. Mashelkar and Anil Gupta, would take on the monumental task of codifying India's vast TMK corpus.

"Prior art," proving that a given discovery was established in the public commons, must be demonstrated either through previous publication—for example, in a scientific journal—or within a database of such knowledge. For the TKDL this involved, for example, translating 35,000 *shoklas* (verses) from ancient texts on Ayurvedic medicine, as well as an equal number from Unani, the traditional medicine descending from ancient Arabic-speaking and Muslim communities. Other indigenous medicine would also be included (Siddha and Yoga). Gupta's background in engineering helped here. The 230,000 initial formulations comprising the TKDL, written in Arabic, Hindi, Persian, Sanskrit, and Urdu, would be translated with the help of an original machine language–driven translation script. These languages and formulations would eventually be translated and codified into English, French, German, Japanese, and Spanish. The work of setting up the TKDL was officially a state-led affair (CSIR, Ministry of Health, Family, and Welfare, and later the new Ministry of AYUSH). Private-sector involvement would entail collaboration with hundreds of traditional medicine scholars, particularly in academic institutions (though the latter are generally considered also to be civil servants). Also included on the project team were information technology specialists—for which India's domestic capacity in this industry came in handy (Ibata-Arens 2019a)—and patent experts (e.g., attorneys) from the private sector.

After an eight-year effort (by 2009), the TKDL had an impressive 30 million pages of searchable data. Previously, Dr. Ragunath Mashelkar, during his term as chief of the CSIR, noted the supposed novel use of turmeric in wound healing, in addition to having been codified in Sanskrit medical reference texts millennia before, was known and used even today by "practically every Indian housewife" (Das 2006). Rajeshwari Hariharan, of the Indian legal firm K&S Partners, which represented India in the fight to keep the traditional knowledge about neem and turmeric in the public commons, supported the aims of the TKDL, saying it was "a way to prevent monopoly patents from being granted" and keeping the information open to the public "because this traditional wealth is for the benefit of mankind."[13]

Dr. Mashelkar saw the establishment of TKDL as just the beginning of India's "defensive protection" movement to guard the innovation commons from commodification. Chakravarty and Mahajan (2010) define defensive protection, referring to the WIPO definition of intellectual property (IP) rights, as a way of "safeguarding against illegitimate IP rights taken out by others over TK subject matter." Not only would traditional medicine be codified in a commons database—though, as of 2020, only accessible by patent examiners under strict nondisclosure agreements—but if all went as planned, the next to be documented in the database would be indigenous architecture techniques, oral tribal knowledge, folklore, and even Indian foods. Echoing the concerns of other government officials not wanting foreigners to "sell our own knowledge to us," Mashelkar recognized that part of the impetus for TKDL was the realization after the protracted battles in the 1990s over turmeric and neem, as well as attempts to patent basmati rice and yoga poses, that India "did not have the time or money to fight each patent" (Jayaraman 1999, 414).

According to Hirwade (2010), discussions of the need to create a global knowledge commons database had been underway in WIPO as early as 1999 at the urging of Indian representatives (referring to Mashelkar and Gupta). It would be much more efficient, members of the Indian task force on the protection of traditional knowledge agreed, to protect traditional knowledge as a "collective human right" by codifying it in a commons database (Hirwade 2010). India, biologically rich but not yet as technologically rich as countries with developed pharmaceutical industries with concomitant legal resources, would wager that positioning its vast TMK in the public domain would be the best bet for maintaining fair and equitable access on a global system level to essential natural medicines. The ideal of fair and equitable access would become a guiding feature of the Indian OSDD project, an emergent innovation platform that became more than a PPP, as discussed below. Worthy aspirations to be sure, but up against the reality of powerful and influential entrenched interests behind leaving the system as is.

Sharma (2017) criticized the efficacy of the TKDL in defending India's traditional knowledge, citing an analysis of data related to patents granted annually by the USPTO (about 2,000). Sharma found that TKDL was ineffective in light of the fact that US patent examiner compensation was tied to the number of applications "disposed of" within a certain amount of time. In other words, despite the effort by India, American patent examiners, incentivized to close applications quickly, would not bother to check the TKDL and, as a result, would grant patents unduly. The European Patent Office, in contrast, had demonstrated consultation with TKDL in the issuing or rejection of patents and, as such, was more likely to reject a patent after referencing the TKDL. India's idea for establishing a global innovation commons had not yet taken root in the United States, which, as of 2020, held on to its position as the seat of political power within the global pharmaceutical industry, obscured within the multilateral WTO TRIPS system.

Furthermore, though the TKDL has about the same number of Ayurvedic (Hindu) and Unani (Muslim) formulations, it has not been immune from accusations that it results from politics of Hindu valorization, itself subordinated under a Western scientific knowledge system (Thomas 2010). Thomas and others (e.g., Gaudillière 2019) have criticized the TKDL project in that, in the process of codification and labeling as "traditional," it removes the formulations from their spiritual, religious, and socioeconomic contexts, placing them in a static point in time. In reality, Ayurveda and other traditional Indian medicines are constantly evolving, adapting to the health needs of patients, not to mention the declining availability of biological materials due to overharvesting and climate pressures (Finetti 2011). In other words, by ensuring they remain in the open commons (TISA upper right), innovations flourish. Codification amounting to commodification of traditional medicine knowledge through the TKDL and the National Registry for Traditional Chinese Medicine

(NRTCM) in China offends many traditional medicine practitioners since, to them, their healing knowledge holds a "sacred value which they would not part with for money" (quoted in Thomas 2010, 661).

Meanwhile, the Indian state has taken on the role of arbiter of what is deserving of codification and thus status. For example, the written is deemed superior to the handed down through oral folkloric practices. Finetti (2011) notes the role that oral traditional knowledge played in the singular ability, in the 2004 tsunami, of the Mokin indigenous people of Thailand to save themselves, having transmitted the knowledge of water movements across generations. As such (as noted in Chapter 2) "traditional" refers to the way knowledge is created, preserved, and transmitted across generations, not the knowledge per se. In sum, traditional medicine knowledge is dynamic, not static, and its codification within the TKDL and other such databases is merely a snapshot at a moment in time of a broader dynamic and continuous innovation process. This is the dilemma in the creation of such sui generis systems—defensive, as in TKDL, or proactive/offensive, as in China's NRTCM—namely, how to preserve and protect traditional knowledge without preventing its evolution (Finetti 2011).

Rather than pursue the proactive (some would say nationalist) path in China via its national traditional Chinese medicine (TCM) registry (still held as a national state secret in 2021), India would pursue a commons approach, consistent with its history in bringing affordable medicines to the developing world—for example, CIPLA and antiretrovirals for the treatment of HIV/AIDS in Africa. China, as discussed in the previous chapter, would also pursue a sui generis system for the protection of its TMK, establishing a national patenting system for traditional medicines and partnering with such designated TCM companies (often state-owned enterprises) as Tong Ren Tang to grant patents.

Defensive protection prevents IP rights from being given to those other than traditional knowledge originators, be they communities or individuals. Proactive or positive protection, on the other hand, confers IP rights to traditional knowledge holders, empowering them to promote their interests, be they economic or otherwise (Ahmad and Godhwani 2012). As such, unlike India's public commons–based framing, China's approach has been closer to the Western "entitlements" approach within standard legal practice. That is, the discourse around IPR involves the granting of exclusive rights "to an individual to exploit particular creations of human ingenuity" (Ahmad and God-hwani 2012, 11). This dilemma is at the crux of challenges involved in governing the fair and equitable use of resources shared in the commons (Ostrom 1990). Traditional knowledge holders believe on the whole that their healing knowledge is not property, as such, but a gift bestowed by nature and thus should not be "alienated in favor of one person" or corporation (Krishna 2019). Similar to indigenous communities in China, within tribal communities in India including an estimated 100 million forest dwellers, knowledge is held by the community and heretofore transmitted and saved across generations orally. Consequently, its codification in TKDL presents a new risk to the community in that, in the wrong hands, it could be exploited by biopirates (e.g., ethnopharmacologists suspected to be in cahoots with Western pharmaceutical companies).

To compensate for such deficiencies in protection by TKDL, some have argued for a different kind of sui generis system in India along the lines of appellation or geographic certification of medicinal plant gene banks, thereby securing the protection of these national biological assets. Others have argued for bolder measures—namely, banning all patents on "life and living organisms including biodiversity, genes, and cell lines" (Hirwade and Hirwade 2012). India's experience has illustrated the difficulty faced by biological and TK resource rich but technologically and legalistically poor communities in protecting their knowledge from unfair expropriation. It has not been uncommon for communities not to become aware of the theft of their IP until years later. Hirwade and Hirwade (2012) have proposed a people's biodiversity register akin to the aforementioned proposals for forest gene bank certifications like appellations.

Multilateral organizations have come a long way toward inclusion of the voices of traditional knowledge holders—for example, in the protection efforts by the UN Convention on Biological Diversity and codification of traditional knowledge by the WHO discussed briefly in Chapters 1 and 2. However, due to the WTO's dominant discourse enabling powerful interests to exploit India's traditional knowledge, backed by the threat of market exclusion of India's products, the market and political power over the exploitation of natural medicine has been concentrated in the WTO. In a 2019 article assessing the success of the TKDL, Krishna notes that in light of the expense (about fifteen crores between 2002 and 2012), in the end the

TKDL succeeded merely in detaching India's traditional medicine knowledge from community and from nature, decontextualizing and destroying its "essence." Further, for Krishna the TKDL is an exercise in hypocrisy, since its aim is to promote transparency as the best deterrent to malfeasance. Patent applicants would know that the TKDL documented prior art in its modern translations of ancient formulations. As of 2019, like the principal investigators for the TCM registry in China (discussed in the previous chapter), CSIR scientists could not access their own creation, even for the purpose of research unrelated to commercialization.[14] Consequently, TKDL's defensive protection model is neither sandbox (promoting open and inclusive innovation; upper-right quadrant of the TISA) nor pool (sharing of codified knowledge on a limited basis; lower-right quadrant of the TISA). Despite its lofty aspirations, TKDL found itself caged in by the Indian government's judicious caution about exposing TKDL data to foreign expropriation. The Honey Bee Network and the Open Source Drug Discovery project have had varying degrees of success at becoming open and inclusive TISA sandboxes of innovation.

Honey Bee Network

Before the turmeric and neem debacles of the mid-1990s, Anil Gupta had envisioned an international network of creative thinkers and innovators to harness the sustainable development potential of managing resources in the commons. Gupta had witnessed, during his decades of community service, the way in which civil servants and NGOs had designed local economic development interventions with the assumption that "poor people are too poor to be able to think and plan on their own" (Gupta 1996). Consequently, despite lip service to participatory governance over local resources, the poor had "seldom been given the opportunity to articulate their own agenda and visions and to determine the terms on which outsiders could participate" (Gupta 1996, 1). Rather, Gupta's experience in Gujarat, India (known worldwide, not incidentally, for its export of diaspora entrepreneurs, such as the TIE network), taught him and development professionals such as himself of the potential in recognizing the experimental creativity of poor people in inventing solutions in adverse environments.

The vision for the HBN originated in the mid-1980s in farming communities in Gujarat. The metaphor of the honeybee was apt because these creatures do things uncommon in the behavior of development professionals. First, honeybees collect pollen from flowers, harnessing precious biological resources with nary a complaint from the flowers themselves. Second, honeybees connect flowers to flowers in the process of pollination. Gupta notes that indigenous people certainly have a right to complain when their knowledge and material resources are "collected" by outsiders without credit or benefit. Further, when development professionals and other outsiders communicate "found" knowledge in English, French, and other languages, local holders of such knowledge cannot connect with one another across national boundaries unless they are also fluent in said international languages. HBN compensates for this international organizational failure by giving credit where credit is due and insisting that knowledge be shared in the vernacular languages of the holders of such knowledge worldwide. It seeks to create an innovation sandbox in that peoples and ideas are included for the purpose of pursuing collaborative innovation supporting sustainable economic development. HBN functions as an innovation pool and links formal and informal science and scientists at the grassroots level sharing well-tested practical knowledge internationally.

Gupta and colleagues established the Society for Research and Initiatives for Sustainable Technologies and Institutions (SRISTI) as a way to provide organizational support to HBN but not impede its open and inclusive architecture for innovation activities. For example, SRISTI developed a database of local innovations, paying particular attention to methods and solutions that could be generalized to national and local contexts elsewhere—for example, in communities facing similar environmental challenges. Criticizing unnamed international organizations, Gupta and his developmental team seized upon the opportunity to engage university students in HBN.[15] Like their counterparts in other countries, Indian university students perform required community service. At some private universities, in order to graduate, students must complete up to 200 hours. During summer vacations they might assist as "innovation scouts," looking for the most eccentric tinkerers in local villages and simply observing them and learning from them in an unobtrusive manner. HBN has also found that a little competition helps to stimulate cross-community collaboration. Students compete (not the local inventors themselves) on the number and ingeniousness of innovations identified. Students are trained to recognize developmental alternatives based on what people have rather than what they do not. In addition to identifying potential to bring innovations from "land to lab to land," students learn humility and respect for local innovators. Born of adversity, HBN has connected primarily farmers but also traditional medicine innovators around the world through "knowledge nodes" in a model of empowerment and sustainable technology development. In this manner, HBN fills the gaps between failures of the state (in protecting indigenous communities from exploitation by multinational corporations and national Ayurvedic pharma companies) and failures of the market, as market incentives are to exploit not cooperate and share. HBN has demonstrated over the years that for a knowledge system to be sustainable, it must be just and fair. That does not mean, however, that it should not be competitive. The stakes in competition can be nonmonetary, honoring contributions or signifying status via nonmaterial incentives, akin to the grander schemes of so-called challenges by deep-pocketed international foundations mentioned in Chapter 2.

HBN competitions have also been a way not only to interest local youth in the innovations of their elders but to transmit this knowledge from old to young. Scaria and Dedeurwaerdere (2012) refer to this as HBN's "contractually created knowledge pool" whereby entrepreneurs and locals benefit from collaborative competition. Akin to the OSDD's crowdsourcing of innovative solutions from volunteer researchers, SRISTI had set up licensing contracts of public-domain-based traditional knowledge. For example, these would be made available as packages of traditional knowledge that could be used across India for a modest fee. For example, SRISTI licensed a package or grouping of traditional medicine knowledge innovations to Matrix Biosciences. In addition to profit sharing, product packaging included the names and photographs of innovators (Scaria and Dedeurwaerdere 2012). In this way, HBN serves as a platform through which local community members can be rewarded in nonmonetary status in addition to monetary compensation. Whereas HBN succeeds at inclusivity at the local level, sharing discoveries among network members (and is thus closer to a pool) in a quasi-open sandbox, OSDD aims for global inclusive innovation in an innovation sandbox for all humanity.

Open Source Drug Discovery

Diseases that have all but been eradicated in the developed world, for example tuberculosis (TB) and malaria, continue to afflict and kill many millions of people globally. Biophysicist Samir Brahmandchari, director general in 2008 of the Indian Council of Scientific and Industrial Research, noted that India had been fighting—partly due to TRIPS, as discussed previously—a war between "health as a right and health as a business" (Singh 2008, 201). Brahmandchari, in announcing in 2008 the establishment of the Open Source Drug Discovery platform, noted that it was designed to compensate for market failure in that the private sector—that is, the global pharmaceutical industry—had yet to step up to the challenge of developing drugs for diseases affecting the poor and the developing world. Neglected tropical diseases, including TB, malaria, and also leishmaniasis—the bacterium better known for causing the affliction leprosy—have been neglected by Big Pharma because these diseases afflict patients in communities that would never become major "profit centers" for the industry. The pharmaceutical industry—in fierce competition in the race to bring to market lucrative "blockbuster" drugs for noncommunicable diseases (diabetes, heart conditions, cancer, obesity)—was notoriously secretive about its research and development and further conducted its research in closed-off silos, avoiding collaboration outside company boundaries or within strict nondisclosure agreements with outside partners. In other words, they were hiding out on the left side of the TISA, closed off from exchanges with broader communities. This was evident in the crisis innovation scenario played out in 2020 in the race to be the first to deploy a worldwide novel coronavirus vaccine, which involved closed and secretive architectures mimicking those in the pharmaceutical industry. With this in mind, such emerging citizen-scientist networks as the Rapid Deployment Vaccine Collaboration and OSDD spin-off Open Source Pharma Foundation developing open-source Covid-19 vaccines in 2021 represent anomalies worthy of further study (Regalado 2020; Reader 2020).

OSDD would be the opposite of a silo: it would be open to any researcher interested in participating, and all findings would be shared across institutional and national boundaries, making it an inclusive innovation sandbox. India in 2008 had two unique capacities: the will to challenge the Western pharmaceutical ways of doing things in order to encourage innovative activity and the wherewithal of explicit government backing coupled with domestic capacity in information technology at the time. For example, Infosys was an early partner in the OSDD project, working with sponsors, including Sun Microsystems, to set up the complex network software platform within which global R&D collaborations would occur. Infosys also designed the user portal for OSDD (Bhardwaj et al. 2011).

New OSDD users would agree, upon signing in for the first time, to a "clickwrap" license, agreeing not to attempt to patent any data obtained through their collaborations on the platform. Users would also receive micro credits for their discrete contributions to project goals, themselves broken down into smaller packets of objectives. Each and every contribution (e.g., annotating genetic code) would be dated and stamped with their username. Work would be peer-reviewed by senior mentor experts. New users would have the opportunity to undergo extensive training and also socialization into the mind-set of open-source communities. Some would describe OSDD more as crowdsourcing (TISA pools) than as open-sourcing (TISA sandboxes) per se in part because students, including undergraduates, are encouraged to contribute but also because OSDD is not purely open in the public commons. That is, in order to access data, users must sign in and accept the licensing terms. The vision for OSDD was inspired by the open-source software movement ignited by Linus Torvalds. Torvalds conceptualized the revolutionary open-source Linux operating system as a communitarian alternative to the operating system duopoly of Microsoft and Apple. Biomedical scientists took the Linux concept and applied it to open-source data sharing, advancing innovations in bioinformatics, visualization, simulation, and data mining for the purpose of biomedical research and development. Hence the potential emerged for in silico modeling in new drug discovery, bringing massive increases in speed in developing new molecular targets for drugs at a fraction of the cost undertaken by the standard closed and siloed pharmaceutical industry model.[16]

Open-source systems are neither markets nor hierarchies. The definition of property in the community of open-source science, for example, focuses on the right to distribute as opposed to the right to exclude others from access.[17] Thus open-source science presented an emergent organizational form very different from the predominant commercial proprietary and secretive value system prevalent in the global pharmaceutical industry at the time (Jha and Nerurkar 2010). "Open" in OSDD, as in HBN, does not, however, mean without competition.

The element of competition within the OSDD is similar to that of the Human Genome Project (HGP), which organized researchers into competing nodes or teams as a way to streamline the process of mapping the human genome.[18] The OSDD would break complex problems down into smaller tasks—more manageable in time and number of participants. Nonmonetary incentives were built into the OSDD collaboration platform whereby contributors would earn credits, moving from learning from training and learning by doing, to signaling their inclusion in a broader community of like-minded others, to ultimately sharing their collaborations across institutional and national boundaries and being recognized for them. OSDD would introduce a bit of hierarchy into its internationally networked peer crowdsourcing platform. Rights and privileges would be earned based on accrued contributions over time. In this manner, some users would eventually earn "gold" or "platinum" status based on their individual contributions.

Zakir Thomas, OSDD project director in 2012, noted that after five years of operation, money had never been an issue—that is, the government funds pledged in 2008 had yet to be exhausted. Rather, the challenge for OSDD was really about "winning hearts and minds." It was about changing the dominant mind-set of secrecy and closedness in global drug development to an embrace of the innovative potential of open-source drug discovery. By 2012 OSDD had attracted 7,000 researchers. Most of them were Indian. OSDD had yet to convince the rest of world that its open and inclusive innovation architecture was worthwhile (Masum et al. 2013). At the same time, leaving a legacy is a powerful motivator. Dr. T. Balganesh, honored in India as a distinguished scientist and twenty-five-year veteran of AstraZeneca Bangalore, had become, in 2011, the new OSDD chief of drug development. For Balganesh, his time in global pharma at AstraZeneca had taught him that if India wanted access to drugs for neglected diseases, it would have to develop them itself (Singh 2012). By 2012 OSDD would have anti-TB molecules nearing clinical trials, while the malaria and leishmaniasis programs were just taking off. Echoing Balganesh's sentiments about the willingness of pharmaceutical companies to neither develop drugs for neglected diseases nor embrace an open-source innovation model, pharma industry veteran entrepreneur and expert in innovation Bernard Munos lamented the devolution of a culture of creativity to one limited to that of "process" in the global drug development pipeline, the innovation silos of the TISA.

This shift in culture for Munos related to the push for me-too drugs that could be sources of reliable revenue streams through monopoly patents. Like the HBN network model, OSDD, and other open and inclusive platforms for drug discovery, alternative models have been emerging "in places like India and China" precisely because, in the face of competition from leading Western economies, they have to do more with less. Alternative drug development models in these countries have arisen out of adversity. In the current global climate, the quick and lean "outside the box" players are the new insurgents. Meanwhile large pharmaceutical companies are the incumbents. OSDD is one among many emerging organizational insurgents challenging the global order. For Munos, incumbents rarely survive successful insurgent-led disruptions unless they adapt or co-opt (e.g., Pfizer acquiring BioNTech discoveries for its co-developed Covid-19 vaccine). A handful of global pharma firms have adapted, as will be discussed in Chapter 5 under the Global Health Innovative Technology Fund NDD initiative in Japan, not to mention previous market disruptions led by Indian pharmaceutical companies including CIPLA and Biocon (Ibata-Arens 2019a).

Through its open, inclusive, and transparent platform, OSDD has, in its first decade, contributed to the global understanding of TB through its Linux-inspired collaboration platform. Its structured play sandbox model has encouraged generations of Indian students to contribute, while socializing them into a mind-set that embraces open innovation. OSDD's sandbox has the potential to expand on a global scale. As of 2010, 80 percent of its users were Indian. Fewer than 4 percent were US-based and even fewer were European (2 percent). By 2020 its user base was somewhat more balanced throughout the world. Nevertheless, OSDD full transparency at all stages created certain vulnerabilities. Its inclusion of undergraduate students would face criticism—for example, the OSDD was admonished for publishing results before proper "peer review" by gatekeepers of international journals.[19]

A hotly debated posting on Nature.com in 2010 (Jayaraman 2010) attacked the OSDD for boasting that it had reannotated (meaning mapped and verified) the entire genome of *Mycobacterium tuberculosis*. Dozens of commentators on the posting (most were supportive of the efforts of OSDD leadership and its volunteer annotators, many of whom were students) also implied that those few posts critical of OSDD must have been "planted" by pharmaceutical companies.[20] Judging by the less than ethical marketing practices of Arthur Sackler (of Purdue Pharma and opioid addiction crisis infamy) and Pfizer as the company built its global empire in the twentieth century, mentioned in Chapter 2, these suspicions may have been warranted (Posner 2020). The OSDD and emerging organizational forms like it present a real threat to the status quo by ensuring that research into cures for disease remains open in terms of access to knowledge as well as no-fee licensing, which essentially amounts to the sharing of discoveries in the open commons. These initiatives have also signaled that there exists an alternative way to engage in new drug discovery that is open and inclusive (TISA sandboxes and pools) instead of closed and exclusive (TISA cages and silos). This presents a countermovement to the tragedy of the anticommons put in place by the global pharmaceutical–backed TRIPS IPR patent-compliance system. The edifice of WTO TRIPS was predicated on the now tenuous claim that patent monopolies are the best way to stimulate innovation— incremental innovation for profit perhaps, but not novel innovations in essential medicines to be sure.

The anticommons in NDD has led to patent proliferation, blocking researchers from accessing critical and foundational tools, leading to the underuse of knowledge. In this regard, by 2011, it was estimated that more than 20 percent of the entire human genome had been patented already. Two-thirds of those human genome patents were held by private firms in the business of health. The right to basic human health is consistent with the open-source approach to NDD. Health is an inalienable right; it cannot be taken out of the commons and owned as private property (Masum et al. 2011). Some would argue that patenting the human genome is tantamount to commodifying the corporal bodies of humans themselves. Like the OSDD with its open-source approach, the HGP had generated a positive economic impact many times the amount invested in the project by participating governments. Nevertheless, there will always be a proportion of people and firms trying to free ride on the knowledge shared in the OSDD and other open innovation platforms. This discrepancy in part explains why access to the Indian TKDL is limited and the Chinese NRTCM is closed entirely. Ideally, in innovation architectures where benefit sharing is easy and transparent, the chances of free riding should be lessened. In other words, a "sharing or shaming" scenario might discourage malfeasance. In social scientific experiments and as is evident in real-world open-source experiments like Linux, HGP, and OSDD, more people cooperate in a "systematic, significant and predictable manner" rather than engage in selfish behavior (Scaria and Dedeurwaerdere 2012, referencing Benkler [2011], find that 50 percent versus 30 percent cooperate or defect, respectively; see also Årdal and Røttingen 2012).

The stage-gate command-and-control (top-down) project management model predominant in Big Pharma and many other manufacturing industries doesn't work so well in open-source boundary-spanning projects encompassing diverse contributors, many of whom may be volunteers (Masum et al. 2013). Others have noted that OSDD might be better suited to the repurposing of failed Big Pharma candidate drugs because there is nothing to lose by sharing them (Allarakhia 2013). The shared drug compound pools discussed in the next chapter are an example of this approach.

One of the most noteworthy features of the OSDD is that it provides a model for future PPPs in its structured-play aspects in its role as innovation sandbox. OSDD training and mentoring of new users enables capacity-building opportunities unavailable through mere open-access platforms. Collins et al. (2019) provide an outline of existing initiatives underway worldwide that are fostering open access and capacity building. Among those exemplar initiatives listed is OSDD. Responding to criticisms like those expressed in the controversial 2010 Nature.com post, Munos said that the open and transparent peer review process within OSDD means that contributors are constantly reviewing each other's contributions. "The glare of scrutiny . . . will keep people honest" (Munos, quoted in Patlak 2010). In 2020, OSDD was comprised of 7,900 contributors from 130 countries, becoming the largest open-source collaboration in the history of drug discovery. Another way communities across India have protected and conserved traditional medicinal knowledge in the (local) commons is through *deo rahati*.

Deo Rahati, Sacred Groves

Maharashtra, in central-west India, south of New Delhi and east of Mumbai—mentioned above in reference to the movement to overturn illegal patents on turmeric and neem—is one of India's most bio-diverse regions. Like Yunnan, China, it is home to a number of ethnic groups. It is also known for the prevalence of protected spaces governed by various religious practices. These protected spaces are known by the Sanskrit term *deo rahati*, meaning "sacred groves." *Deo rahati* have been traced back to the Vedic period (c. 1500–500 BCE), a time of high civilization in which the first recorded Hindu religious texts were written. Sacred and protected natural spaces are prevalent throughout India even today. There are more than 2,800 sacred groves in Maharashtra.

It is estimated that in India as a whole, more than 100,000 sacred groves existed into the 2000s. Ancient Sanskrit texts noted that sacred groves were revered because healing plants were often abundant there (Malhotra, Ravindranath, and Murali 2000). While many of these spaces have come under threat from built infrastructure projects, especially dams and roads—the Center for Biodiversity and Indigenous Knowledge (CBIK) in Yunnan, China, discussed in the previous chapter, contended with similar issues—sacred groves to some extent today still maintain a "social force" protecting the plants within these spaces from interference from the outside. At the same time, *deo rahati* have been largely overlooked in scholarship about plant genetic conservation and traditional medicinal knowledge (Nipunage and Kulkarni 2010). Unlike in China after the 1978 opening under Deng Xiaoping, where the central state allowed innovative and entrepreneurial activities in local communities (as long as they did not pose any threat to the politics of the Chinese Communist Party or to the central state in Beijing, as noted in Chapter 3), efforts in India have been hampered by lack of resources at all levels of government and limited inward-flowing foreign funding. Unlike China, which also allowed (for a time) foreign involvement in local stakeholder institutional and capacity building, as in the Ford Foundation's backing of the CBIK in the 1980s, India closed itself off to the world after its political independence in 1947 and delayed opening to foreign actors (the colonial holdover of Monsanto notwithstanding) until as late as liberalization in the 1990s.

Dr. Dilip K. Kulkarni, renowned expert on the relationship between *deo rahati* and biodiversity and professor emeritus at the Agarkar Research Institute, is an ethnobotanist. He has been working on sacred groves since 1983. He worked at Agarkar Research Institute from 1978 until his retirement in 2010. Prior to his research on sacred groves, for his PhD, he had studied the Mahadev Koli tribe residing in five districts of Maharashtra—Raigad, Thane, Pune, Ahmednagar, and Nasik—during which time he observed the relationship between tribal practices and biodiversity conservation. These areas are located in a geographical belt of high biodiversity called the Western Ghats.[21] Since retirement in 2010, Kulkarni has been working at the BAIF Development Research Foundation outside Pune city.[22]

The sacred groves in Maharashtra are protected in part by local communities and are revered because the spaces have been attributed to different deities, such as Wagzai, Kalubai, Kalkai, Mankai, and Sukai. More than 100 such deities have been documented. Some decades ago, Kulkarni was invited to join a government-sponsored research project studying the food habits of tribal groups. The project was approved by the Indian Council of Medical Research. Kulkarni's mentor, esteemed ethnobotanist and expert on *deo rahati* Dr. V. D. Vartak, encouraged Kulkarni to explore this in the context of sacred groves. During this time, Kulkarni saw that tribal communities were eager to conserve sacred groves, particularly for the maintenance of wild varieties of medicinal plants. Now, unfortunately, the practice is dying out.

Kulkarni noted that while sacred groves were previously well maintained, now there is little awareness of their importance among contemporary locals. Faith in the deities has dwindled, and therefore the associated bond between the groves and the local people is not evident. Developmental pressure has increased. Government authorities seem uninterested in conservation, even those in the Forest Department, according to Kulkarni. He says,

There is no special person to collect information related to sacred groves. There continue to be less qualified persons in the field of botany, zoology and anthropology. There is a need to adopt a multidisciplinary approach to the study of sacred groves. Coordination and collaboration between different disciplines—anthropology, botany, entomology and microbiology—is required. Not many scholars visit the sacred groves. There is a need not only to write papers but also to study the interconnected facets of the various disciplines where sacred groves are concerned.

In addition, it has been a challenge to recruit talented young students to the field of ethnobotany. As India develops technologically, hardly anyone is interested in studying traditional things, according to Kulkarni. Parents encourage their children to become engineers and doctors but not plant scientists. It used to be that youth in village communities would learn the ways of their elders to understand the ecosystem around them on which they depended. Now, according to Kulkarni, young persons "lack knowledge of their own surroundings." Companies bioprospecting have exploited this by paying local youth to collect materials from the wild (e.g., by showing them photos of what they want). In the absence of training in sustainable harvesting practices, the local ecosystems have been damaged, some beyond repair.

Further, younger generations have been lured to cities like Bangalore and Pune, which offer a chance of economic advancement, mostly in information technology call centers, open 24/7, as are these cities now. Young people from rural communities often move to larger cities in search of jobs. As a result, only the elderly have remained in the villages where the sacred groves are located. It is therefore essential to create jobs for young persons in villages. Ecotourism may also help community mobilization, in the absence of state and national government funds to invest in maintaining sacred groves. Unfortunately, recent ecotourism has decimated the ecology of the land, including the failed Valley of Flowers "Kaas Pathar" case in Satara district, Maharashtra. The community allowed tourists to enter the sacred spaces, disturbing the natural environment. The tourists also took plant matter and otherwise disrespected the delicate balance that had been kept between human incursion and nature. One glimmer of hope is in a local organization called the Maharashtra Vruksha Samvardhini, Shaniwar Peth, in Pune, which has, through volunteer and other efforts, begun to study the *deo rahati* in Maharashtra and their critical relation to traditional medicine. This has included the way in which local communities have gone about protecting these shrinking sacred spaces.

Presently, sacred grove areas are divided into a "core zone" and an "eroded zone." While the eroded zone contains loose soil and little vegetation due to overexploitation, the core zone is ideally still rich with plants. Other tribal communities—unlike the community in the Kaas region—keep many things secret. For example, if someone requires raw plant materials that grow in undisclosed locations for medicinals (wild plants have far greater potency than the same plant grown via cultivation, as mentioned elsewhere), the local doctor/*vaidya* (Ayurveda doctor) is sent to check the person. If the *vaidya* confirms the illness, then the tribal community will send its own people to collect the material from its wild ecosystem (Kulkarni 2017). Attesting to the significance of *deo rahati*, in a 2010 article Nipunage and Kulkarni state that the sacred grove "provides an insurance policy for the future. It preserves a reservoir of continually evolving genetic material, representative of [the] natural ecosystem. It preserves a reservoir of wild animals, medicinal and economically important plants, and rare, endangered, and endemic plants" (192).

Conclusion

Of the case studies of emergent organizations in India, some are formal PPPs (TKDL, OSDD), while others are grassroots in origin (HBN, *deo rahati*). All have a stated mission of maintaining natural medicine knowledge in the open innovation commons (TISA sandboxes). India has challenged the status quo in the WTO TRIPS and, by extension, the power and influence of the global pharmaceutical industry, as demonstrated by the turmeric patent war and the fight to bring essential HIV/AIDS medicines to developing countries at affordable prices. As such, it should be recognized for staying the course, guided by a moral compass, of bringing healing innovations in medicine to all humanity. In contrast to China's strategic state intervention and positive protection (e.g., via a sui generis national patenting scheme for natural medicines) and India's commons and defensive protection, Japan's resource dependency has led to a more private-sector approach at home and multilateral efforts abroad.

Notes

1. This is a bit incongruous given the private-sector entrepreneurial acumen in such biologics as those by CIPLA and Biocon. See Ibata-Arens (2019a).

2. The exchange rate is based on yearly exchange rate of 1 USD to Rs. 57.3743 in 2012 (FRED 2020).

3. Regional governments in India are comprised of quasi-independent states having governors and able to make their own laws and subordinate union territories without such rights. As of 2019 there were twenty-nine states and seven union territories, after the state of Jammu and Kashmir were separated into two union territories.

4. Self-help groups are small peer-support groups engaged in economic activity in rural places.

5. Some observers have noted that the alleged preferential treatment of Patanjali by government regulators under the Modi administration is evidence of cronyism in the Indian government. That is, cronyism was evident in the trading of political favors between socially influential Ramdev and politician Modi (Bhatia and Lasseter 2017; Thakurta 2019; PTI 2020).

6. The safety and efficacy of AYUSH drugs were still questioned as late as 2020. Dr. Sumaiya Shaikh, a neuroscientist and the founding editor of *Alt News Science*, a nonprofit fact-checking blog, has argued, "There is limited scientific evidence for the efficacy of BGR-34 and IME 9 in the management of type-2 diabetes." Shaikh criticized the efficacy in existing scientific studies of AYUSH-64 as well by pointing out, "The existing studies are published by CCRAS in their self-owned low-impact journals, further questioning their credibility. In contradiction, the independent study published in a reputed scientific journal opposes the evidence of efficacy proposed by the CCRAS" (Shaikh 2019).

7. Based on the monthly exchange rate in April 2020, 1 USD = Rs. 76.1682 (Board of Governors of the Federal Reserve System 2020).

8. The exchange rate is based on a yearly exchange rate of 1 USD to Rs. 57.3743 in 2012 (FRED 2020).

9. The block (*Tehsil*) is a district subdivision and consists of a cluster of villages (*Gram*). As of 2020, there were 7,184 blocks across India having 664,282 villages. Certain topographical features determine the size and population of block and village (see Local Government Directory 2020).

10. After retiring in 1975, Dr. Mehta donated his Pune bungalow to the government of India. In 1986, the National Institute of Naturopathy was established on the site. Even today, a small one-room house commemorates the time that Gandhi resided there (Satyalakshmi 2017).

11. By 2005 the number of references to individual medicinal plants had risen to 35,000 (Hirwade 2010).

12. "Prior art" refers to proof, typically in a publication or database, of preexisting knowledge comprising the claimed-as-novel aspects of a patent application. Existence of prior art (documenting that someone else had the original idea) undermines the claim of originality by the patent applicant.

13. Chouhan (2012) provides brief summaries of the neem, turmeric, and basmati court cases, among others. See also Hirwade and Hirwade (2012).

14. Gaudillière (2019) implies that the TKDL "can easily be mined" because it has unified—at least in Western metadata terms about medicines—India's corpus of medicinal knowledge. Though he does not mention it, perhaps Gaudillière was assuming that the TKDL would eventually be accessible to the public.

15. Gupta noted that HBN and SRISTI neither use nor approve of the "rapid rural appraisal" or the "participatory rural appraisal" methods prevalent in certain aid organizations. In both methods, outsiders to a given local community evaluate said community with limited inclusion of community members in the process of design and management of the aid.

16. Umashankar and Gurunathan (2015) outline the steps of the drug discovery process: target identification and validation, lead candidate generation, optimization, preclinical studies, clinical trials, and marketing.

17. Robertson et al. (2013) outline six "laws" of open science collaborations based on their collective experience with open-source drug discovery—for example, in malaria treatment. First, all data and ideas are shared. Second, anyone can take part at any level of the project. Third, there will be no patents. Fourth, suggestions are the best form of criticism. Fifth, public discussion is much more valuable than private email. Sixth, the project is bigger than and is not owned by any given laboratory.

18. The node structure of the Human Genome Project PPP itself emerged as a result of a private-sector challenge (Jha and Nerurkar 2010).

19. These kinds of concerns might be interpreted, on the one hand, as elitist but, on the other, as valid in terms of the potential unleashing of dangerous "biohacked" organisms into the environment (see Talbot 2020).

20. Other contributors noted that the identity of at least one commentator who was critical of OSDD research, who had presented themselves as a "concerned scientist," could not be verified as authentic.

21. According to Dr. Kulkarni, "These [Mahadev Koli] tribes are not native to Maharashtra. They hail from the Mahadev hills of Madhya Pradesh and migrated to the Western Ghats after wars that took place in the pre-colonial era" (Kulkarni 2017).

22. The BAIF Development Research Foundation was known previously as the Bharatiya Agro Industries Foundation.

5

Medicine Gardens: Japan's Investment in New Drug Discovery

In 2012, Kyoto University professor Shinya Yamanaka was recognized with the Nobel Prize in Medicine for his advances in inducing adult stem cells to behave more like embryonic ones. These were called induced pluripotent stem cells (iPS). For example, adult cells can be made to regrow damaged tissue in the skin and other organs. The initial discoveries leading to iPS took place not in Japan but at the Gladstone Institute in San Francisco, where Yamanaka was a postdoctoral fellow working with an international collaborative team of researchers (Ibata-Arens 2019a). Since 2013, recognizing the role of these kinds of international research and development (R&D) networks in scientific discovery, the Japanese government has initiated a number of "open innovation" public-private partnerships (PPPs) and also created a new Agency for Medical Research and Development (AMED), established in 2015. Central to Japan's efforts has been a focus on biologics, including stem cells, genomics, and other natural medicines.

The awarding in 2012 of the Nobel Prize to a Japanese biomedical researcher was the proximate stimulus for a pivot in Japan's innovation strategy for new drug discovery and related health care diplomacy—for example, new drug discovery that seeks to alleviate neglected disease conditions in the developing world. Japan's approach differs from the technonationalism of China's approach (typology of innovation system architectures [TISA] cages) to the exploitation of its natural medicine resources and India's public commons approach (TISA sandboxes). It represents a middle ground between seeking high novelty and openness, on the one hand, and making do with fewer novel resources, on the other. What explains Japan's hybrid approach, open in contrast to China's but not as bold as India's in terms of the aim for open innovation sandboxes characterizing that nation's emergent organizations in new drug discovery?

First, it could be argued that Japan's shift to a more open and inclusive approach to innovation in (bio)medicine is simply power politics—that is, Japan wants to counterbalance the rising political influence of China in less developed South and Southeast Asia (not to mention other parts of the Global South). For example, the China-backed Asian Infrastructure Investment Bank (est. 2016) threatens to eclipse the role of the Japan-backed Asian Development Bank (est. 1966). Japanese policymakers and academics also sought to improve Japan's international scientific reputation, part and parcel of international policy influence and global status, after failing to keep up with the speed and accuracy of other international teams (namely, China) in mapping its assigned portion of the human genome in the global Human Genome Project of the 1980s and 1990s. A few vocal critics in Japan have pointed to the cause of Japan's slowness: its closed innovation system (Ikawa 1991; Sakaki 2019).

Second, a market-based argument would say, on the one hand, that Japan is looking decades into the future in a long-term branding and marketing campaign. Once countries develop a positive brand consciousness toward Japanese pharmaceutical firms sponsoring neglected tropical disease (NTD) R&D for health care solutions that are more natural and have less toxicity than synthetic chemical drugs, as these developing economies grow economically, national governments and middle-class consumers will turn to Japanese brand names for their drugs and medicines. On the other hand, Japanese pharmaceutical companies are no different from their Western counterparts in that they have ample stocks of underutilized synthetic chemical compounds that could be useful in treating NTDs. At the same time, experimenting with these compounds domestically is costly and inefficient, due to the aging population and low birth rates, which together have led to dwindling numbers of available able-bodied clinical test subjects.

Third, a norms-based argument would see selfless altruism guiding Japan's promotion of open and inclusive innovation in new drug discovery, a kind of commons. For example, Japan could have merely paid lip service to the UN Convention on Biological Diversity (CBD) Aichi Biodiversity Targets (ABT), which include protection and conservation of medicinal plant biodiversity and traditional knowledge (TK) under the United Nations Nagoya Protocol (2010). Instead, the Japanese government put money behind establishing the Japan Biodiversity Fund (JBF), which has invested through its Satoyama and Satoumi initiatives in ecosystem governance throughout the developing world. Japanese reverence for nature has deep roots in its spirituality and religious practice. For example, in Japan within the religious practice of Shintoism, the concept of *reihō* (霊峰), meaning "sacred mountain," literally "sacred peak," is akin to *deo rahati* (sacred groves) in India.[1] Even though the Japanese state after the Meiji Restoration in 1868 embraced most everything Western, including medicine, the Japanese people never strayed too far away from traditional natural medicine.

Historical-Institutional Background

Kampo or Kampō (漢方) is traditional Japanese medicine first introduced to Japan from China and Korea by the sixth century CE. Its practitioners initially followed traditional Chinese medicine (TCM). Due to the limited availability of biological materials, especially medicinal plants, many formulations were simplified to include primarily plants endogenous to Japan (Sreedhar, Watanabe, and Arumugam 2017). In 1709, Kaibara Ekiken (貝原益軒), a scholar of samurai birth, adapted the Chinese materia medica encyclopedia *Bencao Gangmu* (本草纲目) and compiled *Yamato Honzō* (大和本草), the first original Japanese materia medica. Kaibara excluded many exotic species that did not exist in Japan while recording all then known Japanese medicinals in one single text (Marcon 2015). Over time, the vast pharmacopoeia of many thousands of Chinese crude drugs was reduced to around 300 drugs. Eventually, *kampo* became isolated from TCM. Some *kampo* physicians, like Tōdō Yoshimasu (吉益東洞) (1702–1773), criticized "the highly theoretical and speculative nature of Chinese medicine as being inadequate to meet the problems of every-day practice." TCM was and remains imbued with spiritual and metaphysical ideas—for example, in the practice of Taoist TCM. Japan developed new schools of *kampo*, such as the Koho school (古方派) and the Setchu school (折衷派) (Watanabe et al. 2011; Yakubo et al. 2014). Meanwhile, by the sixteenth century Western medicine was introduced to Japan by Jesuit missionaries and continued even during the Tokugawa era of isolationism known as *sakoku* (鎖国, 1639 to 1854). After 1640, under *sakoku*, Japan only allowed the Dutch to trade with Japan through Dejima island, Nagasaki. The Dutch brought to Japan translations of Western medical texts (Guthrie et al. 2020).

By the time of the Meiji Restoration (1868), Western medical science was recognized for its effectiveness in treating infectious diseases and introducing innovations in surgical techniques. In 1874, the Meiji government had established the first national certification and examination system for medical doctors. By 1879 the Japanese state sanctioned officially Western-style medicine as the de facto national standard in medical treatment and withdrew formal recognition of *kampo*. This decertification led to the decline of *kampo* in favor of the German system of health care and medical education in Japan (Steslicke 1972; Watanabe et al. 2011). At the time, the Meiji restorers had embraced Bismarckian economics and governance, so the emulation of German standards of medicine should be seen in this context.

Kampo medicine would remain out of favor for nearly a century. By the 1970s, Japan had become an affluent society with little incidence of infectious disease still endemic to the developing world. Indeed, like societies in the West, Japan was experiencing increases in noncommunicable afflictions: diabetes, heart disease, and obesity. Japanese consumers had turned to natural medicines like *kampo* as an effective complementary and alternative medicine to prevent and treat these new diseases. The scandal around the synthetic chemical thalidomide in Western Europe reverberated in Japan. The scandal exposed unethical conduct by a German pharmaceutical company in developing and marketing thalidomide even though its own scientists had confirmed damaging side effects. Pregnant women who took thalidomide for morning sickness gave birth to children with severe birth defects, including missing limbs and dwarfism. Due in part to news coverage about thalidomide and still smarting from the nation's own incidences of Minamata disease caused by industrial chemicals, Japanese consumers grew wary of Western synthetic chemical drugs due to the high incidence of adverse side effects. As a result, *kampo* reentered the Japanese lexicon. Nowadays, local pharmacies and convenience stores sell over-the-counter *kampo*—more recently, in pill form. Japanese consumers tend to favor powdered or prepared liquids in mini bottles, believing these to be more rapidly absorbed into the body. For example, "Ukon"—made from wild turmeric and used as a hangover remedy—is a perennial favorite of office workers, who buy a bottle or two on the way out for a night of drinking or on the way home.

After the National Health Insurance (NHI) scheme began covering *kampo* in 1976, its use has risen steadily. However, since 1986, no new *kampo* formulations have been approved by the Japanese government, due to changes in the approval process making it consistent with that for synthetic chemical drugs (i.e., double-blind clinical trials and assays of active chemical ingredients). The impact has been that natural medicines, given their modest profit margins and low patentability, have not been developed by most Japanese pharmaceutical companies (Arai and Kawahara 2018).[2]

A growing body of evidence, discussed in Chapters 1 and 2, has shown that natural medicines have fewer incidences of adverse side effects than the synthetic chemical drugs from Western pharmaceutical companies—prescribed for the same conditions. On the other hand, the spread of viral resistance to synthetic chemical drugs treating such diseases as the influenza virus has indicated a need to develop new antiviral drugs. Natural medicines (*kampo*) became "attractive targets for novel antiviral drugs owing to their wide variety of chemical constituents." The Japanese government began funding researchers involved in the evaluation of the efficacy and safety of *kampo* medicines. Examples include Maoto (麻黄湯), containing ephedra and cinnamon bark, and Daiokanzoto (大黄甘草湯), made of licorice and rhubarb. These have been found effective and safe in treating the influenza virus and strong in viral resistance (Watanabe 2018; Nomura et al. 2019; Tsumura & Co. 2020c, 2020d). Though not utilizing materials endogenous to Japan, the Kyoto University start-up Therabiopharma's cutting-edge extraction methods have resulted in a curcumin injection found to have 10,000 times the potency of the raw rhizome in treating colon cancer, with high efficacy and none of the toxicities associated with the main synthetic chemical drug used in colon cancer treatment, oxaliplatin (*Business Wire* 2018).

All Japanese pharmacy schools currently require that their students demonstrate competency in understanding the natural plant and other biological material origins of all medicines. This includes a national regulation requiring all pharmacy schools to maintain a medicinal plant garden on their premises, comprised of all plant materials listed in the Japan *kampo* pharmacopoeia—a measure supporting experiential learning with said biological materials.

However, unlike with the Indian national government's embrace of Ayurveda, Yoga and Naturopathy, Unani, Siddha, and Homoeopathy (AYUSH), the revival of *kampo* emerged in the context of the dominance of Western medicine. Paradoxically, "the pragmatic and reductive approach of restricting kampo therapy to clinically meaningful components helped to facilitate its gradual integration into modern medicine" (Watanabe et al. 2011). By 2004, all medical schools in Japan would offer courses of some kind on *kampo*. In 2020, unlike China with TCM and India with AYUSH, Japan had yet to formally sanction the practice of *kampo* as an independent field of medicine. Instead, physicians taking the national standard medical school curriculum would continue to be trained and certified in Western medicine only.

Prior to the reaction in the 1970s to the thalidomide scandal, in 1967, the first four *kampo* extracts had been approved for reimbursement by the NHI system (Katayama et al. 2013). In 1976 Japan's then Ministry of Health and Welfare, now the Ministry of Health, Labor, and Welfare (MHLW), approved additional *kampo* drugs for payment under the NHI scheme owing to the "strong political pressure from Taro Takemi," who was the president of the Japanese Medical Association (1957–1982) and the World Medical Association (1975–1976) and a leading advocate of *kampo*. Subsequently, the Japanese government passed the Good Manufacturing Practice law in 1987, including regulations on research and development into *kampo* medicine, ensuring uniformly high quality and standardization of *kampo* products (Katayama et al. 2013). In 2001, the Ministry of Education, Culture, Sports, Science, and Technology (MEXT) decided to put *kampo* education into "the core curriculum of medical schools," and eighty medical schools provide *kampo* medical education (Yakubo et al. 2014). Unlike in China and India, however, Japan lacks government departments dedicated to the promotion and support of traditional and natural medicine.

In 2009, the government indicated it would remove *kampo* from the NHI scheme in an effort to "cap mounting medical expenses." This removal failed due to strong opposition from the private sector and consumers. Advocates argued that without insurance coverage, patients who used *kampo* medicines would face great financial burden and might avoid using them, leading to more severe illness. The Japan Society for Oriental Medicine (JSOM, 日本東洋医学会) and such *kampo* companies as Tsumura & Co. (津村) led a national petition against removing *kampo* from the NHI. A personal plea by a patient on a blog regarding the impending crisis in their health led many thousands to join the petition. The petition received more than 920,000 signatures within three weeks (Fuyuno 2011; *Pharmaceutical Daily* 2010; Sun 2009). As a result, the government dropped the proposal to defund *kampo*. In 2020, a number of private organizations and institutions were engaging in the promotion of *kampo* and the preservation of its medicinal plants. Figure 5.1 outlines the state and private-sector links in promoting natural medicines as a resource for new drug discovery.

Organizations and PPPs

The Japan Society for Oriental Medicine

The Japan Society for Oriental Medicine, established in 1950, is the leading organization of *kampo* medicine in Japan. In 1977 JSOM opened a nonprofit organization to promote the "scientific culture" of *kampo*. It also established a medical certification program of JSOM (専門医資格) (JSOM 2020a). As of March 2020, JSOM had 8,407 members comprised of medical professionals, including physicians (JSOM 2020d). In June 2001, in response to concerns about the purity of crude drugs related to safety and efficacy, JSOM set up an evidence-based medicine (EBM) committee to compile clinical evidence on *kampo* treatment. In 2007, the task force for the Evidence Reports/Clinical Practice Guidelines of EBM committee started collecting "randomized controlled trials" (比較試験) of *kampo* medicines used in Japan and publishing findings as "structured abstracts" (構造化抄録) on the JSOM website. These were also known as Evidence Reports of Kampo Treatment (JSOM 2020c).

Figure 5.1 Inclusive Innovation in New Drug Discovery: Japan State and PPPs

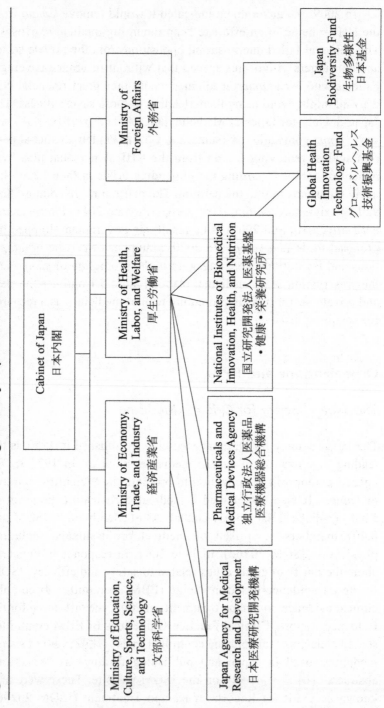

Between 1986 and 2020, 493 structured abstracts had been published by the EBM. For example, JSOM has reported on the efficacy and safety of Rikkunshito (六君子湯), a *kampo* medicine of Japanese ginseng, Japanese ginger, and other herbs, used to treat gastrointestinal weakness, loss of appetite, and other gastric problems. Another report is on the efficacy of Bakumondoto (麦門冬湯), an herbal medicine mainly made up of Japanese ophiopogon tuber to treat dry cough and bronchitis (Tsumura & Co. 2020b, 2020e; JSOM 2020b).

Japanese critics of *kampo* clinical research, echoing counterparts in China and India, note that taking a holistic, patient-focused treatment course inclusive of *kampo* and forcing it into a so-called (Western) scientific disease-centered allopathic clinical-testing methodology is meaningless to improving overall health of patients (Watanabe et al. 2011). Nonetheless, the trend of integrating *kampo* into the Western standard continues, in contrast to the nationalist sui generis strategies in China and the diversity and inclusion in India.

Centers of Kampo *Research*

Aside from the JSOM, universities have also established research centers for *kampo*. For example, the Kitasato University Oriental Medicine Research Center (北里大学東洋医学総合研究所), established in 1972, is "Japan's first comprehensive research institute for kampo medicine" (Kitasato University Oriental Medicine Research Center 2020). Another example is the Institute of Natural Medicine (INM) of the University of Toyama (富山大学和漢医薬学総合研究所), established for basic and applied research about natural medicine. Besides medical care, Toyama INM's mission also includes "the preservation of natural environment" and "securing and preserving natural drug resources." It also conducts research on "advanced natural products and attendant drug discovery" in Japan and elsewhere. R&D foci include discovery of "new antibacterial and antiviral natural products from plants, marine sponges, and bacterial sources" (Institute of Natural Medicine 2020a). Toyama INM has four databases that provide information about crude drugs and *kampo* formulas, including TradMPD (Traditional Medical & Pharmaceutical Database, 伝統医薬データベース), WAKANYAKU Wiki Database (和漢薬 Wikiデータベース), ETHMEDmmm (民族薬物データベース), and kampoDB.[3] Exploratory research projects of the INM include maintaining a library of natural medicines, sponsored by MEXT (2010–2015). As of August 2020, the library contained 96 compounds derived from crude drugs, 120 crude drug extracts, and 42 *kampo* formula extracts (Institute of Natural Medicine 2020b).

In Japan, the closest to India's Traditional Knowledge Digital Library (TKDL) commons database is the Standards of Reporting Kampo Products (STORK, formerly referred to as KCONSORT), hosted by the National Institute of Biomedical Innovation and created in 1996. The site is open access, but users must indicate that they are either researchers or health care professionals. Its coverage is small in comparison to TKDL and China's national registry, only listing ingredients for 148 approved "ethical" *kampo* drugs (in Japanese and English). In Japan, *ethical* refers to drugs prescribed by physicians and excludes over-the-counter drugs. Further, the site merely replicates information listed on the package inserts of these medications. STORK resulted from the shift to so-called evidence-based medicine by the Japanese government and related codification of the active pharmaceutical ingredients in *kampo* medicines. As with the TKDL in India, the Japanese national government oversaw a consortium of government and private-sector professionals to agree on the national standards for measurement and standardization of *kampo* formulations that would be included in the database. Japanese public- and private-sector organizations have been active in protecting the biological materials for natural medicine drug discovery.

National Institutes of Biomedical Innovation, Health, and Nutrition Research Center for Medicinal Plant Resources

Medicinal plants have shown promise in national drug discovery in Japan. However, Japan relies mostly on the import of medicinal plant ingredients from China, upward of 80 percent of the total consumed in Japan (Fuyuno 2011). Japan's Agency for Medical Research and Development focuses on new drug discovery and drug development through PPPs, the design of platform technology, and the breeding and cultivation of medicinal plants (AMED 2017a). Similarly, to promote the cultivation and preservation of medicinal plants domestically, the National Institutes of Biomedical Innovation, Health, and Nutrition (NIBIOHN, 国立研究開発法人医薬基盤・健康・栄養研究所),

established in 2015, has set up the Research Center for Medicinal Plant Resources (薬用植物資源研究センター), which preserves more than 4,000 species and groups of medicinal plants at four locations in Japan (Hokkaido, Tsukuba, Wakayama, and Tanegashima). Its origins are in the National Institute of Nutrition, established in 1920. NIBIOHN also invests in R&D of technology to promote the cultivation of medicinal plants in these locations (NIBIOHN 2020b). These activities accelerated in the 1980s after the Chinese government began setting restrictions on the exports of ephedra and licorice, which are main ingredients for both TCM and *kampo*. As discussed in Chapter 3, China in recent decades has recognized the need to protect its own natural medicine resources from unsustainable use.[4] Table 5.1 outlines specific measures supporting inclusion of natural medicine into new drug discovery.

The Tsukuba division of NIBIOHN includes identifying foreign plant resources yet to be used in medicines (外国産未利用植物資源の開発に関する研究), aimed at discovering new drugs for treating tropical diseases, for example, leishmaniasis (NIBIOHN 2020c). Moreover, this center also has created a Comprehensive Medicinal Plant Database (薬用植物総合情報データベース), in part replicating efforts elsewhere in Japan—in contrast to the centralized national databases in China and India. The database lists 200 medicinal plants, such as Japanese kudzu vine and ephedra, 80 *kampo* formulas, and 157 crude drugs, including jujube and ginseng (NIBIOHN 2020a). No discussion of Japan's *kampo* industry would be complete without referencing Tsumura & Co.

Tsumura & Co.

Tsumura & Co., established in 1893, produces and sells *kampo* formulations, commanding more than 80 percent of total *kampo* market share in Japan. In fiscal year 2019, Tsumura's net sales were ¥123.5 billion (around $1.13 billion) (Tsumura & Co. 2020f).[5] Like its much larger competitors in China and rising challengers in India, Tsumura has a stated business vision of becoming a global leader in the provision of natural medicines. For example, Tsumura has been targeting the US market with its TU-100 (Daikenchuto, 大建中湯), a ginger, ginseng, and pepper formula found to help relieve gastrointestinal bloating and constipation (Kono et al. 2015). Tsumura was banking on apparent rising consumer demand in that country. Tsumura also saw

Table 5.1 Innovation Policies for New Drug Discovery in Japan

Year	Name (English)	Name (Japanese)
2002	National BioResource Project	ナショナルバイオリソースプロジェクト
2005	Research on Development of Foreign Unused Plant Resources	外国産未利用植物資源の開発に関する研究
2005	Research on the Cultivation of Medicinal Plants	薬用植物の栽培に関する研究
2007	Research on Development of New Drugs	創薬基盤推進研究事業
2011	Platform Project for Supporting Drug Discovery and Life Science Research	創薬等ライフサイエンス研究支援基盤事業
2011	Project Promoting Clinical Trials for Development of New Drugs	臨床研究・治験推進研究事業
2013	Drug Discovery Support Network (DDSN)	創薬支援ネットワーク
2014	Act on Promotion of Health Care Policy	健康・医療戦略推進法案
2014	Act on the Independent Administrative Agency of Japan Agency for Medical Research and Development	独立行政法人日本医療研究開発機構法案
2014	Advanced Research and Development Programs for Medical Innovation	革新的先端研究開発支援事業
2014	Basic Science and Platform Technology Program for Innovative Biological Medicine	革新的バイオ医薬品創出基盤技術開発事業

continues

opportunity in the Chinese TCM market through a joint venture with Ping An Insurance Company, which held just under 10 percent of stock in Tsumura as of 2019 (Tsumura & Co. 2020a).

To ensure the supply of the raw material crude drugs used in *kampo* medicines, Tsumura cultivates and procures the medicinal plants transnationally through its overseas affiliates. Based on its estimation, the raw material crude drugs are 80 percent from China, approximately 15 percent from Japan, and around 5 percent from Laos and other countries. Tsumura has expanded cultivation locations within Japan (e.g., Hokkaido). As mentioned previously, Tsumura has been instrumental in ensuring that the NHI continues to cover *kampo* medicines (Tsumura & Co. 2020a).

Table 5.1   Continued

Year	Name (English)	Name (Japanese)
2014	Project Focused on Developing Key Technology for Discovering and Manufacturing Drugs for Next-Generation Treatment and Diagnosis	次世代治療・診断実現のための創薬基盤技術開発事業
2014	Strategy of SAKIGAKE	先駆けパッケージ戦略
2015	Development of a Drug Discovery Informatics System	創薬支援インフォマティクスシステム構築
2015	Drug-Discovery Innovation and Screening Consortium (DISC)	産学協働スクリーニングコンソーシアム（DISC）
2015	Next Generation Drug Discovery Compound Library Project	次世代創薬シーズライブラリー構築プロジェクト
2015	Support Program for Orphan Drug Prior to the Designation	希少疾病用医薬品指定前実用化支援事業
2015	The iD3 Technology Archive	創薬アーカイブ（登録技術・活用事業）
2015	The Program for Technological Innovation of Regenerative Medicine	再生医療実現プロジェクト
2017	Infrastructure Program for Drug Discovery Seeds Development	創薬シーズ実用化支援基盤整備事業
2017	Project for Promoting Clinical Innovation Network	クリニカル・イノベーション・ネットワーク推進支援事業
2019	Science and Technology Platform Program for Advanced Biological Medicine	先端的バイオ創薬等基盤技術開発事業

Health Insurance Coverage

According to the World Health Organization, in 2017, Japan's health expenditure accounted for 10.94 percent of GDP, and health expenditure per capita was around $4,168.99. The out-of-pocket expenditure per capita was $535.62 (WHO 2020d). Between 2016 and 2017, the sales of prescription *kampo* products increased slightly from ¥148.1 billion (around $1.29 billion) in fiscal year 2016 to ¥150.9 billion (around $1.31 billion) by the end of 2017, which was 1.4 percent of total prescription pharmaceutical sales by drug price basis in the NHI (Tsumura & Co. 2020f).

As mentioned above, the first four *kampo* extracts were reimbursed under the National Health Insurance in 1967, and later MHLW

expanded coverage to three categories of *kampo* medicines: drug formulation extracts, crude drugs, and crude drug preparations. The number of *kampo* medicines covered by the NHI had increased to 148
kampo formulation extracts, 241 crude drugs, and 5 crude drug preparations as of July 2020.[6] Even though surveys indicate that the majority of physicians treat patients with *kampo* medicines (80–90 percent),
the overall prescription rates of *kampo* remain low. This situation has
been described as "treatment absent theory."[7] That is, Japanese physicians prescribe *kampo* drugs not based on *kampo* medicine theory
(diagnosing patterns of symptoms in the context of a holistic evaluation
of a patient's whole body) but using Western "biomedical" diagnosis
(the word *myopic* is often mentioned by interview sources in China and
Japan). Katayama and others have argued that to avoid the misuse of
kampo drugs proper "education and clinical evidence based on traditional use of kampo medicine should be established" (Katayama et al.
2013).[8] With this in mind, the MHLW and AMED have pursued *kampo*
natural-medicine-related innovations in new drug discovery.

Natural Medicine Innovation

The Ministry of Health, Labor, and Welfare, overseeing the Japanese
health care system, is responsible for health care policies, welfare
services, and support for innovation in the pharmaceutical industry.
According to a survey in 2014, "Kampo medicines were prescribed for
221 patients out of a total of 487 patients based on patient-centered
kampo diagnosis while continuing Western medical care," and "two-
thirds of the chronic pain patients with the use of kampo medicines
combined with Western medicine experienced further pain improvements" (Arai et al. 2014).

Under the purview of MHLW, the Japan Agency for Medical
Research and Development (AMED) promotes medical R&D. AMED
has organized R&D programs funding drug discovery and development, medical device development, and translational and clinical
research. Further, AMED's investments focus on four disease targets
(cancer, mental health and neurological disorders, infectious diseases,
and rare diseases). Its annual budget is about $1 billion. In 2020, R&D
for new drug discovery based on Japanese *kampo* and natural medicine
on the whole emphasized promoting new methods in breeding and cul-

tivation of medicinal plants. The Science and Technology Platform Program for Advanced Biological Medicine supported advanced biological medicines and gene transfer technologies, gene expression control technologies, and biologics generally (AMED 2020).

In addition to cooperation with universities, private pharmaceutical businesses, and individual experts, AMED launched in 2015 a partnership with the Pharmaceuticals and Medical Devices Agency (PMDA), also under the MHLW. AMED would continue promoting R&D in medicine, while PMDA would review and consult on overall R&D strategy, given its Food and Drug Administration–like position in the drug regulatory approval pipeline (AMED 2017b). Japan's health and health care ministry was doing its level best to stimulate innovations in new drug discovery. AMED director in 2017 Dr. Makoto Suematsu, at an event hosted by the American Chamber of Commerce in Japan that April, was reported to acknowledge the reluctance of Japanese researchers to share information across institutional boundaries. This fragmentation, for Suematsu, had become the biggest obstacle to advancements in medical-related research (Cheyney 2017). Never content to sit back and allow the invisible hand of the market to run its course, the Japanese government has sought public- and private-sector partnerships. Table 5.2 outlines the stages of the innovation process for drug and medicine research and development and Japanese responses to market failure. Japan's inclusive innovation, reflecting the way its innovation architecture is structured within sandboxes and pools, is illuminated through organizational case studies: the Japan Biodiversity Fund Satoyama Initiative (SI), Takeda Garden for Medicinal Plant Conservation, Kyoto (TKG, 武田薬品工業株式会社 京都薬用植物, *Yakuhin Kōgyō Kabushiki Gaisha Kyōto Yakuyō Shokubutsuen*), and the Global Health Innovative Technology Fund (GHIT).

Japan Biodiversity Fund and the Satoyama Initiative

Japan has taken steps to protect biological diversity, including national government support for the United Nations Nagoya Protocol. While there has not been much of a national state-level effort by Japan to protect traditional medicine from biopiracy, in part due to its relative

**Table 5.2   Inclusive Innovation in Drug (Re)Discovery:
State and Private-Sector Responses to Market Failure**

Product/Output	Resource (and related literature)	Remediation of Market Failure	Do Nothing (in response to market failure)	Japan's Health Diplomacy "Sharing to Save" (level)
Medicinal plants (sustainable harvesting)	Biodiversity (environmental science, ecology)	Ecosystem governance, sustainable bioprospecting	Absence of governance, overharvesting, biopiracy, loss of habitat, species extinction	Japan Biodiversiy Fund, Satoyama and Satoumi (state)
Natural/traditional medicines (protection and conservation)	Traditional medicinal knowledge protection and conservation (ethnobotany, ethnopharmacology, history of medicine)	Management of common pool resources, traditional medicine knowledge databases	Irrevocable loss of traditional medicine knowledge	Takeda Garden for Medicinal Plant Conservation, Kyoto (private industry)
New drug discovery	Inclusive innovation architectures (political economy, economic sociology, development economics)	Structuring of incentives to cooperate	Suboptimal human health (pandemic and chronic disease)	GHIT Fund (public-private partnership)

resource scarcity also related to Japan's international activism in environmental policy, private companies, including Takeda Pharmaceutical, have taken initiatives as discussed below.

The Nagoya Protocol was adopted on October 29, 2010, during the Tenth UN Conference of the Parties (COP) to the Convention on Biological Diversity.[9] The Tenth COP had been hosted by Japan in the city of Nagoya, in Aichi Prefecture. The protocol centers on the fair and equitable sharing of benefits derived from the utilization of genetic resources (Ministry of Environment 2019). The Nagoya Protocol was a landmark in biodiversity governance in that, for the first time, the protection of the intellectual property rights of local, often indigenous, traditional knowledge stakeholders would be codified. This codification, if not entirely legally binding, in contrast to the power of the World Trade Organization's Agreement on the Trade-Related Aspects of Intellectual Property Rights, would at the very least include these local stakeholders within the global normative framework around fair use.

Guided by the United Nations' Strategic Plan for Biodiversity 2011–2020, agreed upon at the Nagoya meeting, Japan proposed to the 2010 COP a vision of "Living in Harmony with Nature." Under the "Harmony" vision, the aim was to achieve by 2020 a better balance between human activity and the natural environment. Measures included efforts to halt and reduce the loss of biodiversity globally. Twenty specific targets were outlined by Nagoya 2010, referred to as the Aichi Biodiversity Targets (Convention on Biological Diversity 2014). Among the various goals of ABT were stemming the spread of invasive alien plant and animal species, improving sustainable agricultural practices, and reducing pollution. For example, Target 17 called for a "participatory national biodiversity strategy." Target 18 focused on respecting and maintaining "traditional knowledge" regarding biodiversity and its uses. Pollution and sustainable development targets in particular were reinforced after the devastation of the 2011 earthquake and tsunami in Japan. Between 2010 and 2011, Japan—in part via the $2 billion Japan Biodiversity Fund—led the world in biodiversity-related direct (bilateral) assistance. Together with Germany and the European Union, they provided at least half of all global biodiversity-related aid (Convention on Biological Diversity 2014).

ABT, under "Key Action Goal E-2-1," launched the "Satoyama" sustainable forest (though literally "mountain") and "Satoumi" ocean management of "socioecological production landscapes" (Convention on Biological Diversity 2014, 88) in Japan and internationally. Early projects under these initiatives were in African countries, which has been seen as a diplomatic counterbalance to the resource-mining activities of China in this region of the world. Under Satoyama, the government and private sector should "re-evaluate the wisdom on traditional knowledge and techniques for resource usage that have been cultivated in response to the natural characteristics of local regions, and strive to pass them down and promote their use."

Examples of JBF investments supporting inclusive innovation include sustainable cultivation and harvesting practices of medicinal plants, particularly in developing countries in Southeast Asia and the Global South. Satoyama public relations materials from the Japan Ministry of Environment emphasized three guiding principles for their sustainable development projects in Japan and around the world. First, Satoyama embraces diverse ecosystem values and wisdom. Second, it prioritizes integrating traditional and modern knowledge to promote scientific innovations. In this manner it is similar to the Honey Bee Network in India and the Center for Biodiversity and Indigenous Knowledge in China. Third, it respects traditional communal land rights while recognizing "evolving frameworks of the commons" (International Partnership for the Satoyama Initiative, Ministry of the Environment Japan, and United Nations University 2010). As such, the JBF Satoyama Initiative is situated in the upper-right quadrant of TISA sandboxes, but toward the bottom, less-novel approaches of the TISA, in that Japan is encouraging sharing of novel innovations in a global commons, though slightly less open and drug discovery focused than the Open Source Drug Discovery platform in India.

Satoyama is a quasi-PPP in that the Ministry of Environment and United Nations University, a Tokyo-based affiliate of the United Nations, are the core partners, while private-sector participants have tended to be nongovernmental organizations (NGOs) operating in developing countries rather than through industry, in contrast to GHIT discussed below. The Satoyama Initiative engages indirectly with local communities, sponsoring case study research among network members about socioecological production landscapes best practice as well as supporting donor organization efforts in the field in connecting stakeholders to outside resources. As such the SI has functioned as more of a bird's-eye-level information exchange than as a partner for local sustainable economic development or innovation in new drug discovery. Its main focus has been in documenting best practice among member research sites worldwide. For example, it convenes a researchers' practitioner conference annually in Tokyo.

Case studies highlighted in the annual thematic review reports since 2015 (Volume 1) have included community forests in anonymized areas in China (UNU-IAS and IGES 2015), traditional knowledge in Yunnan, China (UNU-IAS and IGES 2016), and sustainable medicinal plant biodiversity stewardship within *deo rahati* in Western Ghats, India (UNU-IAS and IGES 2017).[10] SI has been particularly active with traditional-knowledge-based classification of genetic resources in Yunnan province, owing to that region's active indigenous community of traditional medicine knowledge (TMK) stakeholders. In the 2018 case study writeups, for example, researchers noted the importance of traditional knowledge in innovations in the use of orchids and tea varieties for the development of medicines (Xue, Zhang, and Yang 2018).

The impact of the JBF has been twofold. First, funds have been invested into capacity building, including country-level support for national clearinghouses (built on taxonomies of traditional knowledge) to recognize and protect TK (akin to tracing the provenance of artwork).[11] Second, efforts at raising public awareness include briefings for key decisionmakers in biodiversity management internationally. Related JBF activities under the SI mentioned above, co-led by the UN University and Japan's Ministry of Environment, focused on the sustainable use of biological resources. Target communities are towns and villages in or near (dependent upon) rural landscapes, including mountainous areas. Nestled in the northern mountains of Kyoto (the city of Kyoto is surrounded by three mountain ranges) is a twenty-three-acre garden enclave called the Takeda Garden for Medicinal Plant Conservation, Kyoto.[12] Field research in 2017 to 2019 confirms that it does much more than serve as a "museum of living herbs" as indicated in its public relations materials.[13]

Takeda Garden for Medicinal Plant Conservation, Kyoto

The chain of islands that comprise Japan, while narrow in width from east to west compared to mega-biodiverse China or India, is long from north to south. Latitudes in the wintery northern island of Hokkaido have vastly different flora and fauna than in the far southern islands of subtropical Okinawa. Still, Japan is a resource-dependent country. Upward of 95 percent of the plant materials for medicinals is imported, mainly from China. While Tsumura—as mentioned above, a traditional herbal medicine *kampoyaku* (漢方薬), or *kampo* producer—holds 80 percent of the domestic market for traditional medicines, it is giant Takeda Pharmaceutical, whose natural medicines comprise less than 1 percent of its annual sales, that has maintained a space for plant conservation through its corporate social responsibility programs. As such, Takeda has contributed to conservation of medicinal plants within Japan and with partners abroad.[14] The TKG maintains a materia medica and pharmacopoeia archive, documenting plant- and other biological-material-based medicinal formulas from Japan and other countries. The garden also tracks threatened species and the causes of species extinction due, for example, to loss of ecosystems.

Activities include annual exchange with medicinal gardens around the world of seeds and rhizomes as part of joint conservation efforts. This exchange occurs so that the biological materials of banks can be protected in the event any one garden is impacted by natural disaster or other exogenous (bio)shock (pesticides, war).[15]

According to former head scientist Dr. Eiichi Kodaira, the garden hosts students at all levels of education—for example, having training programs for pharmacy students (Kodaira, Nozaki, and Matsuoka 2016). The aim of the education programs is to nurture younger generations of scientists to have an understanding of the healing potential of compounds derived from plants in the wild and under cultivation.

The garden was established originally in 1933 as a cultivation area for medicinal plants responding to the loss of plant medicinal knowledge under the march of the Meiji government to modernize and "reject the old ways." As with the "white coat" phenomenon in China in subsequent decades, the adoption of Western scientific methods and the way modern medical doctors were trained led to a neglect between 1868 and the post–World War II period of traditional medicinals, as mentioned above. In 1781, Chobei Takeda started a business selling herbal medicinals in Osaka—acting as middleman between wholesalers of Chinese and Japanese medicinals and medical professionals. His innovation was to buy various materials in bulk, then package and sell them in smaller packets to doctors. In 1871, within years after the Meiji Restoration, Chobei Takeda & Company began importing Western pharmaceuticals.

Though Takeda Pharmaceutical was importing Western drugs, its medicinal garden in Kyoto was a place where experimentation with various plant materials would continue. Though the company gradually moved away from its origins in natural medicines to a portfolio of synthetic chemical drugs, it maintained the space of its garden in Kyoto. Over the years, its role as living museum has included conservation and demonstration of the modern-day uses of traditional compounds from all over the world. It includes gardens dedicated to *kampo* and folk medicine, including a space (fenced off with barbed wire) for such poisonous plants as belladonna, which also have healing properties.

In 2017, the garden had an annual budget of $2 million to support its activities, including maintaining about 2,500 plant species, of which more than 100 are endangered. Its facilities are nondescript and modest given its conservation mission. The TKG has a climate-controlled

seed and rhizome bank of thousands of additional varieties not cultivated within its garden (e.g., from tropical ecosystems).[16] It collabo-
rates with plant conservation gardens in Japan and other parts of Asia.
It should be noted that reflecting this private-sector, corporate-level
sponsorship, the links to local indigenous communities are minimal,
and thus stakeholder-inclusive innovations are limited. It has, however,
made progress in collaborating with botanical gardens in Asia to help
maintain spaces of conservation of the earth's biodiversity, keeping
certain sacred spaces secret. Consequently, the Kyoto garden would
fall into the lower-right quadrant of the typology of innovation architecture, supporting open sharing of existing plant medicinal knowledge
and not necessarily innovating upon that knowledge.

Without a critical mass of local TMK stakeholders with the quotidian understanding of herbal plant biodiversity issues, resource-
dependent Japan's corporate social responsibility efforts have been
attempted within an otherwise vacant local stakeholder space at home.
One exception is noteworthy. Japan is unique in that all universities
with pharmacy schools are required by the government to have medicinal plant gardens. This ensures that future drug scientists and phar-
macists learn about the natural origins of medicines. These gardens are
also required to cultivate all plants listed in the Japanese *kampoyaku*
pharmacopoeia.[17] As discussed above under the JBF, the Japanese government has also engaged in environmental activism abroad, in multilateral bodies including the United Nations. A new PPP, Japan's GHIT,
has contributed to inclusive innovation in new drug discovery, drawing
from knowledge about biologics within natural medicine.

Global Health Innovative Technology Fund

*"Huge unmet medical needs exist for neglected diseases, but the
near total lack of market incentives means that proactive investment
in their R&D is incredibly rare" (GHIT 2019).*

The Global Health Innovative Technology Fund was established in
November 2012, having been conceived in 2011 by two colleagues, B.
T. Slingsby, then at Eisai Pharmaceuticals, and Tachi Yamada of the
Bill and Melinda Gates Foundation. The concept, said to have been
sketched on the back of a napkin, was to create an investment-matching
fund for new drug discovery serving the developing world through a

unique international public-private partnership in Japan. Priority targets for development would be those neglected by market failure—that is, those disease conditions endemic to the poor and underdeveloped world: malaria, tuberculosis (TB), and other NTDs. The idea would be to bring on board key players from the Japanese government and pharmaceutical companies. Slingsby and Yamada soon recruited a core team of members from government, industry, and international foundations. When asked how this could have come together so quickly, observers involved in the early stages noted two things. First, after the Tohoku earthquake in 2011, government officials began a soul-searching process, identifying ways in which the government could work more effectively with communities facing public health crises.[18] Second, Slingsby, an American who holds a doctorate in medicine from Tokyo University (2007) and served as the fund's CEO until March 2019, was known for his ability to "speak the language" of whichever stakeholder he was pitching, in Japanese. One observer noted that he had an uncanny ability to put whomever he was speaking with at complete ease, facilitating the flow of ideas and implementation of them in practice (anonymous interviews 2019).

The name GHIT—a play on the word *hit* used in the pharmaceutical industry to refer to how potential drugs "hit" target disease conditions—was proposed by one of the founding funders, Minori Saito, representing Astellas Pharmaceuticals. Soon thereafter, Takeda Pharmaceutical and Daiichi Sankyo joined the effort. The Ministry of Health, Labor, and Welfare would be the main government source of funds, in conjunction with the Ministry of Foreign Affairs, which would work with the United Nations Development Program on delivery and access in developing countries in the Global South. Coincidentally, the MHLW was undergoing its own transformation, establishing the quasi-independent Agency for Medical Research and Development, a kind of National Institutes of Health for Japan. So, the timing of the proposal of an international matching fund for Japan was fortuitous. An observer at the time noted that for the first time, the customary risk-averse organizational mind-set prevalent in Japanese institutions "totally changed." From the start of GHIT's formation, the Japanese government and industry partners would get out of their domestic "inward-looking" (*uchi muki*, 内向き) comfort zones and seek international partners. GHIT would also help to build bridges between heretofore disparate efforts by the Ministries of

Education, Culture, Sports, Science, and Technology and of Health, Labor, and Welfare. MEXT oversees basic scientific (drug) discovery at universities, while subsequent preclinical-stage research has been the purview of MHLW. Rather than have to navigate the procedures and reporting requirements of two different ministries, for GHIT awardees there is seamless funding from early- to late-stage R&D. A small step toward greater inclusion, to be sure, but bordering on revolutionary in the context of Japan's domestic innovation system heretofore characterized by factionalized, secretive silos (TISA low novelty and closed).

While the concept of public-private partnership is not new to Japan—retired Tokyo University professor Fumio Kodama had led the creation of private sector–(national public) university *sangakurenkei* (産学連携) policies decades prior—two aspects of the GHIT stand out. First, there is a "firewall" between the funders (50 percent is from government, 25 percent from foundations, and 25 percent from industry) and the decisions on which projects get funded. This means in practice that fund sponsors' projects may not be selected for investment in a given round at all. The same goes for teams from universities with close ties to MHLW. Second, the fund governance was to be international at the outset. At all levels, from the board of directors to evaluation panels selecting R&D projects for funding, the aim is to maintain half non-Japanese participants under a "robust and transparent system," according to Catherine Ohura, GHIT CEO as of 2019 (Ohura 2019).

This international and open innovation architecture was revolutionary for Japan at the time. As one executive involved in GHIT noted, "The Japanese prefer to work with themselves, and do things for Japan."[19] GHIT would go on to fund dozens of drug and diagnostic research and development projects whose benefits would accrue primarily to patients and communities beyond Japan's national borders. If the work of GHIT was contextualized into the TISA, it would be in the lower-right quadrant but plotted nearest to the upper right, since its focus on using intellectual property pools is a basis for new drug discovery to be shared with developing countries in a quasi-commons way.

In the first round of funding, Phase 1.0 ($100 million, 2013–2017), thirteen projects were selected, mainly for promising treatments and diagnostics for the aforementioned target diseases. Other projects underway from the beginning were initiatives by Eisai, Takeda, and other lead firms to share their compound libraries in a shared pool, with the aim of using advances in data analysis to identify those with potential for use in TB or malaria treatment. By 2015, GHIT had also launched its first "Grand Challenges" competition, in the image of the Bill & Melinda Gates Foundation funding program of the same name (*Asian Scientist* 2015). Teams of international collaborators would be supported with seed funds to develop drug concepts, vaccines, and diagnostics for the aforementioned NTDs, including leishmaniasis. In its funding, GHIT would focus on three criteria: quality of the science, usability in the field, and affordability. GHIT would not be in the business of developing high-priced boutique medicine, as discussed in Chapter 2.

By 2019, two products had come to fruition: a TB diagnostic and a pediatric praziquantel to treat the parasitic disease schistosomiasis. Reflecting GHIT's early success, Phase 2.0 was launched in 2018 with twice as much in the fund ($200 million, for projects from 2019 to 2022). The fund has also become a platform for uniting efforts across product development partners to standardize data collection and seek a standardized drug-approval process across countries, particularly in Asia. For example, GHIT has been working with partners including the United Nations Development Program in countries throughout Africa, as well as more recent initiatives planned for Indonesia and the Philippines. Bunpei Yamamura, GHIT's senior director of brand communications, has been with GHIT from its inception, having been recruited early on by GHIT cofounder and first CEO Slingsby. Reflecting on the arc of GHIT since its establishment in 2012, Yamamura says that PPPs like GHIT in Japan are at a unique crossroads, where different cultures are coming together with a shared goal of improving human health. In Yamamura's experience dealing with various stakeholders in the process of new drug discovery, the differences between Japanese and non-Japanese ways of approaching research are less noticeable than the differences, regardless of country, in mind-set between people from government, private industry, and NGOs. In this regard, Yamamura is most encouraged when he witnesses corporate CEOs interacting with NGO volunteers in ways completely atypical to C-suites—that is, working with local stakeholders with a profound sense of humility in finding better ways to improve human health together.

Japan has shifted to an open and inclusive innovation system architecture, at least vis-à-vis new drug discovery as part of its health diplomacy in the developing world. Explanations for this evolution, even revolution, in its national government approach range from the political to the altruistic, as discussed above. The corporate-sponsored, yet heretofore small-scale, efforts of the TKG in Japan represent a first step toward connecting theories of inclusive innovation with practices among stakeholder groups, as the Honey Bee Network (HBN) has done successfully in India. At the very least, community engagement at the local level has been an important part of conservation and protection of the plant biological material for medicinals.

Japan's corporate social responsibility supporting the TKG reflects the long-term horizon for Japanese firms in general—its corporate culture prioritizes future potential over the present at hand. This has translated into efforts to protect and conserve plant medicinal biodiversity in part for its own sake and also to maintain these knowledge and biological resources, "just in case" (念の為, *nennotame*), as Japanese are wont to say. In this regard, Japan has demonstrated environmental leadership in addition to stewardship in multilateral bodies including the United Nations. The Japanese have backed promises with billions of dollars of funds invested by the Japan Biodiversity Fund in stakeholder efforts to protect and conserve biodiversity around the world. Japan has also created risk-taking PPPs in new drug discovery, exemplified by GHIT.

Heretofore, the beneficiaries of Japan's inclusive innovation diplomacy have been far away in space (developing countries). Further, the potential economic return on investment is in the distant future, if it materializes at all—for example, in raising the brand consciousness of Japanese companies in target countries. On their own, places that have the most (local, regional, national) stakeholders (traditional medicine practitioners, indigenous groups, cultivators, politicians, and bureaucrats) might struggle to make actionable policy absent these nudges from vetted international partners.

Paradoxically, resource-poor Japan, lacking significant numbers of domestic stakeholders with vested interests and thus the potential to lobby to influence the outcome of national policy, may be best positioned to assume leadership in seeking multilateral solutions that benefit all countries.

Conclusion

Japan's biological resource scarcity has led it to seek international partnerships in supporting innovations in and protection and conservation of genomic materials for natural medicine drug discovery. Through its official development assistance, including the JBF and Satoyama Initiative, Japan has built a global network of researchers connected to local stakeholders in socioecological production landscapes. At the same time, Japan has worked within such multilateral organizations as the United Nations to facilitate international standard setting on sustainable harvesting practices and quality—for example, Good Manufacturing Practice and certifications of origin in the use of medicinal plants. The dependence of its *kampo* medicines primarily on China for raw materials in part explains Japan's multilateral versus bilateral approach, due to its hot-and-cold political relationship with that country. At home, Japanese private industry has collaborated with universities in demonstration gardens and seed and rhizome banking to conserve and maintain bio stocks of medicinal plant genetic biodiversity. The efforts of Takeda Pharmaceutical in its medicinal garden in Kyoto are noteworthy in this regard, considering the miniscule relation to the firm's profit from natural medicines.

The GHIT has built on Japan's strength in *sangakukanrenkei* (産 学官連携)—industry-academic-government relations in its unique PPP structure making early-stage investments in new drug discovery, in a dual innovation sandbox and intellectual property pool architecture. In doing so, GHIT has brought much-needed essential medicines for NTDs and diagnostics closer to market and to patients in the developing world, reflecting an open commons approach (TISA right side).

Japan's inclusive innovation in health diplomacy contradicts assumptions that Japan is largely a closed innovation system, unconcerned with what goes on beyond its borders. Its active international engagement for new drug discovery and related medicinal plant conservation paints a different picture—that is, Japan's material and human (e.g., due to an aging population and low birth rates) resource scarcity has driven an international outlook in its new drug discovery.

As such, Japan's national policy, neither purely nationalist (China) nor framed as a global commons (India), nevertheless has been pragmatic and boundary spanning. In offering solutions to the complex intersections between sustainable use of biodiversity, new drug discovery for human health, and standard setting in the intellectual property rights of such discoveries, Japan could be a model for the future, accomplishing more on a global level with less on a national level. I return to the global context and future possibilities in the last chapter.

Notes

1. During the Heian period (794–1155 CE), indigenous Shinto and imported Buddhist beliefs conjoined, for example, in terms of religious mountain practices (山岳宗教, *sangaku shūkyō*).

2. It should be noted that government approval of *kampo* is predicated on the formula remaining the same over time. This is unlike in China and elsewhere in Asia, where the prescribing physician has flexibility in the crude drugs (natural materials) used within a given prescribed natural medicine.

3. All of these databases are free and open to the public except TradMPD.

4. China has set export restrictions on licorice since 1983, justifying this move on the basis of protecting the environment (Meng, Su, and Zhu 2006). In 2006, the Ministry of Commerce of the PRC and three other ministries/administrations carried out the "Interim Measures for the Check and Ratification of Export Enterprises of Ephedrine Precursor Chemicals" (麻黄素类易制毒化学品出口企业核定暂行办法, *Mahuangsulei Yizhi Duhuaxuepin Chukou Qiye Heding Zanxing Banfa*), whose article 13 stipulated that China must forbid the export of natural (meaning wild) ephedra (天然麻黄草, *Tianran Mahuangcao*) to protect ephedra resources and the natural environment. However, since January 2019, the Chinese Ministry of Commerce and four other ministries/administrations have implemented export quotas to support cultivated ephedra (人工种植麻黄草, *Rengong Zhongzhi Mahuangcao*) business (General Administration of Customs, P. R. China 2006; Ministry of Commerce of the People's Republic of China 2018).

5. According to the IRS, the yearly average exchange rate in 2019 was 1 USD = 109.008 yen (IRS 2020).

6. According to Kotoe Katayama et al. (2013), on the basis of 67,113,579 health care claim records collected by the MHLW in 2009, of the 382 categories of approved drugs covered by the NHI, *kampo* formulation extracts rank as the 28th most prescribed and account for 0.80 percent of the total number of retrieved and prescribed drugs. Crude drugs and crude drug preparations respectively rank 177th and 238th, and each of them accounts for 0.05 percent and 0.02 percent of the total retrieved and prescribed drugs.

7. Physicians might prescribe *kampo* medicines, but most of them only use a very limited number.

8. According to the IRS, the yearly average exchange rate in 2016 was 1 USD to 113.138 yen, and in 2017 it was 1 USD to 116.667 yen (IRS 2020).

9. Japan became a signatory to the CBD in 1993 (Convention on Biological Diversity 2014).

10. Sarnaik et al. (2017) outline the contributions of the "Fairwild" certification system in the Satoyama Initiative Thematic Review drawing from the work of Dr. Kulkarni (interviewed in Chapter 4) in supporting sustainable

harvesting practices of medicinal plants. Established in 2008, Fairwild was developed by a group of NGOs, including the World Wildlife Fund.

11. According to the Organization for Economic Cooperation and Development, Japan has been one of the top sources of biodiversity-related official development assistance (OECD 2016).

12. Not to be confused with the unaffiliated Kyoto Botanical Garden, located in the valley below.

13. It should be noted that Japan (and China) has sacred natural spaces similar to *deo rahati*, associated with folk and Buddhist practices. In Japan the concept of *satoyama* reflects a village-mountain space. Revered mountain habitats, including the Yoshino-Kumano, have been considered as sacred spaces (Iwatsuki 2003).

14. Tsumura has been active in creating quality standards for its suppliers in China, as well as monitoring and auditing activities to ensure purity in plant materials. It has also sponsored, through corporate social responsibility programs, a number of activities supporting youth education about the environment.

15. The US invasion of Iraq is said to have wiped out seed banks that had been preserved since ancient times (Siegel and Betz 2016).

16. By the end of 2019, the budget had declined by an undisclosed amount. Sources cited difficulty the garden was having in recruiting junior scientists to work in its somewhat secluded mountain location. By that time, Dr. Kodaira had decamped for Kitasato University (mentioned above) in order to focus on his own (AMED-sponsored) research into extraction technologies for obtaining active ingredients from medicinal plants.

17. According to the 2015 edition of the 日本植物園協会日本植物園協会員植物園一覧 (Japan Association of Botanical Gardens List of Member Gardens), thirty-one pharmacy-school-related medicinal plant gardens were members of the association (Japan Association of Botanical Gardens 2015).

18. In the initial days after the 2011 earthquake and tsunami, private-sector and nongovernmental organizations (as well as the US military) were better equipped and moved more quickly than the national government in disaster rescue and relief efforts.

19. It should be noted that Japan has partnered with the United States since 1965 via the Cooperative Medical Science Program on finding cures and treatments for infectious diseases of Asia and the Pacific. Further, in 2017 AMED partnered with the National Institute of Allergy and Infectious Diseases (NIAID) of the National Institutes of Health (NIH) for AMED's first international call in English, reviewing applications jointly with NIH/NIAID. Thirteen early-career and/or female-scientist-led projects were selected.

6

A Way Forward: Bringing Innovative Solutions to Global Human Health Problems

After laying out the global context of the current crisis in our innovation system, which left us woefully underprepared for the coronavirus pandemic that emerged in 2020, this book has reviewed the academic and policy literature concerned with inclusive innovation, contextualized within the global intellectual property rights (IPR) regime, itself embedded within larger structures reflecting powerful private interests. It proposed a new conceptual typology of innovation system architectures (TISA) framework of inclusive innovation through innovation sandboxes and intellectual property (IP) pools, created and led by certain change agents. Further, the book examined the current state and future prospects for stakeholder inclusion in the innovation process—for example, harnessing the innovation potential of biological materials (biologics), particularly plant-derived natural medicines and the traditional medical knowledge that goes with it. The cases in this book have challenged the claim by Big Pharma that we need patents for monopoly profits to drive innovation. The commodification of biologics, including parts of the human body, traditional medicinal knowledge, and biological materials upon which medicine depends, amounts to stealing from the open innovation commons (a universal right) in order to enrich patent-protected monopoly profits (granting a right to exclude). The era of nineteenth-century innovators in medicine who shared their discoveries freely in an open innovation commons for

161

the benefit of all humanity has faded—that is, the global pharmaceutical industry has largely neglected investments into developing healing medicines in favor of selling profitable drugs, as long as patent monopolies are held firmly in place. Patients in need have been neglected in favor of patients who can afford to pay. The retreat of a guiding moral compass is happening in an age of spreading epidemics and increasing frequency and severity of pandemics of both communicable and chronic diseases. However, as the cases of inclusive innovation in this book have shown, the embers of noblesse oblige, albeit diminished, shine brightly in countries in Asia.

A revolutionary overthrow of the current global IPR regime aside, in the search for transformational change in the structure and process of innovation inclusive of the needs of humanity, barriers to even modest incremental improvements remain. These include a lack of national compliance with multilateral agreements to protect and conserve natural medicinals, weak acknowledgment and inclusion of local stakeholders, lack of technical access and unfamiliarity with legal rights of the same, and lack of resources to collect, code, store, and protect traditional medicinal knowledge data. These limitations point to the urgent need for additional research to explore new conceptual frameworks and the critical need for a global architecture for an innovation commons, as well as the development of methods to analyze (e.g., taxonomies) existing models and practice on the ground.

What are some immediate steps toward a solution to chronic and infectious epidemic/pandemic crises humanity faces today? Crises include the fact that greater numbers of people are getting sick, and fewer synthetic chemical drugs are effective in treating them. A first step is acknowledging that there is a problem with the way things are structured and implemented in the global innovation system. A second step is collecting evidence on what has been tried and evaluating and considering alternatives to the status quo, including emergent organizations and certain kinds of public-private partnerships (PPPs).

From Tragedy of the Commons to Public Innovation Commons

The divergent state and private-sector initiatives pursued in China, India, and Japan to deal with the twenty-first-century challenges of epidemic and pandemic disease have been most evident in the emergent organizations analyzed herein. The most effective and timely solutions in such times of crisis innovation as the world faced during the global coronavirus pandemic were neither fully state nor purely market based. Emergent organizations in China, India, and Japan instead created structured-play-based incentives to cooperate and also compete within innovation sandboxes. India's arguments for a global innovation commons are nearest to the ideal (upper-right quadrant) of a system reflected in the TISA framework that encourages high levels of novelty and a high degree of openness. China's more nationalistic approach seeks to develop new medicines with high novelty but not necessarily share them in an open commons. This proved problematic in the uncooperative global competition to launch a workable Covid-19 vaccine that was affordable, safe, and effective. Japan has taken a more pragmatic approach, relying on transnational networks to encourage openness and access to existing drugs and medicines while supporting novel essential medicine discovery. Yet Japan has been limited by its national resource dependency and history of fragmentation and silos in its domestic innovation system. Consequently, its ambitions remain modest but actionable as less novel but still open (TISA pools). Figure 6.1 outlines where the case studies of inclusive innovation analyzed in Chapters 3, 4, and 5 fall within the TISA as measured by novelty and openness.

The following recaps the highlights from China, India, and Japan, noting inflection points in the intersection of state politics and private markets, aiming for new drug discovery in essential medicines.

China

Overall, emergent organizations in China have partnered with a national government keen to protect and promote technonational security of knowledge and material assets in domestic industries. Natural medicine development has benefited from a newfound interest in its protection and conservation by the Chinese Communist Party, led in 2020 by Xi Jinping. As such, in recent decades China has taken a more assertive, proactive, and positive approach to the sustainable development of biologics, especially traditional Chinese medicine (TCM)–originated drugs. The coronavirus pandemic prompted expansion in new drug discovery within PPPs already underway with

Figure 6.1 Typology of Innovation Architecture: Cases in TISA Quadrants

	Cages	Sandboxes
High novelty	NRTCM (China)	Public innovation commons HGP (global) Linux (global) OSDD (India) Collaborative competition JBF SI (Japan) HBN (India)
	TKDL (India)	
	Silos	Pools
Low novelty		GHIT (Japan)
	Big Pharma Me-too synthetic drugs Patents in perpetuity	CBIK (China) Takeda Garden (Japan) STORK (Japan)

Low openness ⟶ High openness

the support of private foundations from Ford (Center for Biodiversity and Indigenous Knowledge) to Gates (Global Health Drug Discovery Institute), albeit often stymied by political interference from the central state. Private entrepreneurs at the head of TCM pharma companies, including Yiling Pharma, stepped up to provide medicines effective in the treatment of Covid-19, going so far as to send care packages worldwide to Chinese students studying and, in 2020, trapped abroad. TCM for Covid-19 treatment was also sent by the Chinese government to countries on the western end of its Belt and Road Initiative. Meanwhile, at home, the National Registry for Traditional Chinese Medicine (NRTCM), after collecting thousands of heretofore uncodified TCM formulations—a potential treasure trove of information for drug discovery—remains closed off from sharing in the commons as literally containing "state secrets." Even the national researchers who led the project to collect the data, compiling an unprecedented book of remedies for the twenty-first century, were shut out from accessing their own database creation. Instead, select state-owned or politically connected Chinese pharmaceutical companies would be granted national patents under a national sui generis IP system. China had initiated its national registry after witnessing the way in which Indian traditional medicine had been exploited unfairly by the Western pharmaceutical industry. The turmeric patent war is one among numerous examples discussed in Chapter 4. India would take the opposite approach from China at least in its posturing to the outside world.

India

The Traditional Knowledge Digital Library (TKDL) in India arose in response to blatant intellectual property expropriation in the attempts—some successful—to patent and profit from uses of traditional medicines derived from turmeric (i.e., curcumin) and other ancient Indian traditional formulations and biological materials. As India has among the oldest histories in Asia of medicine, the documented formulations of medicinal use of numerous plant materials were known on a quotidian level by all Indians, at home and in the diaspora.[1]

By placing many hundreds of thousands of formulations from Ayurveda, Unani, and others firmly in the public commons, the Indian government and private-sector partners sought to protect from unfair exploitation the vast corpus of medicinal knowledge and the biological materials providing active ingredients to the global pharmaceutical supply chain. As such, India's approach under TKDL would be defensive, using the database to challenge patent applications before they could be granted erroneously. While the TKDL has been successful on the whole, mainly in European patent denials, patent examiners in the US Patent and Trademark Office (USPTO) in the United States hadn't bothered to check the TKDL for prior art, reflecting regulatory capture of the USPTO in that country, on the one hand, and broader pressures to get "new drugs" with speed to market, on the other. The fact that the TKDL remains closed to all save patent examiners belies its positioning as part of an open public commons.

Emergent organizations in India, led by local actors forging and attempting to forge international stakeholder network connections, have tried to protect and conserve traditional medicine knowledge and biological materials from unfair exploitation. Whereas stakeholders in *deo rahati* (sacred groves) have struggled to recruit younger generations to take on stewardship of local community traditional medicine knowledge and biological materials, the Honey Bee Network (HBN) has succeeded through creative ways in engaging youth, particularly students, in collaborative competition. This has involved, for example, nonmonetary prizes for identifying best practice in sustainable harvesting of plant medicinals and managing these within common, pooled local ecosystem resources supporting local economic development.

The Open Source Drug Discovery (OSDD), another Indian state-led PPP developing essential medicines for neglected tropical diseases (NTDs), was created in the image of open-source coding (Linux) and open-source science (Human Genome Project). Again, through the innovative use of nonmonetary competitive incentives (microcredits earning increasing status for individual, often student contributions), OSDD has continued to innovate drug discovery for essential medicines, while increasing its global reach over time. As important, the OSDD, like HBN, has mentored junior scientists and nascent entrepreneurs within a value system that confirms there is worth in competition driven by purpose rather than profit. Perhaps this will be its long-lasting impact and legacy, as worthwhile as the new medicines developed from its innovative activity. Japan has taken a wholly different approach, reflecting its domestic resource scarcity.

Japan

Biological-resource-scarce Japan, through its international health and biodiversity diplomacy, has acted presciently. Lacking the mega-biodiverse material resources of China and India, Japan, through its Japan Biodiversity Fund and Satoyama Initiative, has built international networks of diplomats, nongovernmental organizations (NGOs), and local stakeholders around the world and put real national money behind protection and conservation of medicinal biodiversity and natural medicine innovation. Its natural medicine (*kampo*) company Tsumura has collaborated with farming communities in China and Southeast Asia in developing sustainable cultivation practices. Takeda Pharmaceutical, via its medicinal garden in Kyoto, has partnered with medicinal gardens around the world to maintain long-term viability of medicinal plants in its seed and rhizome banking exchange, though notably Chinese gardens had ceased sending materials as of 2018 as part of China's national campaign to protect state secrets and national biological assets, while paradoxically continuing to request Japanese materials.

Japan's Standards of Reporting Kampo Products is the most open access among the three national traditional medicine registries, compared to TKDL in India and NRTCM in China. Users merely indicate that they are accessing for noncommercial research purposes on the honor system (I accessed it easily in a few clicks). Its data is limited, however, to merely hundreds of formulations. China's national registry has thousands; India's has hundreds of thousands. This low number in Japan is due in part to its National Health Insurance system's certifying a small proportion of the original thousands of *kampo* medicines brought to Japan from premodern China. On the other hand, the Japanese government still mandates that all university pharmacy schools maintain a plant medicinal garden of living specimens comprising all natural medicines listed in the Japanese pharmacopoeia.

The Global Health Innovative Technology Fund (GHIT) is Japan's most recent (as of this writing) initiative linking new drug discovery to its domestic strengths in biologics, especially genomics and stem cells, and to treatments and cures for NTDs in the developing world. GHIT is perhaps an archetypical inclusive innovation framework. Its IP pool with aspirations as an innovation sandbox draws from state resources and the support of the Ministries of Health, Labor, and Welfare and of Foreign Affairs. It is led by a board backed by private industry (Eisai Pharmaceuticals, Astellas Pharmaceuticals, and Takeda Pharmaceutical) and an NGO (Gates Foundation) that funds projects independent of the potential biases of sponsoring firms and free of political interference. That is, in a given funding round, upending Japan's long-standing deferential hierarchies, product pitches from sponsoring pharma firms' scientists are judged by an independent, external international board of experts. Further, in keeping with the international structure of the Japan Biodiversity Fund's Satoyama Initiative and other PPPs, projects from anywhere in the world are welcome—though applications are accepted only in English and Japanese. Several promising diagnostics and drugs for tuberculosis and malaria were nearing clinical trials as of this writing.

Future research could compare the observed cases in Japan with those in other countries, as well as identify effective bi- and multilateral attempts at inclusive innovation practices.[2] Within these countries, exploring potential variations across domestic regions, ethnic groups, and religions could confirm or challenge the representativeness of the findings herein. The thirteen cases analyzed across three country contexts have provided a lens on the progress of national governments in partnership with private-sector actors in harnessing, in an inclusive and sustainable manner, the innovation potential of such biologics as natural medicines in new drug discovery, especially for essential medicines. We need more progress toward inclusive innovation activities in the open commons, within TISA sandboxes.

Conclusion

In the seventeenth century, international trade was dominated by seagoing countries possessing vessels with the backing of national governments and militaries: the Netherlands, England, Portugal, and Spain. Many of the natural resources were extracted and moved from East and South to West and North. This trade included spices and medicines. Chapter 2 began with a story of the etymology of the word *drug* in this regard. The tables are turning—that is, Asia is on track to become the center of the global economy. For example, China is at the vanguard of extracting material resources from the Global South to the East, via its twenty-first-century Belt and Road Initiative renewal and expansion of its historical Silk Road. China is also on track to become the largest economy in the world in a few decades.

As this book has demonstrated, certain Asian countries have both the vast biological resources and increasing research and development capacity for biologic-based drug discovery. With this in mind, having a patent-centric global IPR regime, which was established in the late twentieth century, may lead to unintended consequences in the twenty-first—that is, as Asian economies, China and India in particular, continue to develop and grow under an all-life-is-patentable global model, they will flourish. It might be prudent to consider the long-term value to Western economies, the national security of their citizens, and their residents' domestic public health of maintaining innovations based on natural medicines within a global innovation commons.

The most virulent and dangerous pathogens threatening human-ity come from the natural world, as they have throughout human his-tory. Perhaps it is hubris that for a mere century, we thought that somehow synthetic chemicals were the solution. From nature come the threats, and it follows that nature is where we will find the cures. As mega-biodiverse China and India continue to rise as international economic and political powers, it would be in the interest of global human health for these countries to share their natural medicine inno-vations in the global innovation commons. The alternative is that pre-ventative treatments and cures for the next pandemic will have potential to emerge from societies that have strategic assets in the applied medical knowledge that Western countries lack. In 2021, China would be among the first to deploy a Covid-19 vaccine—not to mention the successful use of natural traditional Chinese medicine in Covid-19 treatment. It should also be noted that China was the locus of the initial outbreak of the major viral pandemics of the last century—namely, the misnamed Spanish flu of 1918 and the novel coronavirus that emerged in 2019.

Without a sui generis system on a global scale for the protection and conservation of natural medicine in the global innovation com-mons, we might see the patented IPR strength shift from the United States and Europe to countries in Asia that are strong in natural med-icine intellectual and material resources, enriching their pharmaceuti-cal industries. As witnessed during the Covid-19 pandemic, countries competed to launch treatments and vaccines for their citizens first and foremost. In the case of China, when treatments and vaccines were deployed internationally, they targeted certain countries expected to reciprocate by serving China's long-term strategic national interests.

Future research might examine the growing role of such transna-tional actors as private foundations and other open-source communities and networks in facilitating paradigm shifts in the way we think about innovation and further as a source of systemic change in the way we innovate. I have been inspired by the community stakeholders, doctors, scholars, and activists striving to harness the human health potential of biologics, particularly natural medicines, in an age of pandemic disease. The inclusive TISA framework of open innovation sand-boxes and shared intellectual property pools follows from the grounded theorizing of Elinor Ostrom (and others) about the global commons reviewed in Chapters 1 and 2. The guiding critical question has centered on how we can improve the current global innovation system in order to better serve human health through the discovery and development of safe and effective essential medicines.

Chapters 1 and 2 enumerated the innovation failures of the World Trade Organization (WTO) Agreement on the Trade-Related Aspects of Intellectual Property Rights (TRIPS) global intellectual property rights system backed by synthetic drug makers of Big Pharma. Given the entrenched interests behind the WTO TRIPS status quo, is it possible to engender accessible innovations in essential medicines absent a Schumpeterian overthrow of the moribund "me-too," evergreening incremental-innovation system currently protected by patent monopolies? The emergent organizations in Asia, connected to like-minded stakeholders globally, offer a glimpse into a possible future. In contrast, multilateral organizations, namely, the WTO, protecting the status quo are facing scientific, evidence-backed calls for a new system governing the use and exploitation of natural medicine materials and the traditional knowledge about how to innovate with them. That these calls are coming from political and economic leaders in mega-biodiverse countries with deep codified histories of innovation in medicine is significant.

In furthering the aim of inclusive innovation in drug discovery, how do we save what remains of traditional medicinal knowledge, in the dual goals of conserving potential resources for innovations in medicine and protecting the indigenous communities stewarding the knowledge? It may be that neither top-down national state nor bottom-up local approaches are sufficient to either explain activities on the ground or accomplish the immense task at hand. Relying on market-based profit-driven incentives has not produced adequate solutions either. An international PPP model of emergent inclusive innovation architectures may be the best path, as the cases in China, India, and Japan have illustrated.

Embedding these material and human resources into an open innovation commons characterized by sharing discoveries within "sandboxes and pools," examined in depth within the TISA framework herein, is in the interest of humanity. The cases analyzed in this book have also shown that it is possible to cooperate while competing. Incentivizing innovation needs neither to be profit driven nor patent centric, despite the vociferous claims to the contrary by vested interests behind avoiding innovating our innovation system.

Notes

1. Self-made billionaire Kiran Mazumdar-Shaw, founder of BIOCON, India's largest biopharmaceutical company—and undoubtedly able to access any medicine of her choice—when she became ill with Covid-19, reported that she made sure to take *chyavanprash*, an Ayurvedic medicine to improve immunity (Mazumdar-Shaw 2020).

2. For example, more research is needed to understand the intersections of religious and spiritual practice that have made sacred spaces into protected ecosystems characterized by sustainable economic development.

Acronyms

ABT	Aichi Biodiversity Targets
ACE	angiotensin-converting enzyme
AMED	Agency for Medical Research and Development (Japan)
ASU&H	Ayurveda, Siddha and Unani, and Homoeopathy
AYUSH	Ayurveda, Yoga and Naturopathy, Unani, Siddha, and Homoeopathy
BFA	Boao Forum for Asia
BMG	Beijing Municipal Government
BOP	bottom of the pyramid
BRI	Belt and Road Initiative
CBD	Convention on Biological Diversity
CBIK	Center for Biodiversity and Indigenous Knowledge
CCP	Chinese Communist Party
CCRAS	Central Council for Research in Ayurvedic Sciences
COP	Conference of the Parties
Covid-19	coronavirus disease 2019
CSIR	Council of Scientific and Industrial Research (India)
EBM	evidence-based medicine
FDA	Food and Drug Administration
GHDDI	Global Health Drug Discovery Institute
GHIT	Global Health Innovative Technology Fund
HBN	Honey Bee Network
HGP	Human Genome Project
HIV/AIDS	human immunodeficiency virus/acquired immunodeficiency syndrome
ICMR	Indian Council of Medical Research
INM	Institute of Natural Medicine (India)
IP	intellectual property
IPR	intellectual property rights

iPS	induced pluripotent stem cells
ISM	Indian Systems of Medicine
ISM&H	Indian Systems of Medicine and Homoeopathy
JBF	Japan Biodiversity Fund
JSOM	Japan Society for Oriental Medicine
LH	Lianhua Qingwen Capsule
MEXT	Ministry of Education, Culture, Sports, Science, and Technology (Japan)
MHLW	Ministry of Health, Labor, and Welfare (Japan)
NATCM	National Administration of Traditional Chinese Medicine
NDD	new drug discovery
NGO	nongovernmental organization
NHI	National Health Insurance
NHP	National Health Policy (India)
NIAID	National Institute of Allergy and Infectious Diseases (United States)
NIBIOHN	National Institutes of Biomedical Innovation, Health, and Nutrition (Japan)
NIH	National Institutes of Health (United States)
NRTCM	National Registry for Traditional Chinese Medicine
NTD	neglected tropical disease
OECD	Organization for Economic Cooperation and Development
OSDD	Open Source Drug Discovery
PAA	Poverty Alleviation Action (China)
PAB	Poverty Alleviation Board (China)
PMDA	Pharmaceuticals and Medical Devices Agency (Japan)
PPP	public-private partnership
R&D	research and development
SARS	severe acute respiratory syndrome
SI	Satoyama Initiative
SPV	special purpose vehicle
SRISTI	Society for Research and Initiatives for Sustainable Technologies and Institutions
STORK	Standards of Reporting Kampo Products
TB	tuberculosis
TCM	traditional Chinese medicine
TISA	typology of innovation system architectures
TK	traditional knowledge
TKDL	Traditional Knowledge Digital Library
TKG	Takeda Garden for Medicinal Plant Conservation, Kyoto
TM	traditional medicine
TMK	traditional medicine knowledge
TRIPS	Trade-Related Aspects of Intellectual Property Rights
USPTO	US Patent and Trademark Office
WHO	World Health Organization
WIPO	World Intellectual Property Organization
WTO	World Trade Organization
YUM	Yunnan Uplands Management

References

Ackerknecht, Erwin H. 2016. *A Short History of Medicine*. Baltimore: Johns Hopkins University Press.

Agrawal, A., and E. Ostrom. 2006. "Political Science and Conservation Biology: A Dialog of the Deaf." *Conservation Biology* 20 (3): 681–682. http://hdl .handle.net/10535/5892.

Ahmad, Tabrez, and Jaya Godhwani. 2012. "Traditional Knowledge: A New Challenge in Patents." SSRN. https://ssrn.com/abstract=1981642.

Allarakhia, Minna. 2013. "Open-Source Approaches for the Repurposing of Existing or Failed Candidate Drugs: Learning from and Applying the Lessons Across Diseases." *Drug Design, Development and Therapy* 7: 753–766. https://doi.org/10.2147/dddt.s46289.

Alsever, Jennifer. 2020. "Medicine by Machine: Is A.I. the Cure for the World's Ailing Drug Industry?" *Fortune*, January 20. https://fortune.com/longform/ai -artificial-intelligence-medicine-healthcare-pharmaceutical-industry.

Alves, Romulo R. N., and Lerece M. L. Rosa. 2007. "Biodiversity, Traditional Medicine and Public Health: Where Do They Meet?" *Journal of Ethnobiology and Ethnomedicine* 3. https://doi.org/10.1186/1746-4269-3-14.

AMED. 2017a. "Division of Pharmaceutical Research and Development." Last updated July 7. https://www.amed.go.jp/en/program/list/11/01/004.html.

AMED. 2017b. "Overview of the Partnership." Last updated April 7. https:// www.amed.go.jp/en/aboutus/collaboration/pmda.html.

AMED. 2020. "Drug Discovery and Development." Last updated March 13. https://www.amed.go.jp/en/program/index01.html.

Angell, Marcia. 2005. *The Truth About the Drug Companies: How They Deceive Us and What to Do About It*. New York: Random House.

Angell, Marcia. 2015. "Why Do Drug Companies Charge So Much? Because They Can." *Washington Post*, September 25. https://www.washingtonpost.com /opinions/why-do-drug-companies-charge-so-much-because-they-can /2015/09/25/967d3df4-6266-11e5-b38e-06883aacba64_story.html.

Aoki, Keith. 1998. "Neocolonialism, Anticommons Property, and Biopiracy in the (Not-So-Brave) New World Order of International Intellectual Property Protection." *Indiana Journal of Global Legal Studies* 6 (1): 11–58.

Apffel-Marglin, Frederique, and Stephen A. Marglin. 1990. *Dominating Knowledge: Development, Culture, and Resistance.* Oxford, UK: Clarendon Press.

Arai, Ichiro, and Nobuo Kawahara. 2018. "Kampo Pharmaceutical Products in the Japanese Health-Care System: Legal Status and Quality Assurance." *Traditional & Kampo Medicine* 6 (1): 3–11. https://doi.org/10.1002/tkm2.1204.

Arai, Young-Chang P., Hiromichi Yasui, Hideya Isai, Takashi Kawai, Makoto Nishihara, Jun Sato, Tatsunori Ikemoto, et al. 2014. "The Review of Innovative Integration of Kampo Medicine and Western Medicine as Personalized Medicine at the First Multidisciplinary Pain Center in Japan." *EPMA Journal* 5 (1). https://doi.org/10.1186/1878-5085-5-10.

Årdal, Christine, and John-Arne Røttingen. 2012. "Open Source Drug Discovery in Practice: A Case Study." *PLoS Neglected Tropical Diseases* 6 (9). https://doi.org/10.1371/journal.pntd.0001827.

Asian Scientist. 2015. "GHIT Funds Grand Challenges." *Asian Scientist*, February 9. https://www.asianscientist.com/2015/02/topnews/ghit-funds-grand-challenges.

Bach, Peter B. 2019. "No Miracle Drug Should Cost $2.1 Million." *Bloomberg*, May 24. https://www.bloomberg.com/opinion/articles/2019-05-24/check-the-exorbitant-price-of-zolgensma-and-other-orphan-drugs.

Baker, Scott R., Nicholas Bloom, Steven J. Davis, and Stephen J. Terry. 2020. "COVID-Induced Economic Uncertainty." Working Paper 26983, National Bureau of Economic Research, Cambridge, MA, April. https://www.nber.org/papers/w26983.

Baur, Axel, Charlie Chen, Franck Le Deu, Michele Raviscioni, and Jan van Overbeeke. 2019. "Asia on the Move: Five Current Trends Reigniting Growth in the Region's Biopharmaceutical Market." McKinsey & Company, May 15. https://www.mckinsey.com/industries/pharmaceuticals-and-medical-products/our-insights/asia-on-the-move-five-trends-shaping-the-asia-biopharmaceutical-market.

BBC. 2020. "Coronavirus: Trump's WHO De-funding 'as Dangerous as It Sounds.'" *BBC News*, April 15. https://www.bbc.com/news/world-us-canada-52291654.

Beijing Municipal Science & Technology Commission Biomedicine Division. 2018. "全球健康药物研发中心入驻新址, 创新研发全面开展" [Global Health Drug Discovery Institute settled in the new site, the innovative R&D was fully carried out]. Beijing Municipal Science & Technology Commission, November 8. http://kw.beijing.gov.cn/art/2018/11/8/art_6382_563904.html.

Bell, Jacob. 2017. "Pfizer, Roche, Aspen Under Investigation for Cancer Drug Pricing." *BioPharma Dive*, June 14. https://www.biopharmadive.com/news/pfizer-roche-aspen-cancer-pricing-investigation/445004.

Bender, Erin Kathleen. 2003. "North and South: The WTO, Trips, and the Scourge of Biopiracy." *Tulsa Journal of Comparative & International Law* 11: 281–319.

Benkler, Yochai. 2011. *The Penguin and the Leviathan: The Triumph of Cooperation over Self-Interest.* New York: Crown Business.

Berezow, Alex. 2014. "Black Death: The Upside to the Plague Killing Half of Europe." *Forbes*, May 12. https://www.forbes.com/sites/alexberezow/2014/05/12/black-death-the-upside-to-the-plague-killing-half-of-europe.

Bhardwaj, Anshu, Vinod Scaria, Gajendra Pal Singh Raghava, Andrew Michael Lynn, Nagasuma Chandra, Sulagna Banerjee, Muthukurussi V. Raghunandanan, et al. 2011. "Open Source Drug Discovery—a New Paradigm of Collaborative Research in Tuberculosis Drug Development." *Tuberculosis* 91 (5). https://doi.org/10.1016/j.tube.2011.06.004.

Bhatia, Rahul, and Tom Lasseter. 2017. "As Modi and His Right-Wing Hindu Base Rise, So Too Does a Celebrity Yoga Tycoon." Reuters, May 23. https://www.reuters.com/investigates/special-report/india-modi-ramdev.

Bhattacharya, Nandini. 2016. "From Materia Medica to the Pharmacopoeia: Challenges of Writing the History of Drugs in India." *History Compass* 14 (4): 131–139.

Bill & Melinda Gates Foundation. 2020. "Promoting Chinese Innovation/Global Health Drug Discovery Institute." Accessed September 18, 2020. https://www.gatesfoundation.org/Where-We-Work/China-Office/Promoting-Chinese-Innovation/Global-Health-Drug-Discovery-Institute.

Binz, Christian, and Bernhard Truffer. 2017. "Global Innovation Systems—a Conceptual Framework for Innovation Dynamics in Transnational Contexts." *Research Policy* 46 (7): 1284–1298. https://doi.org/10.1016/j.respol.2017.05.012.

Bio. Accessed February 14, 2020. https://www.bio.org.

Bloom, David E., Michael Kuhn, and Klaus Prettner. 2020. "Modern Infectious Diseases: Macroeconomic Impacts and Policy Responses." Working Paper 27757, National Bureau of Economic Research, Cambridge, MA, August. https://www.nber.org/system/files/working_papers/w27757/w27757.pdf.

Board of Governors of the Federal Reserve System. 2020. "Foreign Exchange Rates—G.5." Accessed July 24, 2020. https://www.federalreserve.gov/releases/g5/current/default.htm.

Boldrin, Michele, and David K. Levine. 2008. *Against Intellectual Monopoly*. Cambridge: Cambridge University Press

Boldrin, Michele, and David K. Levine. 2009. "Market Structure and Property Rights in Open Source Industries." *Washington University Journal of Law & Policy* 30: 325–363.

Botha, Louisa, Sara Grobbelaar, and Wouter Bam. 2016. "Towards a Framework to Guide the Evaluation of Inclusive Innovation Systems." *South African Journal of Industrial Engineering* 27 (3): 64–78. http://dx.doi.org/10.7166/27-3-1632.

Boudreau, Kevin. 2010. "Open Platform Strategies and Innovation: Granting Access vs. Devolving Control." *Management Science* 56 (10): 1849–1872. https://doi.org/10.1287/mnsc.1100.1215.

Boyle, James. 2003. "The Second Enclosure Movement and the Construction of the Public Domain." *Law and Contemporary Problems* 66 (1/2): 33–74.

Brant, Robin. 2020. "Coronavirus: Vaccine Front-Runner China Already Inoculating Workers." BBC, August 27. https://www.bbc.com/news/world-asia-china-53917315.

Brenner, Neil, Jamie Peck, and Nik Theodore. 2010. "Variegated Neoliberalization: Geographies, Modalities, Pathways." *Global Networks* 10 (2): 182–222. https://doi.org/10.1111/j.1471-0374.2009.00277.x.

Brimnes, Niels. 2004. "Variolation, Vaccination and Popular Resistance in Early Colonial South India." *Medical History* 48 (2): 199–228.

Brown, Gordon, and Daniel Susskind. 2020. "International Cooperation During the COVID-19 Pandemic." *Oxford Review of Economic Policy* 36 (1): 64–76.

Buck, Matthias, and Clare Hamilton. 2011. "The Nagoya Protocol on Access to Genetic Resources and the Fair and Equitable Sharing of Benefits Arising from Their Utilization to the Convention on Biological Diversity." *Review of European Community & International Environmental Law* 20 (1): 47–61.

Buhner, Stephen Harrod. 2002. *The Lost Language of Plants: The Ecological Importance of Plant Medicines to Life on Earth.* White River Junction, VT: Chelsea Green.

Burke, Adam, Yim-Yu Wong, and Zoe Clayson. 2003. "Traditional Medicine in China Today: Implications for Indigenous Health Systems in a Modern World." *American Journal of Public Health* 93 (7): 1082–1084. https://doi.org/10.2105/ajph.93.7.1082.

Buse, Kent, and Andrew M. Harmer. 2007. "Seven Habits of Highly Effective Global Public-Private Health Partnerships: Practice and Potential." *Social Science and Medicine* 64 (2): 259–271.

Buse, Kent, Nicholas Mays, and Gill Walt. 2012. *Making Health Policy.* Maidenhead, UK: McGraw-Hill.

Buse, Kent, and Gill Walt. 2002. "Globalisation and Multilateral Public-Private Health Partnerships: Issues for Health Policy." In *Health Policy in a Globalising World*, edited by Kelley Lee, Kent Buse, and Suzanne Fustukian, 41–62. Cambridge: Cambridge University Press. https://doi.org/10.1017/CBO9780511489037.005.

Business Insider India Bureau. 2019. "Difference Between States and Union Territories." *Business Insider India*, December 4. https://www.businessinsider.in/india/news/india-news-difference-between-states-and-union-territories/articleshow/71831006.cms.

Business Wire. 2018. "Therabiopharma (Japan Based Bio-Venture) Reports 10,000 Times Higher Curcumin Concentration in Bloodstream Clearly Demonstrates Strong Efficacies With/Without Oxaliplatin in an Animal Study for Colon Cancer." *Business Wire*, August 21. https://www.businesswire.com/news/home/20180821005346/en/Therabiopharma-Japan-Based-Bio-Venture-Reports-10000-Times.

CCRAS. 2014. "AYUSH—64." Central Council for Research in Ayurvedic Sciences. http://www.ccras.nic.in/sites/default/files/viewpdf/IEC_Communication/Ayush%2064.pdf.

CCRAS. 2017. "Vision Document 2030." Central Council for Research in Ayurvedic Sciences. http://www.ccras.nic.in/sites/default/files/viewpdf/Vision%20and%20Mission.pdf.

Chakravarty, Rupak, and Preeti Mahajan. 2010. "Preserving Traditional Knowledge: Initiatives in India." *IFLA Journal* 36 (4): 294–299. https://doi.org/10.1177/0340035210388246.

Chandna, Himani. 2019. "Govt to Begin Hunt for a Commercially Viable New Drug Molecule Made in India." *The Print*, December 26. https://theprint.in/india/govt-to-begin-hunt-for-a-commercially-viable-new-drug-molecule-made-in-india/340626.

Chang, Jung San, Kuo Chih Wang, Chia Feng Yeh, Den En Shieh, and Lien Chai Chiang. 2013. "Fresh Ginger (Zingiber Officinale) Has Anti-viral Activity Against Human Respiratory Syncytial Virus in Human Respiratory Tract Cell Lines." *Journal of Ethnopharmacology* 145 (1): 146–151. https://doi.org/10.1016/j.jep.2012.10.043.

Chaturvedi, Kalpana, and Joanna Chataway. 2009. "The Indian Pharmaceutical Industry: Firm Strategy and Policy Interactions." In *The New Asian Innovation Dynamics,* edited by G. Parayil and A. D'Costa, 138–169. Basingstoke, Hampshire: Palgrave Macmillan.

Checkel, Jeffrey T. 1998. "The Constructivist Turn in International Relations Theory." *World Politics* 50 (2): 324–348. http://www.jstor.org/stable/25054040.

Cheyney, Maxine. 2017. "The Mission of AMED." *ACCJ Journal*, May 2017. https://journal.accj.or.jp/the-mission-of-amed.

Chinese Academy of Sciences. 2003. "非典，教会我们：坚持中西医并重" [SARS, teach us: Insist on equal emphasis on traditional Chinese and Western medicine]. June 10. http://www.cas.cn/zt/kjzt/zykfd/fzdt/200306/t20030610 _1711467.shtml.

Chinese National Bureau of Statistics. 2020. Accessed May 22, 2020. http:// data.stats.gov.cn/english/index.htm.

Chinese State Council. 2015. "中药材保护和发展规划 (2015–2020年)" [The protection and development plan of Chinese herbal medicine (2015– 2020)]. April 14. http://www.gov.cn/zhengce/content/2015-04/27/content _9662.htm.

Chivian, Eric, and Aaron Bernstein, eds. 2008. *Sustaining Life: How Human Health Depends on Biodiversity*. Oxford: Oxford University Press.

Chotiner, Isaac. 2020. "How Pandemics Change History." *New Yorker*, March 3. https://www.newyorker.com/news/q-and-a/how-pandemics-change-history.

Chouhan, Vishwas Kumar. 2012. "Protection of Traditional Knowledge in India by Patent: Legal Aspect." *Journal of Humanities and Social Science* 3 (1): 35–42.

Christakis, Nicholas A., and James H. Fowler. 2013. "Social Contagion Theory: Examining Dynamic Social Networks and Human Behavior." *Statistics in Medicine* 32 (4): 556–577.

Cockburn, Iain M. 2004. "The Changing Structure of the Pharmaceutical Industry." *Health Affairs* 23 (1): 10–22.

Cole, Daniel H., and Michael D. McGinnis. 2014. *Elinor Ostrom and the Bloomington School of Political Economy*. Lanham, MD: Lexington Books.

Collins, Jane Eva, Harriet Harden-Davies, Marcel Jaspars, Torsten Thiele, Thomas Vanagt, and Isabelle Huys. 2019. "Inclusive Innovation: Enhancing Global Participation in and Benefit Sharing Linked to the Utilization of Marine Genetic Resources from Areas Beyond National Jurisdiction." *Marine Policy* 109: 103696. https://doi.org/10.1016/j.marpol.2019.103696.

Connor, Linda H., and Geoffrey Samuel, eds. 2001. *Healing Powers and Modernity: Traditional Medicine, Shamanism, and Science in Asian Societies*. Westport, CT: Greenwood Publishing Group, Inc.

Convention on Biological Diversity. 2010. "About the Japan Biodiversity Fund." https://www.cbd.int/jbf/about.

Convention on Biological Diversity. 2014. "Fifth National Report." March 2014. https://www.cbd.int/doc/world/jp/jp-nr-05-en.pdf.

Convention on Biological Diversity. 2020a. "The Cartagena Protocol on Biosafety." Updated December 24. https://bch.cbd.int/protocol.

Convention on Biological Diversity. 2020b. "Introduction." Accessed December 25, 2020. https://www.cbd.int/intro.

Convention on Biological Diversity. 2020c. "The Nagoya Protocol on Access and Benefit-Sharing." Updated December 24. https://www.cbd.int/abs.

Convention on Biological Diversity. 2020d. "The Nagoya—Kuala Lumpur Supplementary Protocol on Liability and Redress to the Cartagena Protocol on Biosafety." Updated October 15. https://bch.cbd.int/protocol/supplementary.

Convention on Biological Diversity. 2020e. "Strategic Plan for Biodiversity 2011–2020 and the Aichi Targets." Accessed December 25, 2020. https:// www.cbd.int/doc/strategic-plan/2011-2020/Aichi-Targets-EN.pdf.

Cox, Paul Alan. 2009. "Biodiversity and the Search for New Medicines." In *Biodiversity Change and Human Health: From Ecosystem Services to Spread of Disease*, edited by Osvaldo E. Sala, et al., 269–280. Washington, DC: Island Press.

Crampes, Claude, and Corinne Langinier. 2009. "Are Intellectual Property Rights Detrimental to Innovation?" *International Journal of the Economics of Business* 16 (3): 249–268.

Crow, David. 2018. "GSK Director Sued over US Opioid Epidemic." *Financial Times*, July 3. https://www.ft.com/content/b0ebbf32-7ec7-11e8-bc55-50daf1 1b720d.

Dahl, Jordyn. 2017. "How China Is on Course to Unseat U.S. as the Next Leader in Global Health." *Forbes*, April 27. https://www.forbes.com/sites/jordyndahl /2017/04/26/how-china-is-on-course-to-unseat-u-s-as-the-next-leader-in -global-heath.

The Daily Show with Trevor Noah. 2020. "Bill Gates on Fighting Coronavirus | The Daily Social Distancing Show." YouTube, April 2. https://www.youtube .com/watch?v=iyFT8qXcOrM.

Dalevi, Alessandra. 1997. "Green Piracy in the Amazon." RaintreeHealth, September 2, 2011. http://www.raintree-health.com/2011/09/green-piracy-in-the -amazon.

Dalton, Rex. 2000. "Political Uncertainty Halts Bioprospecting in Mexico." *Nature* 408 (6810): 278–278.

Das, Anupreeta. 2006. "India: Breathe In, and Hands Off Our Yoga." *Christian Science Monitor*, February 9. https://www.csmonitor.com/2006/0209/p07 s02-wosc.html.

David, Bruno, Jean-Luc Wolfender, and Daniel A. Dias. 2015. "The Pharmaceutical Industry and Natural Products: Historical Status and New Trends." *Phytochemistry Reviews* 14 (2): 299–315. https://doi.org/10.1007/s11101 -014-9367-z.

DeGeer, Marcia Ellen. 2003. "Biopiracy: The Appropriation of Indigenous Peoples' Cultural Knowledge." *New England Journal of International and Comparative Law* 9: 179–208.

Dhiman, Kamini, Narayanam Srikanth, T. Maheshwar, Shruti Khanduri, Babita Yadav, Ota Sarada, Renu Singh, et al. 2018. *Clinical Research Drug Development*. Vol. 1 of *Glimpses of CCRAS Contributions 50 Glorious Years*. New Delhi: Central Council for Research in Ayurvedic Sciences.

Discovery. 2020. "COVID-19 Vaccine Development Threatens Shark Populations." September 28. https://www.discovery.com/nature/covid-19-vaccine-threatens -shark-population.

Dou, Jie. 2018. "首批经典名方重塑'中药+'全新生态" [The first batch of classic prescriptions reshapes the new ecology of "traditional Chinese medicine +"]. *China Pharmaceutical News*, April 24. http://epaper.cnpharm.com/zgyyb /images/2018-04/24/05/zgyyb2018042405.pdf.

Drahos, Peter. 1999. "Biotechnology Patents, Markets and Morality." *European Intellectual Property Review* 21: 441–449.

Drahos, Peter. 2000. "Indigenous Knowledge, Intellectual Property and Biopiracy: Is a Global Biocollecting Society the Answer." *European Intellectual Property Review* 22 (6): 245–250.

Drahos, Peter. 2003. "Expanding Intellectual Property's Empire: The Role of FTAs." Grain, November 30. https://grain.org/article/entries/3614-expanding -intellectual-property-s-empire-the-role-of-ftas.

Drahos, Peter. 2010. *The Global Governance of Knowledge Patent Offices and Their Clients*. Cambridge: Cambridge University Press.

Drahos, Peter, and John Braithwaite. 2002. "Intellectual Property, Corporate Strategy, Globalisation: TRIPS in Context." *Wisconsin International Law Journal* 20 (3): 452–480.

Dutta, Soumitra, Bruno Lanvin, and Sacha Wunsch-Vincent. 2019. *Global Innovation Index 2019: Creating Healthy Lives—the Future of Medical Innovation.* Ithaca, NY: Cornell University.

Dutz, Mark A. 2007. *Unleashing India's Innovation: Toward Sustainable and Inclusive Growth.* Washington, DC: World Bank, 2007. http://documents .worldbank.org/curated/en/901801468292888364/Unleashing-Indias -innovation-Toward-sustainable-and-inclusive-growth.

Eban, Katherine. 2019. *Bottle of Lies: The Inside Story of the Generic Drug Boom.* New York: Ecco.

Economic Times. 2018. "Indian Ayurvedic Industry to Grow to \$4.4 Billion by the End of This Year." November 19. https://economictimes.indiatimes.com /industry/healthcare/biotech/healthcare/indian-ayurvedic-industry-to-grow -to-4-4-billion-by-the-end-of-this-year/articleshow/66694089.cms.

Editors of *Time.* 2019. *Time: The Science of Addiction.* New York: Meredith Corporation.

Efferth, Thomas, Mita Banerjee, Norbert W. Paul, Sara Abdelfatah, Joachim Arend, Gihan Elhassan, Sami Hamdoun, et al. 2016. "Biopiracy of Natural Products and Good Bioprospecting Practice." *Phytomedicine* 23 (2): 166–173.

Escohotado, Antonio. 1999. *A Brief History of Drugs: From the Stone Age to the Stoned Age.* Rochester, VT: Park Street Press.

European Commission. 2021. "Corona Accelerated R&D in Europe." Last updated January 17. https://cordis.europa.eu/project/id/101005077.

Fabricant, Daniel S., and Norman R. Farnsworth. 2001. "The Value of Plants Used in Traditional Medicine for Drug Discovery." *Environmental Health Perspectives* 109: 69–75.

Falck, Oliver, and Stephan Heblich. 2007. "Corporate Social Responsibility: Doing Well by Doing Good." *Business Horizons* 50 (3): 247–254. https:// doi.org/10.1016/j.bushor.2006.12.002.

Fang, Bitao. 2020. "7月底前出台相关政策促进中医药振兴发展" [Introduce relevant policies by the end of July to promote the revitalization and development of Chinese traditional medicine]. *China Net of Traditional Chinese Medicine,* June 19.

Fang, Lee. 2021. "Pharmaceutical Industry Dispatches Army of Lobbyists to Block Generic Covid-19 Vaccines." *The Intercept.* April 23. https://theintercept.com /2021/04/23/covid-vaccine-ip-waiver-lobbying/.

Fayerman, Jessica J. 2004. "The Spirit of TRIPS and the Importation of Medicines Made Under Compulsory License After the August 2003 TRIPS Council Agreement." *Northwestern Journal of International Law & Business* 25 (1): 257–278.

Findlay, Stephanie, and Jyotsna Singh. 2020. "India's Yogi Tycoon Angers Critics with Coronavirus 'Cure' Kit." *Financial Times,* August 5. https://www.ft.com /content/f4a63ebf-5764-4570-9211-fd76b7e6c614.

Finetti, Claudia. 2011. "Traditional Knowledge and the Patent System: Two Worlds Apart?" *World Patent Information* 33 (1): 58–66. https://doi.org /10.1016/j.wpi.2010.03.005.

Fishenden, Jerry, and Mark Thompson. 2013. "Digital Government, Open Architecture, and Innovation: Why Public Sector IT Will Never Be the Same Again." *Journal of Public Administration Research and Theory* 23 (4): 977–1004.

Forbes. 2020. "Wu Yiling." Accessed May 29, 2020. https://www.forbes.com /profile/wu-yiling/#3e566f7e7480.

Foster, Christopher, and Richard Heeks. 2013. "Conceptualising Inclusive Innovation: Modifying Systems of Innovation Frameworks to Understand

Diffusion of New Technology to Low-Income Consumers." *European Journal of Development Research* 25 (3): 333–355. https://doi.org/10.1057/ejdr.2013.7.

Fowler, J. H., and N. A. Christakis. 2010. "Cooperative Behavior Cascades in Human Social Networks." *Proceedings of the National Academy of Sciences* 107 (12): 5334–5338. https://doi.org/10.1073/pnas.0913149107.

Frankenfield, Jake. 2020. "Which Industry Spends the Most on Lobbying?" *Investopedia*, updated May 7. https://www.investopedia.com/investing/which-industry-spends-most-lobbying-antm-so.

FRED. 2020. "India/U.S. Foreign Exchange Rate." Accessed July 8, 2020. https://fred.stlouisfed.org/series/AEXINUS.

Freeman, Chris. 2002. "Continental, National and Sub-national Innovation Systems—Complementarity and Economic Growth." *Research Policy* 31 (2): 191–211. https://doi.org/10.1016/s0048-7333(01)00136-6.

Fung, Hon-Ngen, and Chan-Yuan Wong. 2015. "Exploring the Modernization Process of Traditional Medicine: A Triple Helix Perspective with Insights from Publication and Trademark Statistics." *Social Science Information* 54 (3): 327–353.

Fuyuno, Ichiko. 2011. "Japan: Will the Sun Set on Kampo?" *Nature* 480 (7378). https://doi.org/10.1038/480s96a.

Galkina Cleary, Ekaterina, Jennifer M. Beierlein, Navleen Surjit Khanuja, Laura M. McNamee, and Fred D. Ledley. 2018. "Contribution of NIH Funding to New Drug Approvals 2010–2016." *Proceedings of the National Academy of Sciences* 115 (10): 2329–2334. doi:10.1073/pnas.1715368115.

Garcia, Javier. 2007. "Fighting Biopiracy: The Legislative Protection of Traditional Knowledge." *Berkeley La Raza Law Journal* 18: 5–28.

Gaudillière, Jean-Paul. 2019. "From Crisis to Reformulation: Innovation in the Global Drug Industry and the Alternative Modernization of Indian Ayurveda." In *Innovation Beyond Technology: Science for Society and Interdisciplinary Approaches*, edited by S. Lechevalier, 121–139. Creative Economy. Singapore: Springer. https://doi.org/10.1007/978-981-13-9053-1_6.

Gawer, Annabelle. 2014. "Bridging Differing Perspectives on Technological Platforms: Toward an Integrative Framework." *Research Policy* 43 (7): 1239–1249. https://doi.org/10.1016/j.respol.2014.03.006.

General Administration of Customs, P. R. China. 2006. "商务部、公安部、海关总署、药品监督管理局2006年第9号令 (麻黄素类易制毒化学品出口企业核定暂行办法)" [Order of the Ministry of Commerce, Ministry of Public Security, General Administration of Customs and the State Food and Drug Administration (No. 9 [2006]) (the interim measures for the check and ratification of export enterprises of ephedrine precursor chemicals)]. October 10. http://www.customs.gov.cn/customs/302249/302266/302267/356382/index.html.

George, Gerard, Anita M. Mcgahan, and Jaideep Prabhu. 2012. "Innovation for Inclusive Growth: Towards a Theoretical Framework and a Research Agenda." *Journal of Management Studies* 49 (4): 661–683. https://doi.org/10.1111/j.1467-6486.2012.01048.x.

GHDDI. 2018. "In China and for the World: Global Health Drug Discovery Institute (GHDDI) Embarks on a New Journey of Innovative Drug Discovery." November 7. Accessed August 28, 2020. http://www.ghddi.org/en/node/186.

GHDDI. 2019. "GHDDI Joins Global Initiative to Seek Rapid Cure to Reduce TB Treatment Time to One Month." October 24. Accessed August 28, 2020. http://www.ghddi.org/en/node/219.

GHDDI. 2020a. "Beijing Municipal Leadership Visits GHDDI amid COVID-19 Crisis." April 1. http://www.ghddi.org/zh/node/243.

GHDDI. 2020b. "Our Partners." Accessed August 28, 2020. http://www.ghddi.org/en/partner.

GHDDI. 2020c. "This Is GHDDI." Accessed August 28, 2020. http://www.ghddi.org/en/about.

GHIT. 2019. "GHIT Fund Leaflet." https://www.ghitfund.org/assets/other media/GHIT_Fund_Leaflet_eng.pdf.

Gibson, Rosemary, and Janardan Prasad Singh. 2018. *China Rx: Exposing the Risks of America's Dependence on China for Medicine*. Lanham, MD: Rowman & Littlefield.

Gill, Stephen. 2002. "Globalization, Market Civilization and Disciplinary Neoliberalism." In *Globalization of Liberalism*, edited by E. Hovden and E. Keene, 123–151. Millennium Series. London: Palgrave Macmillan. https://doi.org/10.1057/9780230519381_7.

Grifo, Francesca, and Joshua Rosenthal, eds. 1997. *Biodiversity and Human Health*. Washington, DC: Island Press.

Grover, Anand, Brian Citro, Mihir Mankad, and Fiona Lander. 2012. "Pharmaceutical Companies and Global Lack of Access to Medicines: Strengthening Accountability Under the Right to Health." *Journal of Law, Medicine & Ethics* 40 (2): 234–250.

Gundeti, Manohar S., Laxman W. Bhurke, Pallavi S. Mundada, Sanjay Murudkar, Ashita Surve, Ramavatar Sharma, Sunita Mata, et al. 2020. "AYUSH 64, a Polyherbal Ayurvedic Formulation in Influenza-like Illness: Results of a Pilot Study." *Journal of Ayurveda and Integrative Medicine*, May 14. https://doi.org/10.1016/j.jaim.2020.05.010.

Gupta, Anil K. 1996. "The Honey Bee Network: Voices from Grassroots Innovators." *Cultural Survival*, March 1. https://www.culturalsurvival.org/publications/cultural-survival-quarterly/honey-bee-network-voices-grassroots-innovators.

Gupta, Anil K. 2004. "The Role of Intellectual Property Rights in the Sharing of Benefits Arising from the Use of Biological Resources and Associated Traditional Knowledge." Study jointly commissioned by WIPO and UNEP, Geneva, Nairobi. https://www.wipo.int/edocs/pubdocs/en/tk/769/wipo_pub_769.pdf.

Gupta, R. K. 2003. "Managing Intellectual Property." In *Synergy of R & D and Marketing*, 61–66. Jamshedpur, India: National Metallurgical Laboratory, Council of Scientific & Industrial Research. http://eprints.nmlindia.org/2553/1/59-78.PDF.

Gupta, R. K., and L. Balasubrahmanyam. 1998. "The Turmeric Effect." *World Patent Information* 20 (3–4): 185–191.

Gupta, V. K., and Vibha Varshney. 2015. "Protecting the Nation's Patents." *DownToEarth*, July 4. https://www.downtoearth.org.in/interviews/protecting-the-nations-patents-15344.

Gustavsen, Bjørn. 2011. "Innovation, Participation and 'Constructivist Society.'" In *Learning Regional Innovation*, edited by M. Ekman, B. Gustavsen, B. T. Asheim, and Ø. Pålshaugen, 1–14. London: Palgrave Macmillan. https://doi.org/10.1057/9780230304154_1.

Guthrie, Douglas James, Robert G. Richardson, William Archibald, Robson Thomson, E. Ashworth Underwood, and Philip Rhodes. 2020. "History of Medicine." *Encyclopædia Britannica*, January 23. https://www.britannica.com/science/history-of-medicine.

Hager, Thomas. 2019. *Ten Drugs: How Plants, Powders, and Pills Have Shaped the History of Medicine*. New York: Abrams Press.

Hall, Peter A., and David Soskice. 2001. "An Introduction to Varieties of Capitalism." *Varieties of Capitalism*, edited by Peter A. Hall and David Soskice, 1–68. Oxford: Oxford University Press. https://doi.org/10.1093/0199247 757.003.0001.

Hammond, Edward. 2015. "Amid Controversy and Irony, Costa Rica's INBio Surrenders Biodiversity Collections and Lands to the State." *Third World Network*, April 2. https://www.twn.my/title2/biotk/2015/btk150401.htm.

Hannon, Paul. 2020. "Global Economy Faces Hard Winter Despite Covid-19 Vaccine Hopes." *Wall Street Journal*, December 1. https://www.wsj.com /articles/global-economy-faces-difficult-winter-despite-covid-19-vaccine -hopes-11606822321.

Hardt, Michael, and Antonio Negri. 2001. *Empire*. Cambridge, MA: Harvard University Press.

Harman, Sophie. 2012. *Global Health Governance*. London: Routledge.

Harvard School of Public Health and World Economic Forum. 2011. "The Global Economic Burden of Non-communicable Diseases." World Economic Forum, September. http://www3.weforum.org/docs/WEF_Harvard _HE_GlobalEconomicBurdenNonCommunicableDiseases_2011.pdf.

Hawthorne, Fran. 2003. *The Merck Druggernaut: The Inside Story of a Pharmaceutical Giant*. Hoboken, NJ: John Wiley & Sons.

Heeks, Richard, M. Amalia, R. Kintu, and N. Shah. 2013. "Inclusive Innovation: Definition, Conceptualisation and Future Research Priorities." Informatics Working Paper 53. Manchester Centre for Development. http://www .mspguide.org/sites/default/files/resource/di_wp53.pdf.

Heeks, Richard, Christopher Foster, and Yanuar Nugroho. 2014. "New Models of Inclusive Innovation for Development." *Innovation and Development* 4 (2): 175–185. https://doi.org/10.1080/2157930x.2014.928982.

Heller, Michael A. 1998. "The Tragedy of the Anticommons: Property in the Transition from Marx to Markets." *Harvard Law Review* 111 (3): 621. https://doi.org/10.2307/1342203.

Heller, Michael A., and Rebecca S. Eisenberg. 1998. "Can Patents Deter Innovation? The Anticommons in Biomedical Research." *Science* 280 (5364): 698–701.

Hewitt, Don, dir. 1955. "The Salk Vaccine." Episode no. 32. *See It Now*. New York.

Hiltzik, Michael. 2020. "The Colossal Problem of Publicly Funded Vaccines in Private Hands." *Los Angeles Times*, November 17.

Hirwade, Mangala Anil. 2010. "Protecting Traditional Knowledge Digitally: A Case Study of TKDL." In *National Workshop on Digitization Initiatives and Applications in Indian Context*, Dhanwate National College, Nagpur, India. http://eprints.rclis.org/14020/1/TKDL_paper.pdf.

Hirwade, Mangala, and Anil Hirwade. 2012. "Traditional Knowledge Protection: An Indian Prospective." *DESIDOC Journal of Library & Information Technology* 32 (3).

Ho, Cynthia M. 2006. "Biopiracy and Beyond: A Consideration of Socio-cultural Conflicts with Global Patent Policies." *University of Michigan Journal of Law Reform* 39 (3): 433–542.

Hoareau, Lucy, and Edgar J. DaSilva. 1999. "Medicinal Plants: A Re-emerging Health Aid." *Electronic Journal of Biotechnology* 2 (2): 56–70.

Hoffman, Jan. 2019. "Purdue Pharma and Sacklers Reach $270 Million Settlement in Opioid Lawsuit." *New York Times*, March 26. https://www.nytimes.com/2019/03/26/health/opioids-purdue-pharma-oklahoma.html.

Holtz, Colin. 2016. "Who Is to Blame for the EpiPen Hike? Drug Monopolies—Not Evil CEOs." *The Guardian*, August 29. https://www.theguardian.com/commentisfree/2016/aug/29/epipen-price-drug-monopolies-mylan.

Hu, Huabin. 2003. "Sacred Natural Sites in Xishuangbanna, in South-Western China." In *The Importance of Sacred Natural Sites for Biodiversity Conservation*, edited by Cathy Lee and Thomas Schaaf, 127–133. Proceedings of the International Workshop Held in Kunming and Xishuangbanna Biosphere Reserve, People's Republic of China, February 17–20. Paris: United Nations Educational, Scientific and Cultural Organization.

Hu, Ke, Wei-Jie Guan, Ying Bi, Wei Zhang, Lanjuan Li, Boli Zhang, Qingquan Liu, et al. 2020. "Efficacy and Safety of Lianhuaqingwen Capsules, a Repurposed Chinese Herb, in Patients with Coronavirus Disease 2019: A Multicenter, Prospective, Randomized Controlled Trial." *Phytomedicine*, May 16. https://doi.org/10.1016/j.phymed.2020.153242.

Huanqiu. 2019. "政府扶持 中药材产业成脱贫 '利器'" [The government's support for the Chinese herbal medicine industry becomes a "good tool" for poverty alleviation.] January 14. https://quality.huanqiu.com/article/9CaKrnKh11x.

Ibata-Arens, Kathryn. 2005. *Innovation and Entrepreneurship in Japan: Politics, Organizations, and High Technology Firms*. Cambridge: Cambridge University Press.

Ibata-Arens, Kathryn C. 2019a. *Beyond Technonationalism: Biomedical Innovation and Entrepreneurship in Asia*. Stanford, CA: Stanford University Press.

Ibata-Arens, Kathryn C. 2019b. "How Asia Can Avoid the Lifestyle Drug Trap." *AsiaGlobal Online*, May 15. https://www.asiaglobalonline.hku.hk/how-asia-can-avoid-the-lifestyle-drug-trap.

IBM. 2010. "Capitalizing on Complexity: Insights from the Global Chief Executive Officer Study." https://www.ibm.com/downloads/cas/1VZV5X8J.

Ikawa, Yoji. 1991. "Human Genome Efforts in Japan." *FASEB Journal* 5 (1): 66–69. https://doi.org/10.1096/fasebj.5.1.1991587.

Im, Kyungtaek, Jisu Kim, and Hyeyoung Min. 2016. "Ginseng, the Natural Effectual Antiviral: Protective Effects of Korean Red Ginseng Against Viral Infection." *Journal of Ginseng Research* 40 (4): 309–314. https://doi.org/10.1016/j.jgr.2015.09.002.

IME-9. 2020. "Ingredients." Accessed July 8, 2020. http://www.ime9.in/ingredients.asp.

Institute of Natural Medicine. 2020a. "Research Area." Accessed August 10, 2020. https://www.inm.u-toyama.ac.jp/en/research/natural.

Institute of Natural Medicine. 2020b. "WAKANYAKU Database Portal." Accessed August 14, 2020. https://www.inm.u-toyama.ac.jp/en/database.

Insurance Regulatory and Development Authority of India. 2016. "Insurance Regulatory and Development Authority of India Notification." July 12, 2016. https://main.ayush.gov.in/sites/default/files/Health%20Insurance%20Regulations%202016.pdf.

International Intellectual Property Institute (IIPI). 2004. "Is a Sui Generis System Necessary?" January 14. https://iipi.org/wp-content/uploads/2010/07/NewYork011404.pdf.

International Partnership for the Satoyama Initiative (IPSI), Ministry of the Environment Japan, and United Nations University. 2010. "The Satoyama Initiative." October. https://satoyama-initiative.org/wp-content/uploads/2011/09/satoyama_leaflet_web_en_final.pdf.

IRS. 2020. "Yearly Average Currency Exchange Rate." Accessed August 14, 2020. https://www.irs.gov/individuals/international-taxpayers/yearly-average-currency-exchange-rates.

Iwatsuki, Kunio. 2003. "Japan's Sacred Mountains." In *The Importance of Sacred Natural Sites for Biodiversity Conservation*, edited by Cathy Lee and Thomas Schaaf, 89–90. Proceedings of the International Workshop Held in Kunming and Xishuangbanna Biosphere Reserve, People's Republic of China, February 17–20. Paris: United Nations Educational, Scientific and Cultural Organization.

Jaffe, Adam B., and Josh Lerner. 2011. *Innovation and Its Discontents: How Our Broken Patent System Is Endangering Innovation and Progress, and What to Do About It.* Princeton, NJ: Princeton University Press.

Jakubczyk, Dorota, and Francois Dussart. 2020. "Selected Fungal Natural Products with Antimicrobial Properties." *Molecules* 25 (4): 911. https://doi.org/10.3390/molecules25040911.

Japan Association of Botanical Gardens. 2015. 日本の植物園 [Japan's botanical gardens]. Tokyo: YASAKA SHOBO.

Jayaraman, K. S. 1999. ". . . and India Protects Its Past Online." *Nature* 401 (6752): 413–414. https://doi.org/10.1038/46622.

Jayaraman, K. S. 2010. "India's Tuberculosis Genome Project Under Fire." *Nature*, last updated June 15. https://doi.org/10.1038/news.2010.285.

Jha, Shishir K., and Amrutaunshu Nerurkar. 2010. "Expanding Open Source into Other Domains: Analysis of Open Source Biomedical Research." In *Conference Proceedings of JITP 2010: The Politics of Open Source*, edited by Stuart W. Shulman and Charles M. Schweik, 160–185. Amherst: University of Massachusetts, Amherst.

Jin, Yantao, Xin Wang, Zhengwei Li, Ziqiang Jiang, Huijun Guo, Zhibin Liu, and Liran Xu. 2015. "Survival of AIDS Patients Treated with Traditional Chinese Medicine in Rural Central China: A Retrospective Cohort Study, 2004–2012." *Evidence-Based Complementary and Alternative Medicine* 2015: 1–7. https://doi.org/10.1155/2015/282819.

Johnson, Chalmers A. 1982. *MITI and the Japanese Miracle: The Growth of Industrial Policy, 1925–1975.* Stanford, CA: Stanford University Press.

Johnson, Ian. 2015. "Nobel Renews Debate on Chinese Medicine." *New York Times*, October 10. Accessed June 3, 2020. https://www.nytimes.com/2015/10/11/world/asia/nobel-renews-debate-on-chinese-medicine.html.

Jones, Alan Wayne. 2011. "Early Drug Discovery and the Rise of Pharmaceutical Chemistry." *Drug Testing and Analysis* 3 (6): 337–344.

Jonge, Bram De. 2013. "Towards a Fair and Equitable ABS Regime: Is Nagoya Leading Us in the Right Direction." *Law, Environment and Development Journal* 9: 241–255.

Joseph, K. J., ed. 2014a. *Innovation and Development* 4 (1).

Joseph, K. J., ed. 2014b. *Innovation and Development* 4 (2).

Joseph, Reji K. 2010. "International Regime on Access and Benefit Sharing: Where Are We Now?" *Asian Biotechnology and Development Review* 12 (3): 77–94.

JSOM. 2020a. "About JSOM." Accessed August 7, 2020. http://www.jsom.or.jp/english/index.html.

JSOM. 2020b. "Evidence Reports of Kampo Treatment (EKAT) Appendix 2018." June 1. http://www.jsom.or.jp/medical/ebm/pdf/EKATJ_Appendix _2018.pdf.

JSOM. 2020c. "Notes on the Current Version." Accessed August 10, 2020. http://www.jsom.or.jp/medical/ebm/ere/version.html.

JSOM. 2020d. "日本東洋医学会の現状" [Current status of the Japan Society for Oriental Medicine]. Accessed August 10, 2020. http://www.jsom.or.jp /about/genjou.html.

Kamau, Evanson Chege, Bevis Fedder, and Gerd Winter. 2010. "The Nagoya Protocol on Access to Genetic Resources and Benefit Sharing: What Is New and What Are the Implications for Provider and User Countries and the Scientific Community?" *Law & Development Journal (LEAD)* 6 (3): 248–263.

Kanagarathinam, D. V. 2018. "Indigenous and Western Medicines in Colonial South India: Nature of Discourses and Impact." *Indian Journal of History of Science* 53 (2): 182–204.

Kantarjian, Hagop, and S. Vincent Rajkumar. 2015. "Why Are Cancer Drugs So Expensive in the United States, and What Are the Solutions?" *Mayo Clinic Proceedings* 90 (4): 500–504. https://doi.org/10.1016/j.mayocp.2015.01.014.

Katayama, Kotoe, Tetsuhiro Yoshino, Kaori Munakata, Rui Yamaguchi, Seiya Imoto, Satoru Miyano, and Kenji Watanabe. 2013. "Prescription of Kampo Drugs in the Japanese Health Care Insurance Program." *Evidence-Based Complementary and Alternative Medicine* 2013: 1–7. https://doi.org/10 .1155/2013/576973.

Kelley, Edward. 2013. "Medical Tourism." WHO Patient Safety Programme lecture. WHO, October 2. https://www.who.int/global_health_histories /seminars/kelley_presentation_medical_tourism.pdf.

Khair, Helmi. 2016. "Is the Right to Health Undermined by the Agreement of Trade-Related Aspects of Intellectual Property Rights?" *Journal of Academia* 4 (1): 28–33.

Kidd, Ian James. 2012. "Biopiracy and the Ethics of Medical Heritage: The Case of India's Traditional Knowledge Digital Library.'" *Journal of Medical Humanities* 33 (3): 175–183. https://doi.org/10.1007/s10912-012-9179-3.

Kingston, David G. I. 2011. "Modern Natural Products Drug Discovery and Its Relevance to Biodiversity Conservation." *Journal of Natural Products* 74 (3): 496–511.

Kitasato University Oriental Medicine Research Center. 2020. "Greetings from the Director General." Accessed August 7, 2020. https://www.kitasato-u.ac .jp/toui-ken/english/greetings.html.

Kodaira, Eiichi, Koujyu Nozaki, and Shirou Matsuoka. 2016. "京都薬用植物園 における植物を利用した体験型プログラム" [Experience-based learning program using plants in Takeda Garden for Medicinal Plant Conservation, Kyoto]. 日本植物園協会誌 [Bulletin of Japan Association of Botanical Gardens] 51: 101–107.

Kong, De-Xin, Xue-Juan Li, and Hong-Yu Zhang. 2009. "Where Is the Hope for Drug Discovery? Let History Tell the Future." *Drug Discovery Today* 14 (3–4): 115–119. https://doi.org/10.1016/j.drudis.2008.07.002.

Kono, Toru, Mitsuo Shimada, Masahiro Yamamoto, Atushi Kaneko, Yuji Oomiya, Kunitsugu Kubota, Yoshio Kase, et al. 2015. "Complementary and Synergistic Therapeutic Effects of Compounds Found in Kampo Medicine: Analysis of Daikenchuto." *Frontiers in Pharmacology* 6. https://doi.org /10.3389/fphar.2015.00159.

Kotecha, Vaidya Rajesh. 2020. "Advisory from Ministry of AYUSH for Meeting the Challenge Arising out of Spread of Corona Virus (Covid-19) in India." Ministry of AYUSH, March 6. https://www.ayush.gov.in/docs/125.pdf.

Kozarich, Daniel. 2016. "Mylan's EpiPen Pricing Crossed Ethical Boundaries." *Fortune*, September 27. https://fortune.com/2016/09/27/mylan-epipen-heather-bresch.

Krishna, Ananye. 2019. "Is Traditional Knowledge Digital Library a Success?" *Journal of Intellectual Property Rights* 24 (5–6) (September–November): 132–139.

Kulkarni, Dilip K. 2017. Interview by author. Pune. September.

Kumar, Ruchi. 2020. "Face It: The Indian Government Is Peddling Pseudoscience." *The Wire Science*, April 27. https://science.thewire.in/health/indian-government-pseudoscience-covid-19.

Landers, Peter, and Miho Inada. 2020. "Japan Tests Coronavirus Drug Despite Danger of Birth Defects." *Wall Street Journal*, March 6. https://www.wsj.com/articles/japan-tests-coronavirus-drug-despite-danger-of-birth-defects-11583492886.

Latha, S. 2009. "Biopiracy and Protection of Traditional Medicine in India." *European Intellectual Property Review* 31 (9): 465–477.

Le, Tung Thanh, Zacharias Andreadakis, Arun Kumar, Raúl Gómez Román, Stig Tollefsen, Melanie Saville, and Stephen Mayhew. 2020. "The COVID-19 Vaccine Development Landscape." *Nature Reviews Drug Discovery* 19 (5): 305–306. https://doi.org/10.1038/d41573-020-00073-5.

Lee, Sungjoo, Hakyeon Lee, and Changyong Lee. 2020. "Open Innovation at the National Level: Towards a Global Innovation System." *Technological Forecasting and Social Change* 151: 119842. https://doi.org/10.1016/j.techfore.2019.119842.

LePan, Nicholas. 2020. "Visualizing the History of Pandemics." *Visual Capitalist*, March 14. https://www.visualcapitalist.com/history-of-pandemics-deadliest.

Leydesdorff, Loet, and Henry Etzkowitz. 1996. "Emergence of a Triple Helix of University-Industry-Government Relations." *Science and Public Policy* 23: 279–286.

Li, Hua. 2015. "Analysis on Industry Chain and Product Chain of Traditional Chinese Medicine." *World Science and Technology—Modernization of Traditional Chinese Medicine Year* 1: 292–295. http://en.cnki.com.cn/Article_en/CJFDTOTAL-SJKX201501057.htm.

Li, Jie Jack. 2014. *Blockbuster Drugs: The Rise and Fall of the Pharmaceutical Industry*. Oxford: Oxford University Press.

Li, Qinayu. 2017. "我国启动中药材产业扶贫行动" [China initiates the Poverty Alleviation Action of Chinese herbal medicine industry]. *Xinhua*, September 1. http://m.xinhuanet.com/2017-09/01/c_1121588149.htm.

Liu, Changhua. 2016. Interview by author. Guangzhou.

Liu, Changhua. 2018. Interview by author. Beijing. January.

Liu, Changhua, and Man Gu. 2011. "Protecting Traditional Knowledge of Chinese Medicine: Concepts and Proposals." *Frontiers of Medicine* 5 (2): 212–218. https://doi.org/10.1007/s11684-011-0142-x.

Liu, Lihong. 2020. "The Role of Chinese Medicine in the COVID-19 Epidemic (Transcript)." ClassicalChineseMedicine.org, March 19. Accessed June 4, 2020. https://classicalchinesemedicine.org/role-chinese-medicine-covid-19-epidemic.

Local Government Directory. 2020. Accessed July 24, 2020. https://lgdirectory.gov.in.

Lock, Margaret, and Vinh-Kim Nguyen. 2018. *An Anthropology of Biomedicine.* Hoboken, NJ: John Wiley & Sons.

Lucchi, Nicola. 2013. "Understanding Genetic Information as a Commons: From Bioprospecting to Personalized Medicine." *International Journal of the Commons* 7 (2): 313–338.

Lundvall, Bengt Åke. 1992. *National Systems of Innovation: Towards a Theory of Innovation and Interactive Learning.* London: Pinter Publishers.

Lundvall, Bengt-Åke. 2007. "National Innovation Systems—Analytical Concept and Development Tool." *Industry and Innovation* 14 (1): 95–119. https://doi.org/10.1080/13662710601130863.

Lundvall, Bengt-Åke, ed. 2010. *National Systems of Innovation: Toward a Theory of Innovation and Interactive Learning.* London: Anthem Press.

Madhav, Nita, Ben Oppenheim, Mark Gallivan, Prime Mulembakani, Edward Rubin, and Nathan Wolfe. 2017. "Pandemics: Risks, Impacts, and Mitigation." In *Disease Control Priorities: Improving Health and Reducing Poverty*, edited by Dean T. Jamison et al., 315–345. 3rd ed. Washington, DC: International Bank for Reconstruction and Development/The World Bank. https://doi.org/10.1596/978-1-4648-0527-1/pt5.ch1.

Mahoney, Richard, and Carlos Morel. 2006. "A Global Health Innovation System (GHIS)." *Innovation Strategy Today* 2 (1): 1–12.

Malhotra, K. C., N. H. Ravindranath, and K. S. Murali. 2000. *Joint Forest Management and Community Forestry in India: An Ecological and Institutional Assessment.* New Delhi: Oxford & IBH Publishing.

Mansfield, Edwin. 1986. "Patents and Innovation: An Empirical Study." *Management Science* 32 (2): 173–181.

Marcon, Federico. 2015. "The First Japanese Encyclopedias of Nature: Yamato honzō and Shobutsu ruisan." In *The Knowledge of Nature and the Nature of Knowledge in Early Modern Japan.* Chicago: University of Chicago Press.

Maskus, Keith E. 2000. *Intellectual Property Rights in the Global Economy.* Washington, DC: Institute for International Economics.

Mason, Paul. 2010. *Meltdown: The End of the Age of Greed.* London: Verso.

Mason, Peter. 2016. *Postcapitalism: A Guide to Our Future.* London: Penguin Books.

Masum, Hassan, Aarthi Rao, Benjamin M. Good, Matthew H. Todd, Aled M. Edwards, Leslie Chan, Barry A. Bunin, et al. 2013. "Ten Simple Rules for Cultivating Open Science and Collaborative R&D." *PLoS Computational Biology* 9 (9): e1003244. https://doi.org/10.1371/journal.pcbi.1003244.

Masum, Hassan, Karl Schroeder, Myra Khan, and Abdallah Daar. 2011. "Open Source Biotechnology Platforms for Global Health and Development: Two Case Studies." *International Technologies & International Development* 7 (1): 61–69.

Matsuzawa, S. 2016. "A Donor Influenced by Local Dynamics: Unintended Consequences of Capacity Building in China." *Sociology of Development* 2 (1): 51–69. https://doi.org/10.1525/sod.2016.2.1.51.

Matthews, Duncan. 2002. *Globalising Intellectual Property Rights: The TRIPS Agreement.* Florence, KY: Taylor and Francis.

May, Christopher. 2009. *The Global Political Economy of Intellectual Property Rights: The New Enclosures.* 2nd ed. Florence, KY: Taylor and Francis.

Mazumdar-Shaw, Kiran. 2020. "Kiran Mazumdar's Covid-19 Diary." *Business India*, September 18. https://businessindia.co/magazine/kiran-mazumdars-covid-19-diary.

Mazzucato, Mariana, Henry Lishi Li, and Els Torreele. 2020. "Designing Vaccines for People, Not Profits." *Project Syndicate*, December 1. https://www.project-syndicate.org/commentary/covid-vaccines-for-profit-not-for-people-by-mariana-mazzucato-et-al-2020-12.

McAfee, Kathleen. 2003. "Neoliberalism on the Molecular Scale: Economic and Genetic Reductionism in Biotechnology Battles." *Geoforum* 34 (2): 203–219. https://doi.org/10.1016/s0016-7185(02)00089-1.

McManis, Charles R. 2009. "Introduction: Open Source and Proprietary Models of Innovation: Beyond Ideology." *Washington University Journal of Law & Policy* 30: 1–15.

McNeil, Donald G. 2001. "Indian Company Offers to Supply AIDS Drugs at Low Cost in Africa," *New York Times*, February 7. https://www.nytimes.com/2001/02/07/world/indian-company-offers-to-supply-aids-drugs-at-low-cost-in-africa.html.

Meneguzzi, Justin. 2020. "Why a COVID-19 Vaccine Could Further Imperil Deep-Sea Sharks." *National Geographic*, November 13. https://www.nationalgeographic.com/animals/2020/11/why-covid-19-vaccine-further-imperil-deep-sea-sharks.

Meng, Xianze, Yonghua Su, and Dezeng Zhu. 2006. "科学利用甘草，保护我国生态环境和药材资源" [Sustainable utilization of Radix Glycyrrhizae for protection of ecology environment and herbal resources]. *Journal of Chinese Integrative Medicine* 4 (6): 556–559.

Menzies, Nicholas K. 2005. "The Center for Biodiversity and Indigenous Knowledge (CBIK): An Institutional Review." CBIK, November 1.

Menzies, Nicholas K. 2016. Interview by author. Kunming. July.

Merriam-Webster. Accessed February 14, 2020. https://www.merriam-webster.com/dictionary/pharmaceutical.

Mgbeoji, Ikechi. 2006. *Global Biopiracy: Patents, Plants, and Indigenous Knowledge*. Vancouver: University of British Columbia Press.

Mgbeoji, Ikechi. 2014. *Global Biopiracy: Patents, Plants, and Indigenous Knowledge*. Vancouver: University of British Columbia Press.

Ministry of AYUSH. 2002. "National Policy on Indian Systems of Medicine & Homoeopathy—2002." https://ayush.assam.gov.in/sites/default/files/swf_utility_folder/departments/dirayush_lipl_in_oid_9/menu/information_and_services/7870046089-Ayush%20%20n%20policy%20ISM%20and%20H%20Homeopathy_0.pdf.

Ministry of AYUSH. 2016. "Ayurveda Treatment Expenditure Guidelines." September. https://main.ayush.gov.in/sites/default/files/Guidelines%20for%20Insurance%20Coverage%20to%20Ayurvedic%20Treatment_0_0.pdf.

Ministry of AYUSH. 2020a. "Background." Accessed June 24, 2020, https://main.ayush.gov.in/about-us/background.

Ministry of AYUSH. 2020b. "Insurance Companies That Are Offering Products Covering One or More Systems of AYUSH Treatment." Accessed July 10, 2020. https://main.ayush.gov.in/sites/default/files/Insurance_companies_offering_products_covering_AYUSH.pdf.

Ministry of AYUSH. 2020c. "Scheme for Development of AYUSH Clusters." Accessed July 17, 2020. http://ayurvedah.in/content/attachment/rules/25_Cluster_Scheme.pdf.

Ministry of AYUSH. 2020d. "Siddha Treatment Expenditure Guidelines." Accessed August 24, 2020. https://main.ayush.gov.in/sites/default/files/Guidelines_For_Reimbursement_Settlement_of_Siddha_Treatment_Expenditure_Claims_Under_Insurance_Coverage%20%281%29_0_0.pdf.

Ministry of AYUSH. 2020e. "Unani Treatment Expenditure Guidelines." Accessed August 24, 2020. https://main.ayush.gov.in/sites/default/files /Guidelines_For_Reimbursement_Settlement_of_Unani_Treatment _Expenditure_Claims_Under_Insurance_Coverage_0_0.pdf.

Ministry of AYUSH. 2020f. "Yoga and Naturopathy Treatment Expenditure Guidelines." Accessed August 24, 2020. https://main.ayush.gov.in/sites /default/files/Guidelines_for_reimbursementsettlement_of_Yoga_and _Naturopathy_treatment_expenditure_claims_under_insurance_coverage_0 _0.pdf.

Ministry of Commerce of the People's Republic of China. 2018. "商务部 公安部 生态环境部 海关总署 国家药品监督管理局公告2018年第83号 关于调整麻黄草出口管理政策的公告" [Announcement of the Ministry of Commerce, Ministry of Public Security, Ministry of Ecology and Environment, General Administration of Customs, and the State Drug and Drug Administration No. 83 of 2018 on adjusting the export management policy of ephedra]. October 18. http://www.mofcom.gov.cn/article/b/e /201810/20181002796543.shtml.

Ministry of Environment. 2019. Accessed January 24, 2019. https://www.env.go .jp/index.html.

Ministry of Foreign Affairs of the People's Republic of China. 2015. "Xi Jinping Meets with Co-Chair of Bill & Melinda Gates Foundation Bill Gates of US." March 29. https://www.fmprc.gov.cn/mfa_eng/topics_665678/xjpcxbayzlt 2015nnh/t1250549.shtml.

Ministry of Health and Family Welfare. 1983. "National Health Policy 1983." https://www.nhp.gov.in/sites/default/files/pdf/nhp_1983.pdf.

Ministry of Health and Family Welfare. 2002. "National Health Policy 2002." https://www.nhp.gov.in/sites/default/files/pdf/NationaL_Health_Pollicy.pdf.

Ministry of Health and Family Welfare. 2017. "National Health Policy 2017." https://www.nhp.gov.in/nhpfiles/national_health_policy_2017.pdf.

Mondillo, Vincent, dir. 2017. *Big Pharma: Market Failure*. Easton, PA: Unfinished Business Foundation.

Morgera, Elisa, and Elsa Tsioumani. 2010. "The Evolution of Benefit Sharing: Linking Biodiversity and Community Livelihoods." *Review of European Community & International Environmental Law* 19 (2): 150–173. https://doi .org/10.1111/j.1467-9388.2010.00674.x.

Morris, David, and Jacqui Morris, dir. 2014. *Attacking the Devil: Harold Evans and the Last Nazi War Crime*. British Film Company, Frith Street Films, and Rankin Film Productions.

Morrow, Thomas, and Linda Hull Felcone. 2004. "Defining the Difference: What Makes Biologics Unique." *Biotechnology Healthcare* 1 (4): 24–29.

Moser, Petra. 2013. "Patents and Innovation: Evidence from Economic History." *Journal of Economic Perspectives* 27 (1): 23–44.

Moynihan, Ray, and Alan Cassels. 2005. *Selling Sickness: How the World's Biggest Pharmaceutical Companies Are Turning Us into Patients*. Vancouver: Greystone Books.

Mukherjee, Sy. 2018. "Viagra Just Turned 20. Here's How Much Money It Makes." *Fortune*, March 27. https://fortune.com/2018/03/27/viagra-anniversary -pfizer.

Mulla, Ghazala. 2017. Interview by author. Pune. September.

Nair, M. D. 2010. "TRIPS, WTO and IPR—TRIPS & Affordable Healthcare: The Concept of OSDD & Patent Pools." *Journal of Intellectual Property Rights* 15: 74–76.

NATCM. 2017. "中药材产业扶贫行动计划 (2017–2020年)" [The Poverty Alleviation Action of Chinese herbal medicine Industry (2017–2020)]. *China Net of Traditional Chinese Medicine*, September 27. http://www.cntcm.com.cn/2017-09/27/content_34857.htm.

NATCM. 2019a. "壮丽70年·党领导中医药发展历程①：团结中西医，共克时艰" [Magnificent 70 years, the development of TCM under the leadership of the CCP①: Unity of traditional Chinese medicine and Western medicine, overcome difficulties]. National Administration of Traditional Chinese Medicine, April 12. http://www.satcm.gov.cn/hudongjiaoliu/guanfangweixin/2019-04-15/9556.html.

NATCM. 2019b. "壮丽70年·党领导中医药发展历程⑫:探索建立健全中医药管理体系" [Magnificent 70 years, the development of TCM under the leadership of the CCP⑫: Explore to establish and improve the management system of traditional Chinese medicine]. National Administration of Traditional Chinese Medicine, July 12. http://www.satcm.gov.cn/hudongjiaoliu/guanfangweixin/2019-07-17/10280.html.

NATCM. 2019c. "壮丽70年·党领导中医药发展历程⑮：宏伟战略引领振兴发展新征程" [Magnificent 70 years, the development of TCM under the leadership of the CCP⑮: Magnificent strategy leads a new journey of revitalization and development]. National Administration of Traditional Chinese Medicine, August 9. http://www.satcm.gov.cn/hudongjiaoliu/guanfangweixin/2019-08-12/10601.html.

NATCM. 2020. "国家中医药管理局的主要职责" [The major responsibilities of the National Administration of Traditional Chinese Medicine]. National Administration of Traditional Chinese Medicine. Accessed May 22, 2020. http://www.satcm.gov.cn/zhengcewenjian/zhengwugongkaimulu/2018-03-25/7070.html.

National Ayurvedic Medical Association. 2020. "History of Ayurveda." Accessed June 19, 2020. https://www.ayurvedanama.org/history-of-ayurveda.

National Healthcare Security Administration of the PRC. 2019. "国家基本医疗保险、工伤保险和生育保险药品目录" [Catalogue of national basic medical insurance, industrial injury insurance and maternity insurance drugs]. August 20. http://www.nhsa.gov.cn/art/2019/8/20/art_37_1666.html.

National Institution for Transforming India. 2017. "Appraisal Document of Twelfth Five Year Plan 2012–17." The Hindu Centre, July 26. https://www.thehinducentre.com/multimedia/archive/03189/Appraisal_Document_3189085a.pdf.

National Medicinal Plants Board. 2020a. "National AYUSH Mission." Accessed July 17, 2020. https://nmpb.nic.in/sites/default/files/downloads/4197396897-Charakasamhita_ACDP_english_0.pdf

National Medicinal Plants Board. 2020b. "Voluntary Certification Scheme for Medicinal Plant Produce (VCSMPP)." Accessed July 22, 2020. https://nmpb.nic.in/sites/default/files/QCI-NMPB-VCS-Brochure8.pdf.

Neergheen-Bhujun, Vidushi, Almas Taj Awan, Yusuf Baran, Nils Bunnefeld, Kit Chan, Thomas Edison Dela Cruz, Dilfuza Egamberdieva, et al. 2017. "Biodiversity, Drug Discovery, and the Future of Global Health: Introducing the Biodiversity to Biomedicine Consortium, a Call to Action." *Journal of Global Health* 7 (2). https://doi.org/10.7189/jogh.07.020304.

Nelson, Richard. 2004. "The Challenge of Building an Effective Innovation System for Catch-Up." *Oxford Development Studies* 32 (3): 365–374. https://doi.org/10.1080/1360081042000260575.

Nelson, Richard R. 1993. *National Innovation Systems: A Comparative Analysis*. New York: Oxford University Press.

Nelson, Richard R., and Nathan Rosenberg. 1993. "Technical Innovation and National Systems." *National Innovation Systems: A Comparative Analysis* 1: 3–21.

NIBIOHN. 2020a. "Comprehensive Medicinal Plant Database." Accessed August 14, 2020. http://mpdb.nibiohn.go.jp/mpdb-bin/top.cgi?lang=.

NIBIOHN. 2020b. "Research Center for Medicinal Plant Resources." Accessed August 14, 2020. https://www.nibiohn.go.jp/en/activities/medical-herb.html.

NIBIOHN. 2020c. "筑波研究部" [Tsukuba Division]. Accessed August 17, 2020. http://wwwts9.nibiohn.go.jp/saibaiken.html.

Nijar, Gurdial Singh. 2013a. "An Asian Developing Country's View on the Implementation Challenges of the Nagoya Protocol." In *The 2010 Nagoya Protocol on Access and Benefit-Sharing in Perspective*, edited by Elisa Morgera, Matthias Buck, and Elsa Tsioumani, 247–268. Leiden: Brill.

Nijar, Gurdial Singh. 2013b. "Traditional Knowledge Systems, International Law and National Challenges: Marginalization or Emancipation?" *European Journal of International Law* 24 (4): 1205–1221.

Nilsson, Adriana. 2017. "Making Norms to Tackle Global Challenges: The Role of Intergovernmental Organisations." *Research Policy* 46 (1): 171–181. https://doi.org/10.1016/j.respol.2016.09.012.

Nipunage, D. S., and D. K. Kulkarni. 2010. "Deo-rahati: An Ancient Concept of Biodiversity Conservation." *Asian Agri-History* 14 (2): 185–196.

Nomura, Toshihito, Masaya Fukushi, Kosuke Oda, Akifumi Higashiura, Takashi Irie, and Takemasa Sakaguchi. 2019. "Effects of Traditional Kampo Drugs and Their Constituent Crude Drugs on Influenza Virus Replication in Vitro: Suppression of Viral Protein Synthesis by Glycyrrhizae Radix." *Evidence-Based Complementary and Alternative Medicine* 2019: 1–12. https://doi.org/10.1155/2019/3230906.

Ochs, Shelley, and Thomas Avery Garran, eds. 2020. *Chinese Medicine and COVID-19: Results and Reflections from China*. Beijing City: Passiflora Press.

Odell, John S., and Susan K. Sell. 2003. "Reframing the Issue: The WTO Coalition on Intellectual Property and Public Health, 2001." Paper prepared for the Conference on Developing Countries and the Trade Negotiation Process, UNCTAD, Geneva, Switzerland, November 6–7.

OECD. 2012. "Innovation and Inclusive Development." Revised February 2013. https://www.oecd.org/sti/inno/oecd-inclusive-innovation.pdf.

OECD. 2016. "Biodiversity-Related Official Development Assistance 2015." November. https://www.oecd.org/dac/environment-development/Biodiversity-related-ODA.pdf.

Ohmae, Kenichi. 1995. *The End of the Nation State: The Rise of Regional Economies*. New York: Simon & Schuster.

Ohura, Catherine. 2019. Interview by author. Tokyo. December.

OpenSecrets.org. 2021. "Pharmaceuticals/Health Products: Lobbying, 2020." Accessed April 2, 2021. https://www.opensecrets.org/industries/lobbying.php?ind=H04++.

Ostrom, Elinor. 1990. *Governing the Commons: The Evolution of Institutions for Collective Action*. Political Economy of Institutions and Decisions. Cambridge: Cambridge University Press.

Oyewunmi, Adejoke O. 2013. "Sharpening the Legal Tools to Overcome Biopiracy in Africa Through Pro-development Implementation of Normative International Standards: Lessons from Brazil, South Africa and India." *African Journal of International and Comparative Law* 21 (3): 447–466.

Pandey, Neelam. 2020. "Patanjali Intent Behind 'Covid Cure' Not Wrong but Should've Followed Protocol: Ayush Minister." *The Print*, June 24. https://theprint.in/india/patanjali-intent-behind-covid-cure-not-wrong-but -shouldve-followed-protocol-ayush-minister/447833.

Patlak, Margie. 2010. "Open-Source Science Makes Headway." *JNCI: Journal of the National Cancer Institute* 102 (16): 1221–1223. https://doi.org/10 .1093/jnci/djq321.

Patwardhan, Bhushan. 2005. "Ethnopharmacology and Drug Discovery." *Journal of Ethnopharmacology* 100 (1–2): 50–52.

Patwardhan, Bhushan. 2017. Interview by author. Pune. September.

Patwardhan, Bhushan, and Manish Gautam. 2005. "Botanical Immunodrugs: Scope and Opportunities." *Drug Discovery Today* 10 (7): 495–502.

Patwardhan, Bhushan, and Ashok Vaidya. 2010. "Natural Products Drug Discovery: Accelerating the Clinical Candidate Development Using Reverse Pharmacology Approaches." *Indian Journal of Experimental Biology* 48: 220–227.

Paun, Carmen. 2020. "Closing the Covid Treatment Gap." *POLITICO*, November 25. https://www.politico.com/newsletters/global-pulse/2020/11/25/closing -the-covid-treatment-gap-490986.

Pharmaceutical Daily. 2010. "漢方薬問題とは何だつたのか-「保険外し」反対運動を振り返る" [What was the *kampo* problem—looking back against "out of insurance" opposition]. January 5. https://www.yakuji.co.jp/entry 17682.html.

Planning Commission, Government of India. 2013. "Twelfth Five Year Plan (2012–2017): Social Sectors." Vol. 3. Ministry of Human Resource Development. https://mhrd.gov.in/sites/upload_files/mhrd/files/document-reports /XIIFYP_SocialSector.pdf.

Plotkin, Mark J. 2020. "Could the Amazon Save Your Life?" *New York Times*, October 2. https://www.nytimes.com/2020/10/02/opinion/amazon-novel -species-medicine.html.

Polanyi, Karl. 1944. *The Great Transformation: The Political and Economic Origins of Our Time*. New York: Rinehart.

Pordié, Laurent. 2010. "The Politics of Therapeutic Evaluation in Asian Medicine." *Economic and Political Weekly* 45 (18): 57–64.

Posner, Gerald L. 2020. *Pharma: Greed, Lies, and the Poisoning of America*. New York: Avid Reader Press.

Prathapan, K. D., and Priyadarsanan Dharma Rajan. 2011. "Biodiversity Access and Benefit-Sharing: Weaving a Rope of Sand." *Current Science* 100 (3): 290–293.

Preuss, Lutz. 2011. "Innovative CSR: A Framework for Anchoring Corporate Social Responsibility in the Innovation Literature." *Journal of Corporate Citizenship* 42: 17–33.

PTI. 2020. "Patanjali's Plea for Ayurvedic Medicine Trials Raises Eyebrows." *Economic Times*, May 27. https://economictimes.indiatimes.com/industry /healthcare/biotech/healthcare/patanjalis-plea-for-ayurvedic-medicine-trials -raises-eyebrows/articleshow/76039940.cms.

Raghavan, Mukundan, Karuna Jain, and Shishir K. Jha. 2013. "Technology and Intellectual Property Strategy of a Firm: A View Through the Commons Theory Lens." *IIMB Management Review* 25 (4): 213–227. https://doi.org /10.1016/j.iimb.2013.07.003.

Raghupathi, Wullianallur, and Viju Raghupathi. 2018. "An Empirical Study of Chronic Diseases in the United States: A Visual Analytics Approach to Public

Health." *International Journal of Environmental Research and Public Health* 15 (3): 431. https://doi.org/10.3390/ijerph15030431.

Raju, K. V., B. Hemalatha, Sharon Poornima, and K. K. Prasanna Rashmi. 2016. *Alternative Medicine Approaches as Healthcare Intervention: A Case Study of AYUSH Programme in Peri Urban Locales.* Bangalore: The Institute for Social and Economic Change.

Ramdas, Sagari R. 2012. "Whose Access and Whose Benefit? Securing Customary Rights in India." In "Biodiversity and Culture: Exploring Community Protocols, Rights and Consent," edited by Krystyna Swiderska with Angela Milligan, Kanchi Kohli, Harry Jonas, Holly Shrumm, Wim Hiemstra, and Maria Julia Oliva. Special issue, *Participatory Learning and Action* 65: 55–64.

Rapaka, Rao S., Vishnudutt Purohit, Paul Schnur, and Joni Rutter. 2014. "Emerging Trends in the Abuse of Designer Drugs and Their Catastrophic Health Effects: Update on Chemistry, Pharmacology, Toxicology and Addiction Potential." *Life Sciences* 97 (1): 1. https://doi.org/10.1016/j.lfs .2014.01.074.

Rauniyar, Ganesh P., and Ravi Kanbur. 2010. "Inclusive Development: Two Papers on Conceptualization, Application, and the ADB Perspective." Working Papers 57036, Cornell University, Department of Applied Economics and Management.

Ravishankar, B., and V. J. Shukla. 2008. "Indian Systems of Medicine: A Brief Profile." *African Journal of Traditional, Complementary and Alternative Medicines* 4 (3): 319. https://doi.org/10.4314/ajtcam.v4i3.31226.

Reader, Ruth. 2020. "How Open-Source Medicine Could Prepare Us for the Next Pandemic." Fast Company, April 30. https://www.fastcompany.com /90498448 /how-open-source-medicine-could-prepare-us-for-the-next-pandemic.

Regalado, Antonio. 2020. "Some Scientists Are Taking a DIY Coronavirus Vaccine, and Nobody Knows If It's Legal or If It Works." *MIT Technology Review,* July 29. https://www.technologyreview.com/2020/07/29/1005720 /george-church-diy-coronavirus-vaccine/.

Reich, Michael. 2002. *Public-Private Partnerships for Public Health.* Boston: Harvard School of Public Health.

Reset. 2020. "Argonne Lab Researchers Working to Develop Coronavirus Vaccine." *Reset* (audio blog). *WBEZ,* March 11. https://www.wbez.org/stories/argonne -lab-researchers-working-to-develop-coronavirus-vaccine/2ea944a4-c1fe-4b 85-98ed-5da8894d4627.

Riddle, John M. 2002. "History as a Tool in Identifying 'New' Old Drugs." In *Flavonoids in Cell Function,* edited by B. S. Buslig and J. A. Manthey, 89–94. Advances in Experimental Medicine and Biology 505. Boston: Springer. https://doi.org/10.1007/978-1-4757-5235-9_8.

Roberts, David J., and Matti Siemiatycki. 2015. "Fostering Meaningful Partnerships in Public-Private Partnerships: Innovations in Partnership Design and Process Management to Create Value." *Environment and Planning C: Government and Policy* 33 (4): 780–793. https://doi.org/10.1068/c12250.

Robertson, Murray N., Paul M. Ylioja, Alice E. Williamson, Michael Woelfle, Michael Robins, Katrina A. Badiola, Paul Willis, et al. 2013. "Open Source Drug Discovery—a Limited Tutorial." *Parasitology* 141 (1): 148–157. https:// doi.org/10.1017/s0031182013001121.

Robertson, W. 1976. "Merck Strains to Keep the Pots Aboiling." *Fortune,* March 1976.

Robinson, Daniel. 2010. *Confronting Biopiracy: Challenges, Cases, and International Debates.* London: Routledge.

Rosenthal, Joshua. 2007. "Politics, Culture and Governance in the Development of Prior Informed Consent and Negotiated Agreements with Indigenous Communities." In *Biodiversity and the Law: Intellectual Property, Biotechnology and Traditional Knowledge*, edited by Charles R. McManis, 373–393. London: Routledge.

Rudra, Shalini, Aakshi Kalra, Abhishek Kumar, and William Joe. 2017. "Utilization of Alternative Systems of Medicine as Health Care Services in India: Evidence on AYUSH Care from NSS 2014." *PLoS One* 12 (5). https://doi.org/10.1371/journal.pone.0176916.

Runge, C. Ford, and Edi Defrancesco. 2006. "Exclusion, Inclusion, and Enclosure: Historical Commons and Modern Intellectual Property." *World Development* 34 (10): 1713–1727.

Saha, Amrita. 2016. "Inclusive Innovation, Development and Policy: Four Key Themes." *IDS Bulletin* 47 (2). https://doi.org/10.19088/1968-2016.184.

Sahai, Suman, Prasmi Pavithran, and Indrani Barpujari. 2007. *Biopiracy: Imitations Not Innovation*. New Delhi: Gene Campaign.

Sakaki, Yoshiyuki. 2019. "A Japanese History of the Human Genome Project." *Proceedings of the Japan Academy, Series B* 95 (8): 441–458. https://doi.org/10.2183/pjab.95.031.

Sala, Osvaldo E., Laura A. Meyerson, and Camille Parmesan. 2009. *Biodiversity Change and Human Health: From Ecosystem Services to Spread of Disease*. Washington, DC: Island Press.

Samuels, Richard J. 1994. *"Rich Nation, Strong Army": National Security and the Technological Transformation of Japan*. Ithaca, NY: Cornell University Press.

Sarnaik, Jayant, Ian G. Bride, Archana Godbole, Mallika Sardeshpande, Umesh Hiremath, and Yogesh Giri. 2017. "FairWild Certification: An Approach for Linking Biodiversity Conservation with Sustainable Livelihoods in the Northern Western Ghats, India." Case Study. In *Sustainable Livelihoods in Socio-ecological Production Landscapes and Seascapes*, edited by UNU-IAS and IGES, 90–101. Satoyama Initiative Thematic Review 3. Tokyo: United Nations University Institute for the Advanced Study of Sustainability.

Sarnoff, Joshua D., and Carlos M. Correa. 2006. "Analysis of Options for Implementing Disclosure of Origin Requirements in Intellectual Property Applications—a Contribution to UNCTAD's Response to the Invitation of the Seventh Conference of the Parties of the Convention on Biological Diversity." Seventh Conference of the Parties of the Convention on Biological Diversity, UNCTAD/DITC/TED/2004/14. *SSRN Electronic Journal*. https://doi.org/10.2139/ssrn.2278629.

Satyalakshmi, K. 2017. Interview by author. Pune. September.

Saxena, Shweta Awasthi. 2009. *Mainstreaming AYUSH and Revitalizing Local Health Traditions Under NRHM: An Appraisal of the Annual State Programme Implementation Plans 2007–10 and Mapping of Technical Assistance Needs*. New Delhi: National Health System Resource Centre.

Saxenian, AnnaLee. 1990. "Regional Networks and the Resurgence of Silicon Valley." *California Management Review* 33 (1): 89–112. https://doi.org/10.2307/41166640.

Scannell, Jack W., Alex Blanckley, Helen Boldon, and Brian Warrington. 2012. "Diagnosing the Decline in Pharmaceutical R&D Efficiency." *Nature Reviews Drug Discovery* 11 (3): 191–200. https://doi.org/10.1038/nrd3681.

Scaria, Arul George, and Tom Dedeurwaerdere. 2012. "Towards a Contractually Created Commons in Traditional Knowledge and Genetic Resources for Scientific Research and Innovation in India: Scope and Challenges." *The*

Knowledge Commons in Action: Application to Genetic Resource Commons and Cultural Commons of the International Journal of the Commons (Forthcoming). https://ssrn.com/abstract=2180780.

Schumpeter, Joseph. A. 1934. *The Theory of Economic Development: An Inquiry into Profits, Capital, Credit, Interest and the Business Cycle.* London: Oxford University Press.

Schumpeter, Joseph A. 2005 (1942). "The Process of Creative Destruction." In *Capitalism, Socialism and Democracy,* introduction by Richard Swedberg, 81–86. London: Routledge.

Schwartz, Casey. 2016. "Generation Adderall." *New York Times,* October 12. https://www.nytimes.com/2016/10/16/magazine/generation-adderall -addiction.html.

Secretariat of the CBD. 2005. *Handbook of the Convention on Biological Diversity: Including Its Cartagena Protocol on Biosafety.* Quebec: Secretariat of the Convention on Biological Diversity.

Secretariat of the CBD. 2016. "2011–2020 United Nations Decade on Biodiversity— Fact Sheets." Convention on Biological Diversity. Accessed October 15, 2016. https://www.cbd.int/undb/media/factsheets/undb-factsheets-en-web.pdf.

Sell, Susan K. 2002. "TRIPS and the Access to Medicines Campaign." *Wisconsin International Law Journal* 20 (3): 481–522.

Sell, Susan K. 2003. *Private Power, Public Law: The Globalization of Intellectual Property Rights.* Cambridge Studies in International Relations. Cambridge: Cambridge University Press.

Sell, Susan K., and Owain D. Williams. 2020. "Health Under Capitalism: A Global Political Economy of Structural Pathogenesis." *Review of International Political Economy* 27 (1): 1–25.

Sen, Saikat, and Raja Chakraborty. 2017. "Revival, Modernization and Integration of Indian Traditional Herbal Medicine in Clinical Practice: Importance, Challenges and Future." *Journal of Traditional and Complementary Medicine* 7 (2): 234–244. https://doi.org/10.1016/j.jtcme.2016.05.006.

Sengupta, Nirmal. 2019. "Global Mechanisms of Protection and Sharing." In *Traditional Knowledge in Modern India,* 31–51. New Delhi: Springer.

Shadlen, Kenneth C., Bhaven N. Sampat, and Amy Kapczynski. 2019. "Patents, Trade and Medicines: Past, Present and Future." *Review of International Political Economy* 27 (1): 75–97. https://doi.org/10.1080/09692290.2019 .1624295.

Shaikh, Sumaiya. 2019. "Under the Microscope: Questionable Claims About Ayurvedic Drugs for Diabetes, Malaria," *Scroll.in,* April 15. https://scroll.in /article/919424/how-manufacturers-of-ayurvedic-drugs-make-claims -backed-by-ayush-ministry.

Shaikh, Sumaiya. 2020. "Homeopathic Drugs Such as Arsenicum Album 30, Promoted by AYUSH, Do Not Boost Immunity Against COVID." *Alt News,* June 30. https://www.altnews.in/homeopathic-drugs-such-as-arsenicum-album -30-promoted-by-ayush-do-not-boost-immunity-against-covid.

Shapiro, Carl. 2000. "Navigating the Patent Thicket: Cross Licenses, Patent Pools, and Standard Setting." *Innovation Policy and the Economy* 1: 119–150.

Sharma, Seemantani. 2017. "Traditional Knowledge Digital Library: 'A Silver Bullet' in the War Against Biopiracy?" *John Marshall Review of Intellectual Property Law* 17.

Shen-Nong Limited. 2020. "Collateral of the Meridian System." Accessed May 29, 2020. http://www.shen-nong.com/eng/treatment/acupuncture_collaterals.html.

Shi, Wentong. 2014. "吴以岭: '我就是一个大夫'" [Wu Yiling: "I am a doctor"]. Chinese Academy of Engineering, originally published in *Hebei Daily*

News, December 25. https://www.cae.cn/cae/html/main/col36/2015-01/08/20150108172756697362941_1.html.

Shu, Chengli, Albert L. Page, Shanxing Gao, and Xu Jiang. 2012. "Managerial Ties and Firm Innovation: Is Knowledge Creation a Missing Link?" *Journal of Product Innovation Management* 29 (1): 125–143.

Siegel, Taggart, and Jon Betz, dir. 2016. *Seed: The Untold Story*. Portland, OR: Collective Eye Films.

Simpson, R. David. 2019. "The Problem with Making Nature Pay for Itself." *Anthropocene*, June. https://anthropocenemagazine.org/2019/06/the-problem-with-making-nature-pay-for-itself.

Simpson, R. David, Roger A. Sedjo, and John W. Reid. 1996. "Valuing Biodiversity for Use in Pharmaceutical Research." *Journal of Political Economy* 104 (1): 163–185.

Singer, Hans, Charles Cooper, R. C. Desai, Christopher Freeman, Oscar Gish, Stephen Hill, and Geoffrey Oldham. 1970. *The Sussex Manifesto: Science and Technology for Developing Countries During the Second Development Decade*. Brighton, UK: IDS Reprints.

Singh, Seema. 2008. "India Takes an Open Source Approach to Drug Discovery." *Cell* 133 (2): 201–203. https://doi.org/10.1016/j.cell.2008.04.003.

Singh, Seema. 2012. "How Open Source Drug Discovery Is Helping India Develop New Drugs." *Forbes India*, April 9. https://www.forbesindia.com/article/breakpoint/how-open-source-drug-discovery-is-helping-india-develop-new-drugs/32668/1.

Skocpol, Theda. 1977. "Wallerstein's World Capitalist System: A Theoretical and Historical Critique." *American Journal of Sociology* 82 (5): 1075–1090. Accessed October 9, 2020. http://www.jstor.org/stable/2777814.

Sneader, Walter. 2005. *Drug Discovery: A History*. Hoboken, NJ: John Wiley & Sons.

Song, Ge. 2016. "Progress Report on Nationwide Survey and Registration for Traditional Knowledge of Traditional Chinese Medicine in China." Unpublished.

Sorensen, Olav Jull, and Jizhen Li. 2016. "Towards a Global Innovation System in a Firm and Nation Perspective." In *Innovation at Business, Regional/National and Global Levels—in a Collaborative Perspective*. CICALICS Workshop, Beijing, China, August 27.

Soto, Hernando De. 2000. *The Mystery of Capital: Why Capitalism Triumphs in the West and Fails Everywhere Else*. London: Civitas Books.

Sreedhar, Remya, Kenichi Watanabe, and Somasundaram Arumugam. 2017. "Introduction to Japanese Kampo Medicines." In *Japanese Kampo Medicines for the Treatment of Common Diseases: Focus on Inflammation*, edited by Somasundaram Arumugam and Kenichi Watanabe, 1–11. Cambridge, MA: Academic Press. https://doi.org/10.1016/b978-0-12-809398-6.00001-9.

Srikanth, N., Sulochana Bhat, Arjun Singh, and Renu Singh. 2015. "Healthcare Seeking Attitude and Utilization of Traditional Medicine in India—an Overview." *World Journal of Pharmaceutical Research* 4 (7): 722–738.

Srinivas, Krishna Ravi. 2012. "Protecting Traditional Knowledge Holders' Interests and Preventing Misappropriation—Traditional Knowledge Commons and Biocultural Protocols: Necessary but Not Sufficient?" *International Journal of Cultural Property* 19 (3): 401–422.

Srinivasan, Padma. 1995. "National Health Policy for Traditional Medicine in India." *World Health Forum* 16 (2): 190–193.

Standing Committee of the National People's Congress. 2016. "中华人民共和国中医药法" [Law of the People's Republic of China on traditional Chinese medicine]. National Administration of Traditional Chinese Medicine, December 26. http://fjs.satcm.gov.cn/zhengcewenjian/2018-03-24/2249.html.

State Council Information Office of the People's Republic of China. 2016. "Traditional Chinese Medicine in China." January 17. http://english.scio.gov.cn/whitepapers/2017-01/17/content_40621689.htm.

State Council Information Office of the People's Republic of China. 2020. "抗击新冠肺炎疫情的中国行动" [Fighting Covid-19: China in action]. June 7. http://www.scio.gov.cn/ztk/dtzt/42313/43142/index.htm.

Stenton, Gavin. 2003. "Biopiracy Within the Pharmaceutical Industry: A Stark Illustration of Just How Abusive, Manipulative and Perverse the Patenting Process Can Be Towards Countries of the South." *Hertfordshire Law Journal* 1 (2): 30–47.

STEPS Centre. 2010. *Innovation, Sustainability, Development: A New Manifesto.* Brighton, UK: STEPS Centre.

Steslicke, William E. 1972. "Doctors, Patients, and Government in Modern Japan." *Asian Survey* 12 (11): 913–931. https://doi.org/10.2307/2643113.

Stevens, Ashley J., Jonathan J. Jensen, Katrine Wyller, Patrick C. Kilgore, Sabarni Chatterjee, and Mark L. Rohrbaugh. 2011. "The Role of Public-Sector Research in the Discovery of Drugs and Vaccines." *New England Journal of Medicine* 364 (6): 535–541. https://doi.org/10.1056/nejmsa 1008268.

Stiglitz, Joseph E. 2006. "Give Prizes Not Patents." *New Scientist*, September 16. https://www8.gsb.columbia.edu/faculty/jstiglitz/sites/jstiglitz/files/2006 _New_Scientist.pdf.

Sun, Ying. 2009. "中药被排除出日本医保体系 27万人签名反对" [*Kampo* medicines are excluded from the Japan national health insurance system 270,000 people signed against]. *news.ifeng.com*, December 7. http://news .ifeng.com/world/200912/1208_16_1465947.shtml.

't Hoen, Ellen F. M., Jacquelyn Veraldi, Brigit Toebes, and Hans V. Hogerzeil. 2018. "Medicine Procurement and the Use of Flexibilities in the Agreement on Trade-Related Aspects of Intellectual Property Rights, 2001–2016." *Bulletin of the World Health Organization* 96 (3): 185–193. https://doi.org /10.2471/blt.17.199364.

Talbot, Margaret. 2020. "The Rogue Experimenters." *New Yorker*, May 18. https://www.newyorker.com/magazine/2020/05/25/the-rogue-experimenters.

Thakurta, Paranjoy Guha. 2019. "Crony Capitalism Is Alive and Kicking." *National Herald*, August 15. https://www.nationalheraldindia.com/opinion /crony-capitalism-is-alive-and-kicking.

Thaler, Richard H., and Cass R. Sunstein. 2003. "Libertarian Paternalism." *American Economic Review* 93 (2): 175–179.

Thaler, Richard H., and Cass R. Sunstein. 2008. *Improving Decisions About Health, Wealth and Happiness.* New Haven, CT: Yale University Press.

Thomas, Pradip N. 2010. "Traditional Knowledge and the Traditional Knowledge Digital Library: Digital Quandaries and Other Concerns." *International Communication Gazette* 72 (8): 659–673. https://doi.org/10.1177 /1748048510380799.

Thompson, Jonathan Marshall, dir. 2018. *DRUG$: The Price We Pay.* Los Angeles, CA: AIDS Healthcare Foundation.

Tianyancha. 2020. "石家庄以岭药业股份有限公司" [Shijiazhuang Yiling Pharmaceutical Co., LTD.]. Accessed June 19, 2020. https://www.tianyancha .com/company/15587508.

Tomizawa, Aki, Li Zhao, Geneviève Bassellier, and David Ahlstrom. 2020. "Economic Growth, Innovation, Institutions, and the Great Enrichment." *Asia Pacific Journal of Management* 37 (1): 7–31.

Tripp, Simon, and Martin Grueber. 2011. "Economic Impact of the Human Genome Project." *Battelle Memorial Institute* 58: 1–58.

Tsujimoto, Masaharu, Yoichi Matsumoto, and Kiyonori Sakakibara. 2014. "Finding the 'Boundary Mediators': Network Analysis of the Joint R&D Project Between Toyota and Panasonic." *International Journal of Technology Management* 66 (2–3): 120–133.

Tsumura & Co. 2020a. "Integrated Report." Accessed August 17, 2020. https://www.tsumura.co.jp/english/info/pdf/report2019.pdf.

Tsumura & Co. 2020b. "Tsumura-Kampo Bakumondoto [麦門冬湯] Extract Granules." Accessed August 10, 2020. https://www.tsumura.co.jp/products/qr_lp/images/pdf/english/029_otc.pdf.

Tsumura & Co. 2020c. "Tsumura-Kampo Daiokanzoto [大黄甘草湯] Extract Granules." Accessed September 4, 2020. https://www.tsumura.co.jp/products/qr_lp/images/pdf/english/084_otc.pdf.

Tsumura & Co. 2020d. "Tsumura-Kampo Maoto [麻黄湯] Extract Granules." Accessed September 4, 2020. https://www.tsumura.co.jp/products/qr_lp/images/pdf/english/027_otc.pdf.

Tsumura & Co. 2020e. "Tsumura-Kampo Rikkunshito [六君子湯] Extract Granules." Accessed August 10, 2020. https://www.tsumura.co.jp/products/qr_lp/images/pdf/english/043_otc.pdf.

Tsumura & Co. 2020f. "Tsumura's Business." Accessed August 26, 2020. https://www.tsumura.co.jp/english/ir/business.

Umashankar, V., and S. Gurunathan. 2015. "Drug Discovery: An Appraisal." *International Journal of Pharmacy and Pharmaceutical Sciences* 7 (4): 59–66.

UNU-IAS and IGES, eds. 2015. *Enhancing Knowledge for Better Management of Socio-ecological Production Landscapes and Seascapes (SEPLS).* Satoyama Initiative Thematic Review 1. Tokyo: United Nations University Institute for the Advanced Study of Sustainability.

UNU-IAS and IGES, eds. 2016. *Mainstreaming Concepts and Approaches of Socio-ecological Production Landscapes and Seascapes into Policy and Decision-Making.* Satoyama Initiative Thematic Review 2. Tokyo: United Nations University Institute for the Advanced Study of Sustainability.

UNU-IAS and IGES, eds. 2017. *Sustainable Livelihoods in Socio-ecological Production Landscapes and Seascapes.* Satoyama Initiative Thematic Review 3. Tokyo: United Nations University Institute for the Advanced Study of Sustainability.

Utkarsh, Ghate. 2003. "Documentation of Traditional Knowledge: People's Biodiversity Registers." In *Trading in Knowledge: Development Perspectives on TRIPS, Trade and Sustainability*, edited by Christophe Bellmann, Graham Dutfield, and Ricardo Melendez-Ortiz, 190–195. New York: Routledge.

Viswanathan, Serena. 2020. "SuperHealthGuard and Loyal Great International Ltd." US Food and Drug Administration, June 26. https://www.fda.gov/inspections-compliance-enforcement-and-criminal-investigations/warning-letters/superhealthguard-and-loyal-great-international-ltd-608633-06262020.

Vu, Jonathan T., Benjamin K. Kaplan, Shomesh Chaudhuri, Monique K. Mansoura, and Andrew W. Lo. 2020. "The Challenging Economics of Vaccine Development in the Age of COVID-19, and What Can Be Done About It." *DIA*, May

1. https://globalforum.diaglobal.org/issue/may-2020/the-challenging-economics -of-vaccine-development-in-the-age-of-covid19-and-what-can-be-done -about-it.

Wallerstein, Immanuel. 1974. "The Rise and Future Demise of the World Capitalist System: Concepts for Comparative Analysis." *Comparative Studies in Society and History* 16: 387–415.

Wallerstein, Immanuel. 1987. "World Systems Theory." In *Social Theory Today*, edited by A. Giddens and J. Turner. Cambridge: Polity.

Walters, Joanna. 2016. "Drug Company Boss Martin Shkreli Refuses to Testify to Congress." *The Guardian*, February 4. https://www.theguardian.com/business /2016/feb/04/martin-shkreli-refuses-to-testify-congress-drug-daraprim.

Wang, Shujun. 2003. "中医药防治SARS科研新进展, 临床疗效进一步证实" [New progress in scientific research on the prevention and treatment of SARS by traditional Chinese medicine, clinical efficacy is further confirmed]. Chinese Academy of Sciences, July 3. http://www.cas.cn/zt/kjzt /zykfd/zl/200307/t20030703_1711488.shtml.

Wang, Yifei, Fujun Jin, Qiaoli Wang, and Zucai Suo. 2017. "Long-Term Survival of AIDS Patients Treated with Only Traditional Chinese Medicine." *Alternative and Complementary Therapies* 23 (2): 60–62. https://doi.org/10.1089 /act.2017.29106.ywa.

Wareham, Jonathan, Paul B. Fox, and Josep Lluís Cano Giner. 2014. "Technology Ecosystem Governance." *Organization Science* 25 (4): 1195–1215. https:// doi.org/10.1287/orsc.2014.0895.

Warnke, Philine, Knut Koschatzky, Ewa Dönitz, Andrea Zenker, Thomas Stahlecker, Oliver Som, Kerstin Cuhls, et al. 2016. "Opening Up the Innovation System Framework Towards New Actors and Institutions." Discussion Papers "Innovation Systems and Policy Analysis" 49. Fraunhofer Institute for Systems and Innovation Research. https://ideas.repec.org/p/zbw/fisidp/49.html.

Watal, Jayashree. 2000. "Intellectual Property and Biotechnology: Trade Interests of Developing Countries." *International Journal of Biotechnology* 2 (1–3): 44–55.

Watanabe, Ken. 2018. "Drug-Repositioning Approach for the Discovery of Anti-Influenza Virus Activity of Japanese Herbal (Kampo) Medicines in Vitro: Potent High Activity of Daio-Kanzo-To." *Evidence-Based Complementary and Alternative Medicine* 2018: 1–9. https://doi.org/10.1155/2018/6058181.

Watanabe, Kenji, Keiko Matsuura, Pengfei Gao, Lydia Hottenbacher, Hideaki Tokunaga, Ko Nishimura, Yoshihiro Imazu, et al. 2011. "Traditional Japanese Kampo Medicine: Clinical Research Between Modernity and Traditional Medicine—the State of Research and Methodological Suggestions for the Future." *Evidence-Based Complementary and Alternative Medicine* 2011: 1–19. https://doi.org/10.1093/ecam/neq067.

Watts, Jonathan. 2010. "Japan Offers Hope to Biodiversity Summit with $2bn Conservation Fund." *The Guardian*, last modified October 27, 2010. https://www.theguardian.com/environment/2010/oct/27/japan-biodiversity -conference-conservation.

WHO. 2002. *WHO Traditional Medicine Strategy, 2002–2005*. Geneva: World Health Organization. https://apps.who.int/iris/bitstream/handle/10665/67163 /WHO_EDM_TRM_2002.1.pdf?sequence=1.

WHO. 2004. *SARS: Clinical Trials on Treatment Using a Combination of Traditional Chinese Medicine and Western Medicine: Report of the WHO International Expert Meeting to Review and Analyse Clinical Reports on*

Combination Treatment for SARS, 8–10 October 2003, Beijing, People's Republic of China. Geneva: World Health Organization.

WHO. 2013. *WHO Traditional Medicine Strategy, 2014–2023.* Geneva: World Health Organization.

WHO. 2017. *Improving Access to Medicines in the South-East Asia Region: Progress, Challenges, Priorities.* Geneva: World Health Organization. https://apps.who.int/iris/handle/10665/258750.

WHO. 2020a. "A Coordinated Global Research Roadmap: 2019 Novel Coronavirus." March 2020. https://www.who.int/blueprint/priority-diseases/key-action/Coronavirus_Roadmap_V9.pdf?ua=1.

WHO. 2020b. "The Doha Declaration on the TRIPS Agreement and Public Health." Accessed December 25, 2020. https://www.who.int/medicines/areas/policy/doha_declaration/en.

WHO. 2020c. "Essential Medicines and Health Products." Accessed October 9, 2020. https://www.who.int/medicines/en.

WHO. 2020d. "Global Health Expenditure Database." Accessed July 10, 2020. https://apps.who.int/nha/database/Select/Indicators/en.

WHO. 2020e. "The Global Strategy and Plan of Action on Public Health, Innovation and Intellectual Property." Accessed December 25, 2020. https://www.who.int/phi/implementation/phi_globstat_action/en.

WHO, WTO, and WIPO. 2013. "Promoting Access to Medical Technologies and Innovation: Intersections Between Public Health, Intellectual Property and Trade." World Trade Organization. https://www.wto.org/english/res_e/booksp_e/pamtiwhowipowtoweb13_e.pdf.

WIPO. 2020. "WIPO Re:Search." World Intellectual Property Organization. Accessed December 25, 2020. https://www.wipo.int/research/en.

The Wire. 2020. "Will COVID-19 Change AYUSH Research in India for the Better?" May 15. https://science.thewire.in/the-sciences/ministry-of-ayush-task-force-clinical-trials-herbs-prophylactics.

Woodward, Aylin, and Shayanne Gal. 2020. "One Chart Shows How the Wuhan Coronavirus Compares to Other Major Outbreaks and Pandemics in the Last 50 Years." *Business Insider*, January 30. https://www.businessinsider.com/how-wuhan-coronavirus-compares-to-other-outbreaks-pandemics-2020-1.

World Bank. 2020. "The Global Economic Outlook During the COVID-19 Pandemic: A Changed World." June 8. https://www.worldbank.org/en/news/feature/2020/06/08/the-global-economic-outlook-during-the-covid-19-pandemic-a-changed-world.

Worth, Robert F. 2018. "The Billionaire Yogi Behind Modi's Rise." *New York Times*, July 26. https://www.nytimes.com/2018/07/26/magazine/the-billionaire-yogi-behind-modis-rise.html.

WTO. 2020. "Overview: The TRIPS Agreement." World Trade Organization. Accessed December 25, 2020. https://www.wto.org/english/tratop_e/trips_e/intel2_e.htm.

Xu, Jing. 2020. "种下'致富'草 走上'脱贫'路" [Planting "get rich" grass and embarking on the road of "get rid of poverty"]. *China Net of Traditional Chinese Medicine*, June 19. http://www.cntcm.com.cn/2020-06/19/content_77233.htm.

Xu, Wen. 2020. "50万份'健康包'将由我驻外使领馆分发至留学生" [500,000 "health kits" will be distributed to international students by our embassies and consulates abroad]. *Beijing News*, April 3. http://www.bjnews.com.cn/news/2020/04/03/712574.html.

Xue, Dayuan, Yuanyuan Zhang, and Jingbiao Yang. 2018. "Facilitating the Implementation of Nagoya Protocol Through Documentation of Traditional Knowledge Associated with Biological and Genetic Resources in China." In *Summary Report and Abstracts: The Seventh Global Conference of the International Partnership for the Satoyama Initiative (IPSI-7)*. International Partnership for the Satoyama Initiative. https://satoyama-initiative.org/wp-content/uploads/Final-IPSI-7-report-1.pdf.

Yakubo, S., M. Ito, Y. Ueda, H. Okamoto, Y. Kimura, Y. Amano, T. Togo, et al. 2014. "Pattern Classification in Kampo Medicine." *Evidence-Based Complementary and Alternative Medicine* 2014: 1–5. https://doi.org/10.1155/2014/535146.

Yang, Zhaohui, Changhua Liu, Ge Song, and Yiwen Zhang. 2015. "Investigation Report on General Information of Intangible Cultural Heritage of Traditional Chinese Medicine in China." *Chinese Journal of Information on TCM* 22 (6): 18–20. https://doi.org/10.3969/j.issn.1005-5304.2015.06.006.

Yeola, Gunvant. 2017. Interview by author. Pune. September.

Yiling Pharmaceutical. 2020a. "About Us." Accessed May 8, 2020. http://en.yiling.cn/ylen/channels/2191.html.

Yiling Pharmaceutical. 2020b. "Lianhua Qingwen Capsules." Accessed May 8, 2020. http://en.yiling.cn/YLEN/contents/2131/38.html.

Yiling Pharmaceutical. 2020c. "TCM Medicine on Way to Italy." April 25. http://en.yiling.cn/ylen/contents/2205/263.html.

Yiling Pharmaceutical. 2020d. "连花清瘟胶囊在三次抗疫中均发挥重大作用" [Lianhua Qingwen Jiaonang plays a significant role in the three anti-epidemics]. May 27. http://www.yiling.cn/news/gsyw/20200527/9278.html.

Yiling Pharmaceutical. 2020e. "石家庄以岭药业股份有限公司2020年第一季度报告正文" [Shijiazhuang Yiling Pharmaceutical Co., LTD. 2020 Q1 report]. April 30. http://www.yiling.cn/tzz/gsgg/2020/0430/9247.html.

Yiling Pharmaceutical. 2020f. "石家庄以岭药业股份有限公司2019年年度报告摘要" [Summary of Shijiazhuang Yiling Pharmaceutical Co., LTD. 2019 annual report]. April 30. http://www.yiling.cn/tzz/gsgg/2020/0430/9246.html.

Yip, Ka-che. 2009. *Disease, Colonialism, and the State: Malaria in Modern East Asian History*. Hong Kong: Hong Kong University Press.

Yu, Peter K. 2007. "The International Enclosure Movement." *Indiana Law Journal* 82 (4): 827–908.

Yu, Yanhong, Boli Zhang, Luqi Huang, and Qingquan Liu. 2020. "国新办举行中医药防治新冠肺炎重要作用及有效药物发布会" [The Conference of the State Council Information Office of the People's Republic of China on the Important Role of Traditional Chinese Medicine in Preventing and Treating Covid-19]. State Council Information Office of the People's Republic of China, March 23. http://www.scio.gov.cn/xwfbh/xwbfbh/wqfbh/42311/42768/index.htm.

Zakrzewski, Peter A. 2002. "Bioprospecting or Biopiracy? The Pharmaceutical Industry's Use of Indigenous Medicinal Plants as a Source of Potential Drug Candidates." *University of Toronto Medical Journal* 79 (3): 252–254.

Zehavi, Amos, and Dan Breznitz. 2017. "Distribution Sensitive Innovation Policies: Conceptualization and Empirical Examples." *Research Policy* 46 (1): 327–336. https://doi.org/10.1016/j.respol.2016.11.007.

Zhang, Hongwu, and Wenlong Huang. 2020. "Overview of the Inheritance and Development of TCM from the Status of Chinese Medicine Enterprises." *Chinese Health Service Management*, 37: 193–196.

Zhao, Yongxin. 2014. "吴以岭: 中医药创新 '拓荒牛' (关注·寻找最美科学家)" [Wu Yiling: "Pioneer cattle" of Chinese medicine innovation (focus: find the most beautiful scientist)]. *People.cn*, May 19. http://scitech.people.com.cn/n/2014/0519/c1007-25032034.html.

Zimmer, Carl, Katie Thomas, and Benjamin Mueller. 2020. "AstraZeneca Partly Resumes Coronavirus Vaccine Trial After Halting It for Safety." *New York Times*, September 12. https://www.nytimes.com/2020/09/12/health/astrazeneca-coronavirus-vaccine-trial-resumes.html.

Index

About the Book

Despite a century of advances in modern medicine, as
well as the rapid development of Covid vaccines, the global pharmaceutical industry has largely failed to bring to market drugs that actually
cure disease. Why? And looking further . . . How can government
policies stimulate investment in the development of curative drugs?
Is there an untapped potential for "natural medicines" in new drug
discovery? How have private–public sector partnerships transformed
the ways we innovate? To what extent are medicinal plant biodiversity
and human health codependent?

Addressing this range of increasingly critical questions, Kathryn
Ibata-Arens analyzes the rise and decline of the global innovation
system for new drug development and proposes a policy framework
for fast-tracking the implementation of new discoveries and preparing
for future pandemics.

Kathryn C. Ibata-Arens is Vincent de Paul Professor of Political
Economy at DePaul University.